BASIC COMMUNICATION SKILLS

BASIC COMMUNICATION SKILLS

Sonu Marwah

ANMOL PUBLICATIONS PVT. LTD.
NEW DELHI-110 002 (INDIA)

ANMOL PUBLICATIONS PVT. LTD.

Regd. Office: 4360/4, Ansari Road, Daryaganj,
New Delhi-110002 (India)
Tel.: 23278000, 23261597, 23286875, 23255577
Fax: 91-11-23280289
Email: anmolpub@gmail.com
Visit us at: www.anmolpublications.com

Branch Office: No. 1015, Ist Main Road, BSK IIIrd Stage
IIIrd Phase, IIIrd Block, Bangalore-560 085 (India)
Tel.: 080-41723429 • Fax: 080-26723604
Email: anmolpublicationsbangalore@gmail.com

Basic Communication Skills,

First Edition, 2010

ISBN 978-81-261-4496-9

PRINTED IN INDIA

Printed at Mehra Offset Press, Delhi.

Contents

Preface

The ability to communicate well is a critical managerial skill. Being able to put your ideas across in a concise, meaningful, interesting and influential way is fundamental to your success in organizational life. The book provides you with the demonstration of thinking, writing, and speaking effectively. But how do you write assignments, analyse case studies, provide executive summaries, reference appropriately and avoid plagiarism.

The Communication Skills book shows you how. It is a key resource for communicating effectively, both in writing and in speaking. You should refer to it whenever you begin to prepare an assignment or a presentation. The book is tailor-made for all students at University level. The book tells you what our lecturers expect and how you can meet their standards.

This Communication Skills book is a useful resource to consult whenever you are preparing an assignment or wondering how to improve your marks. It covers the major aspects of information for students as it gives detailed information about how to structure assignments, research essays and presentations, and what to include in those types of assignments. also it gives guidance on professional writing. Next it examines aspects of university study, such as academic argument, good style, and referencing. It also has a section on cultural differences in learning and teaching.

Author

Chapter 1

Communication as Skilled Performance

The interpersonal process is complex, ever-changing, and directly affected by a large number of interrelated factors. This means that in order to make sense of, and systematically investigate, social encounters, some form of interpretive framework is usually employed. In fact, numerous alternative frameworks have been developed for this purpose. For example, interpersonal encounters have been conceptualized variously as:

- A form of joint economic activity or social exchange in which both sides seek rewards and try to minimise costs, which may be in the form of money, services, goods, status, or affection.
- Transactional episodes during which individuals play roles akin to acting as either parent, adult, or child, and respond to others at one of these three levels.
- A type of dramatic performance composed of major scenes, in which everyone has a role to play with expected lines, some have more prominent roles than others, the actors behave differently 'front stage' as opposed to 'back-stage', there are various 'props' in the form of furniture and fittings, there is a storyline, and all of his changes from one 'production' to the next.

These are just three of the approaches that have been developed as templates for the interpretation of interpersonal communication. In this chapter and in Chapter 2, another such approach will be resented, namely, the perspective that social behaviour can be conceptualised as a form of skilled performance, and that it is therefore meaningful to compare socially skilled behaviour (such as interviewing or negotiating) with motor skill behaviour (such as playing tennis or operating a machine).

In further pursuit of this analogy, it is argued that the models and methods successfully employed for over 100 years in the study of motor skill can usefully be applied to interpersonal skill. The validity of this comparison, and the accompanying implications for the study of social behaviour, will be investigated.

This chapter is concerned with an examination of the nature of skill, and in particular with the perspective that interpersonal communication can be viewed as a form of skill. In order to evaluate this perspective, it is necessary to relate the history of the study of interpersonal skill directly to the study of motor skill, since it was from the latter source that the concept of communication as skill eventually emerged.

The extent to which this analogy can be pursued is then discussed, together with an analysis of the nature of social skill per se. Overall, therefore, this chapter provides a reference point for the entire book, by delineating the nature and defining features of interpersonal skill.

MOTOR SKILLS

The study of perceptual-motor skill has a long and rich tradition within psychology. Such skills, which involve coordinated physical movements of the body, are widely employed in human performance, and they include, for example, eating, dressing, walking, writing, riding a bicycle, and playing golf.

Welford traced the scientific study of motor skill back to 1820, when the astronomer Bessel examined differences between individuals in a task that involved the recording of star-transit times. However, direct psychological interest in the nature of motor skill really began with explorations by Bryan and Harter into the learning of Morse code, followed by studies on movement by Woodworth, and investigations by Book into the learning of typewriting skills. Since this early research, the literature on perceptual-motor skill has become voluminous, and indeed this area remains an important focus of study. Numerous definitions of 'motor skill' have been put forward.

As these definitions indicate, while there are commonalities, theorists tend to emphasise different features, so that Irion, in tracing the history of this research, concluded: 'The field of motor skills does not suffer from a lack of variety of approach.

Indeed, the approaches and methods are so extremely various that there is some difficulty in defining, in a sensible way, what the field of motor skills is.' Robb, in discussing the acquisition of motor skill, reached a similar conclusion, stating: 'The problems associated with how one acquires skill are numerous and complex. For that matter, the term skill is itself an illusive and confusing word.'

However, the study of this field as being encapsulated in the question: 'When we look at a man working, by what criteria in his performance can we tell whether he is skilled and competent or clumsy and ignorant?' In other words, his basic distinction was between skilled and unskilled behaviour (although, in fact, these two concepts represent opposite ends of a continuum of skilled performance, with individuals being more or less skilled in relation to one another). In his investigations of the nature of skill, Welford identified the following three main characteristics.

- They consist of an organised, coordinated activity in relation to an object or a situation and, therefore, involve a whole chain of sensory, central, and motor mechanisms, which underlie performance.
- They are learnt, in that the understanding of the event or performance is built up gradually with repeated experience.
- They are serial in nature, involving the ordering and coordination of many different processes or actions in sequence. Thus, the skill of driving involves a pre-

set repertoire of behaviours, which must be carried out in temporal sequence (put gear into neutral, switch on ignition, and so on).

INTERPERSONAL SKILLS

Given the vast amount of attention devoted to the analysis and evaluation of motor skill performance, it is rather surprising that it was some considerable time before psychologists began to investigate seriously the nature of social skill.

In one sense, this is a term that is widely employed and generally comprehended, since it has already been used in this chapter and presumably understood by the reader. Indeed, the terms 'communication skill', 'social skill', and 'interpersonal skill' have entered the lexicon of everyday use. For example, many job advertisements stipulate that applicants should have high levels of social, or communication, skill. In this global sense, social skills can be defined as the skills employed when communicating at an interpersonal level with other people.

This definition is not very illuminating, however, since it describes what these skills are used for rather than what they are. It is rather like defining a bicycle as something that gets you from one place to another. As illustrated in the next section, attempts to provide a more technical, insightful definition of social skill are manifold.

DEFINITIONS OF INTERPERSONAL SKILL

In reviewing this field, it is concluded that a person was socially skilled according to 'The extent to which he or she can communicate with others, in a manner that fulfils one's rights, requirements, satisfactions, or obligations to a reasonable degree without damaging the other person's similar rights, satisfactions or obligations, and hopefully shares these rights, etc. with others in free and open exchange'.

This definition emphasized the microelements' of social encounters, in terms of reciprocation between participants, and focused upon the outcome of behaviour rather than the skills per se (although Phillips also noted that knowing how to behave in a range of situations was part of social skill). A similar approach was adopted by Combs and Slaby, who defined social skill as 'the ability to interact with others in a given social context in specific ways that are socially acceptable or valued and at the same time personally beneficial, mutually beneficial, or beneficial primarily to others'.

'To perform skillfully, the individual must be able to identify the emotions or intent expressed by the other person and make sophisticated judgments about the form and timing of the appropriate response.' Thus, the skilled individual needs to take cognisance of the others involved in the encounter. This involves perceptual acumen and perspective-taking ability, together with a capacity to mesh one's responses meaningfully, and at apposite moments, with those of others. An evaluation of these definitions reveals a remarkable similarity with the position relating to motor skill, in that there are common elements, but no uniform agreement about the exact nature of interpersonal skill.

One problem here is that any detailed study of higher-order skill will involve a long process. There is a well established '10-year rule' in relation to the learning of complex skill routines, in that the highest level of performance in any field is only attained after 10 years of concerted practice and training.

Top chess players, Olympic athletes, international soccer players, celebrated musicians, etc., will all have engaged in at least a decade of intensive practice. It is very probable that the 10-year rule also applies to complex social skills (negotiating, teaching, counselling, etc.). This makes analysis and synthesis problematic.While there has been study of how various types of motor skill performance change over time, there is a paucity of such research in relation to interpersonal skill. In the interpersonal domain, Spitzberg and Dillard concluded that 'what constitutes skill, even in well-defined contexts, is difficult to specify'.

Trying to define social skills in a sentence is like trying

to define some complex motor skill, such as being a good baseball player, in one sentence. There are many components to these skills.

Skilled performance is not a unitary activity. There is a large variety of different types of skill, some of which involve basic activities that are simple to execute, while others incorporate a range of intricate subelements, making them much more complicated to master.

It is hardly surprising therefore that differing definitions of what constitutes social skill have proliferated within the literature. Any definition must, of necessity, be a simplification of what is an intricate, multifarious, and multifaceted process.

This is not to say that definitions are without value: at the very least, they set parameters as to what should be included in the study of social skill and, therefore, act as a template for legitimate investigation in this field. Moreover, while definitions vary in emphasis, the defining features of skill can be charted. Thus, the six main elements as being central to the concept of social skills; namely, that they:

- Are learned
- Are composed of specific verbal and non-verbal behaviours
- Entail appropriate initiations and responses
- Maximise available rewards from others
- Require appropriate timing and control of specific behaviours
- Are influenced by prevailing contextual factors.

PROCESS

While behaviour is a key aspect of skill, it is in turn shaped by a range of other features. As such, motoric behaviour represents the overt part of an overall process in which the individual pursues goals, devises implementation plans and strategies, continually monitors the environment, considers the position of others involved in the encounter, responds appropriately in that situation, estimates the likelihood of goal success, and adjusts future behaviour accordingly (the operationalisation of these process elements of skilled performance will be discussed.

In this way, interaction is a transactional process in which each person's response is guided and shaped by the responses of others. In fact, a common analogy is made between interacting and dancing. Both are carried out for a wide variety of reasons, some of which overlap.

Thus, one may dance or interact to express oneself, to impress others, to help to develop a relationship, to pass the time, to seduce a partner, and so on. Interacting, like dancing a tango or waltz, depends on the coordinated intermeshing of learned repertoires between the two parties. Both are forms of performance wherein certain 'moves' are expected and anticipated, and the people involved complement one another in a fluid pattern of co-responding.

If one partner is unskilled, the encounter becomes much more difficult. One of the process dimensions to have attracted considerable attention within the interpersonal communication literature is the notion of competence. Indeed, Spitzberg and Cupach argued that 'Competence is an issue both perennial and fundamental to the study of communication.' Some theorists have conceptualised skill as being subsumed by competence.

For instance, Samter concluded that 'Social competence can thus be regarded as the manifestation of the various social skills a person possesses.' Likewise, Ridge defined competence as the ability 'to choose a strategy, then select among skills appropriate to that context and employ these skills', given that 'a strategy is a plan derived from a context that determines which skills to apply'.

Here, competence is regarded as the ability to choose appropriate strategies and implement these in terms of skilled performance. Spitzberg argued, 'Competence can be viewed as an evaluative judgment of the quality of a skill.' He also concluded that appropriateness (the extent to which behaviour meets standards of acceptability and legitimacy) and effectiveness (the degree to which desired outcomes are achieved) were the two main criteria used to guide such judgements. In a comprehensive review of this area, there are three qualities associated with competence.

- *Knowledge:* This relates to the information that is necessary for the person to be able to communicate in a way that is perceived to be competent (e.g. what one should say in this situation, how others might feel about this, what the alternative responses are).
- *Motivation*: This concerns the desire of the person to behave in ways that will be judged as competent.
- *Skill*: This refers to the individual's ability to act in such a way as to promote the perception of competence.

However, it is also possible to argue that skill subsumes competence. Thus, the Dictionary defines skill as 'aptitudes and competencies appropriate for a particular job'. In this way, skilled soccer players or skilled negotiators would be regarded as highly competent in many separate facets of the process in which they are engaged. Likewise, it makes sense to describe someone as 'competent but not highly skilled' at performing a particular action. Furthermore, the terms are often combined.

Thus, Daly asserted, 'Those who exhibit socially competent skills are preferred in interactions.' If all of this is confusing, it reflects the confusion that is rife in the deliberations of some theorists who grapple with this issue. For example, the distinction proffered by Sanders was that competence involves the acquisition of an apparently higher-order 'system of computation and reasoning' whereas skill is of a lower-order nature and concerned with having 'acquired a set of methods and techniques'.

But Sanders failed to explain how one could be skilled without being competent. Moreover, his definition of competence implies that it is an abstract ability. Thus, by Sanders' distinction, someone who could provide a fluent rationale (reasoning) as to how one should be, for example, a good soccer player or negotiator, yet who in practice is disastrous at playing soccer or negotiating, would be highly competent in these contexts, yet also highly unskilled.

GOAL-DIRECTED

Social interaction is now widely recognised as goal-directed activity. A defining feature of skilled performance is therefore intentionality. As expressed Communication skill refers to an individual's ability to achieve communicative goals. Skilled behaviours are selected by the individual to achieve a desired outcome, and as such are purposeful as opposed to chance or unintentional. The importance of goals has long been recognised.

An unskilled person may have ambitious goals, but without carefully related action plans nothing is likely to be achieved. It is illustrated that how, in turn, the execution of plans depends on a range of resources, such as money, access to relevant others, interpersonal skills, and cognitive ability.

Four main theories for explaining and predicting goal-directed intentions and behaviours have been proposed.

- The theory of reasoned action purports that behaviour is determined directly by one's intentions to carry it out, and these are influenced by one's attitudes positive or negative toward the behaviour and by perceived social pressure to perform it.
- The theory of planned behaviour extends this by adding the notion of perceived behavoural control as an important predictor of intention and action. Perceived behavoural control refers both to the presence of facilitating situational conditions and to feelings of self-efficacy (personal confidence in one's ability to execute the behaviour successfully).
- The theory of self-regulation emphasises the centrality of motivational commitment, or desire, to act (this aspect will be further discussed).
- Finally the theory of trying interprets goal-directed behaviour within three domains – trying and succeeding, trying but failing, and the process of striving per se. This theory emphasises the importance of personal attitudes to success and failure as predictors of intentions and actions, as well as attitudes to the process involved en route to the

goal. For example, one may decide not to try to lose weight because of a personal belief that one would fail anyway, or because the process of dieting and exercising is not viewed as desirable. The frequency and recency of past behaviour is also seen as important. Thus, one is likely to be less hesitant about asking a member of the opposite sex for a date if one has had lots of dates (frequency), the last of which was two days ago (recency), than if one has only ever dated three people and the last date was 10 years ago. Although the processes of goal setting, goal implementation, and goal abandonment are affected by a range of variables, in essence the decision to pursue particular goals seems to be determined by two overarching factors:

- Desirability (the attractiveness of goal attainment)
- Feasibility (the strength of belief that the goal can be achieved).

Another distinction has been made between learning goals and performance goals. Those who see themselves as pursuing learning goals (e.g. to learn how to be a better salesperson) view setbacks as opportunities for learning and future development.

On the other hand, those who are guided by performance goals (to sell 'x' number of products today) are more negatively affected by failure.

Learning goals therefore lead to better achievements than performance goals. In their comprehensive analysis of the nature, role, and functions of goals as regulators of human action, Locke and Latham demonstrated how goals both give incentive for action and act as guides to provide direction for behaviour. They reviewed studies to illustrate the following principles:

- People working toward a specific goal outperform those working with no explicit goal.
- Performance level increases with goal difficulty (providing the person is committed to the goal).

- Giving people specific goals produces better results than vague goals (such as 'do your best').

A distinction needs to be made between long-term and short-term goals. In order to achieve a long-term goal, a number of related short-term ones must be devised and executed. Our moment-by-moment behaviour is guided by the latter, since if these are not successfully implemented the long-term goal will not be achieved.

Sloboda used the term 'goal stacks' to refer to a hierarchy of goals through which one progresses until the top of the stack is reached. In this way, skilled behaviour is hierarchically organised with larger goal-related tasks comprising smaller component subunits.

For example, a long-term goal may be to appoint an appropriate person for a job vacancy. In order to do so, there is a range of subgoals which must be achieved – advertising the position, drawing up a short-list of candidates, interviewing each one, and so on. These subgoals can be further subdivided.

At the interview stage, the chief goal is to assess the suitability of the candidate, and this, in turn, involves subgoals such as welcoming the candidate, making introductions, and asking relevant questions.

In this way, the short-term, behavioural goals provide a route to the achievement of the long-term, strategic goal. Another aspect of skilled action is that goals are usually subconscious during performance. The skilled soccer player is not consciously aware of objectives when running with the ball, but these nevertheless govern behaviour. Those involved in the process of successful learning of new skills progress through the following four sequential stages:

- Unconscious incompetence. At this stage, we are blissfully unaware of the fact that we are acting in an unskilled way.
- Conscious incompetence. Here we know how we should be performing but also know that we are not able to produce the level of performance required.
- Conscious competence. At the early stage of skill

acquisition, we are aware of behaving in a skilled manner as we act.

- Unconscious competence. Once a skill has been fully assimilated, we successfully execute it without having to think about it.

INTERRELATED BEHAVIOUR

Social skills are defined in terms of identifiable units of behaviour, and actual performance is in many ways the acid test of effectiveness. In recognising the centrality of behaviour, Millar, Crute and Hargie pointed out: Judgements about skill are directly related to behavioural performance.

We do not judge soccer players on their ability to discuss the game or analyse their own performance, but rather we regard them as skilful or not based upon what they do on the field of play. Similarly, we make judgements about social skill based upon the behaviour of the individual during social encounters.

Therefore, a key aspect of skilled performance is the ability to implement a smooth, integrated, behavioural repertoire. In a sense, all that is ever really known about others during social interaction is how they actually behave.

All kinds of judgements (boring, humorous, warm, shy, and so on) are inferred about people from such behaviours. As mentioned earlier, skilled behaviour is hierarchical in nature, small elements such as changing gear or asking questions combining to form larger skill areas such as driving or interviewing, respectively.

This viewpoint has guided training in social skills, whereby the emphasis is upon encouraging the trainee to acquire separately smaller units of behaviour before integrating them to form the larger response elements – a technique that has long been employed in the learning of motor skills (this issue of skills training is further discussed. Socially skilled behaviours are interrelated in that they are synchronised and employed in order to achieve a common goal.

As this book illustrates, there is a wide range of differing behavioural routines, each of which can usefully be studied separately.

However, to be skilled, the individual must combine appropriate elements of these as required, so as to respond appropriately in a particular interaction. As noted by Stivers, 'Social interaction requires that many different practices and systems of practices be brought together.' This is similar to the tennis player who, to improve performance, focuses on separate aspects of the game (serve, volley, lob, backhand, etc.) during training, but, to be skilled, must combine these during actual matches.

In this sense, while our understanding is informed by a microanalysis of particular elements, for a fuller appreciation of skilled performance the complete picture must also be taken into consideration.

One example of this is that an analysis of aspects of the channels of verbal and non-verbal behaviour combined has been found to be more effective in accurately detecting whether or not someone is being deceptive than the scrutiny of either channel on its own.

Skilled performance has been likened to an orchestra. All of the instruments (behaviours) must be synchronised, and if any one is out of synch the entire performance is adversely affected. In this respect, Bellack highlighted how performance needs to be viewed as a whole when making judgements about skill, pointing out that in social presentation:

Skill therefore involves a coordinated meshing of behaviour, and 'is said to have been acquired when the behaviour is highly integrated'. The car driver needs simultaneously to operate the clutch, accelerator, gear lever, brakes, steering wheel, and light switches.

Similarly, someone wishing to provide reward to another concurrently uses head nods, eye contact, smiles, attentive facial expressions, and statements such as 'That's very interesting.' These latter behaviours are all interrelated in that they are indicative of the skill of rewardingness. Conversely, if someone does not look at us, yawns, uses no head nods, and yet says, 'That's very interesting', these behaviours are contradictory rather than complementary, and the person would not be using the skill of rewardingness effectively.

An individual who adopted such a pattern of mixed response over a prolonged period would be judged to be low in interpersonal skills. People who always act in a socially incompetent fashion are deemed to be unskilled regardless of the depth of theoretical knowledge they may possess about interpersonal behaviour. In skill, it is performance that counts. Noel Coward, recognising his own performance deficit, once said that he could not sing although he knew how to.

An important criterion for judging skill is accuracy. Highly skilled individuals make fewer performance errors than those less skilled. Just as a highly skilled golfer misses fewer putts than one less skilled, so, too, a skilled orator makes fewer speech dysfluencies than a less skilled public speaker. The errors are divided into:

- Errors of omission. Here an action that should have been executed is omitted. For example, a driver forgets to put the gear in neutral before switching on the engine, or a salesperson fails to get the client's commitment to buy before attempting to close a sale.
- Errors of commission. In this instance, the person carries out a behaviour that detracts from performance. For example, a learner driver releases the clutch too quickly and the car engine stalls, or an individual discloses too much deeply negative personal information on a first date and the other person terminates the encounter.

This behavioural aspect of the skills definition has been misunderstood by some theorists. For example, Sanders presented a critique of the skills approach from his background as a 'language and social interaction' scholar. In a misinterpretation of the skills perspective, Sanders made the rather absurd deduction that 'all speakers of a language are equally able to produce grammatical sentences, and thus must be equally skilled'.

Unfortunately, he does not explain how precisely he reached this conclusion, as it is the exact opposite of what is being proposed in the skills perspective. It is completely illogical to make the leap from individuals being able to produce grammatical sentences to being equally skilled, and no skills analyst would make such an error.

While behaviour (both verbal and non-verbal – although the latter domain is almost entirely ignored by Sanders) is recognised as being important, it is how this behaviour is contextually employed that determines the extent to which it is deemed to be skilful.

SITUATIONALLY APPROPRIATE

The importance of contextual awareness for the effective operation of motor skill has long been recognised. In his analysis of motor skill, Welford pointed out that 'skills represent particular ways of using capacities in relation to environmental demands, with human beings and external situation together forming a functional "system" '. There is firm evidence that certain behaviours are situationally determined.

For example, Hargie, Morrow and Woodman carried out a study of effective communication skills in community pharmacy, in which they videotaped 350 pharmacist–patient consultations. They found that skills commonly employed when dealing with over-the-counter items were not utilised by the pharmacist when handling prescription-related consultations.

For instance, the skill of suggesting/advising, which was defined as the offer of personal/professional opinion as to a particular course of action while simultaneously allowing the final decision to lie with the patient, fell into this category. When dealing with prescription items, suggestions or advice were not given, probably because these patients had already been advised by their doctor and the pharmacist did not wish to interfere.

Individuals skilled in one context may not be skilled in another. For example, an excellent midfielder in soccer may be a terrible goalkeeper. Likewise, experienced teachers have been shown to have difficulties in becoming skilled school counsellors. In essence, the more similarity there is between the demand characteristics of situations, the higher the probability that skills will transfer.

Thus, a professional tennis player is usually good at other racquet sports. In the same way, a successful car salesperson is likely to be effective in other related selling contexts. One similarity between motor and social skill is that they are both sequential in nature. Thus, the skill of driving involves a pre-set sequence of behaviours that must be carried out in the correct order.

In social interaction, there are also stages that tend to be followed sequentially. Checking into a hotel usually involves interacting in a set way with the receptionist, being shown to one's room and giving a tip to the porter who delivers one's cases.

Likewise, going to the doctor, the dentist, or church involves sequences of behaviour that are expected and which are more or less formalised, depending upon the setting. In the case of the doctor's surgery, the sequence would be:

- Patient enters the surgery.
- Doctor makes a greeting.
- Patient responds and sits down.
- Doctor seeks information about the patient's health.
- Patient responds and gives information.
- Doctor makes a diagnosis.
- Doctor prescribes and explains treatment.
- Doctor makes closing comments.
- Patient responds, stands up, and leaves the surgery.

This sequence is expected by the patient, who would be most unhappy if the doctor moved straight from (1) to (7) without going through the intervening steps. It can be disconcerting and embarrassing if one is in a situation where the sequence is not as expected or has not been learned (for example, attending a church service of a different religious denomination).

In such situations, however, we usually cope and, unlike the sequence of behaviours in, for example, driving a car, these behaviours are expected rather than essential. It is only in certain rituals or ceremonies that a pre-set sequence is essential (for example, weddings in church) and responses are demanded in a fixed temporal order.

Interpersonal skills are more fluid and individualised than most motor skills. Different people employ varying combinations of behaviours, often with equal success, in social contexts. This process, whereby the same goal can be achieved through the implementation of differing strategies, is referred to as equifinality. These strategies, in turn, have alternative yet equally effective behavioural approaches. While there are common stages in social episodes (e.g. opening, discussion, closing), the behaviours used within each stage vary from one person to another.

However, 'knowing' the social situation is clearly an important aspect of social skill, in order to relate behaviours successfully to the context in which they are employed. Further aspects of the situational context will be explored in Chapter 2.

LEARNING

The fifth aspect of the definition is that skills comprise behaviours that can be learned. Some theorists purport that not all skilled behaviour is learned. For example, Sanders argued, 'There are species of behaviour for which persons can produce desired results "naturally" because the skills are acquired in the course of bodily or mental development.'

As an example, he cites 'speaking and understanding one's native language'. However, most skills analysts would find the view that language just occurs 'naturally' (whatever that means) to be a rather unusual perspective. Does it mean, for example, that children reared in isolation acquire their 'native' language 'naturally'?

Of course, the answer is no, they do not. While most humans are hard-wired to learn language (an exception being those suffering from cognitive impairments), all social behaviour (including non-verbal as well as verbal) still has to be learned. We know that if children are reared in isolation they do not develop 'normal' interactive repertoires and certainly will not acquire their 'native' language. In addition, it has been shown that the interactive skills of parents are key components in the development of social competence in children.

Thus, mothers who encourage their children to talk, and make elaborations on the child's responses, produce enhanced language development in the child. Indeed, there is evidence that the degree of deprivation of appropriate learning experiences from other people differentially affects the social behaviour of individuals. In this way, children from socially deprived home backgrounds are more likely to develop less appropriate social behaviours, whereas children from culturally richer home environments tend to be more socially adept.

The social learning theory posited that all repertoires of behaviour, with the exception of elementary reflexes (eye blinks, coughing, etc.), are learned. This social learning process involves the modelling and imitation of significant others, such as parents, peers, media stars, siblings, and teachers.

The individual observes how others behave and then follows a similar behavioural routine. By this process, from an early age, children may walk, talk, and act like their same-sex parent.

At a later stage, however, they may begin to copy and adopt the behaviour of people whom they see as being more significant in their lives by, for example, following the dress and accents of peers regardless of those of parents. A second major element in social learning theory is the reinforcement of behaviour. As a general rule, people tend to employ more frequently responses that are positively reinforced or rewarded, and to display less often those that are punished or ignored.

This is not to say that there are not innate differences in individual potential, since some people may be more talented than others in specific areas. While most behaviours are learned, it is also true that people have different aptitudes for certain types of performance.

Thus, although it is necessary to learn how to play musical instruments or how to paint, some may have a better 'ear' for music or 'eye' for art and so will excel in these fields. Likewise, certain individuals have a 'flair' for social interchange and find interpersonal skills easier to learn and perfect. However, as discussed earlier, practice is also essential for improvement. Comparisons of highly skilled people with those less skilled, across a wide variety of contexts, show that the former engage in significantly more practice.

COGNITIVE CONTROL

The final element of social skill is the degree of cognitive control that the individual has over behaviour. Thus, a socially inadequate person may have learned the basic behavioural elements of interpersonal skill but may not have developed the appropriate thought processes necessary to control their utilisation.

If skill is to have its desired effect, timing is a crucial consideration. Behaviour is said to be skilled only if it is employed at the opportune moment. For example, smiling and saying 'How funny' when someone is relating details of a personal bereavement would certainly not be a socially skilled response. Indeed, saying the right thing at the wrong time is a characteristic of some social inadequates.

Learning when to employ socially skilled behaviours is every bit as important as learning what these behaviours are, where to use them, and how to evaluate them. In his discussion of the notion of interpersonal competence, Parks highlighted the importance of hierarchical control theory, which conceives of personal action as a process controlled by nine linked and hierarchical levels. From lower to higher, these levels are as follows.

- *Intensity Control:* This is the level just inside the skin involving sensory receptors, muscle movements, and spinal responses. Damage at this basic level has serious consequences for communication. For example, impairments to vision, hearing or to the vocal chords can dramatically impede interpersonal ability.
- *Sensation Control:* Here, the sensory nuclei collected at level 1 are collated and organised into meaningful

packages. The ability to portray a certain facial expression would be dependent upon activity at this level.

- *Configuration Control:* The basic packages developed at level 2 are in turn further organised into larger configurations, which then control movements of the limbs, perception of visual forms, and speech patterns. The ability to decode verbal and non-verbal cues occurs at this level.
- *Transition Control:* This level further directs the more basic configurations into fine-grained responses, such as changing the tone of voice, pronouncing a word, or using head nods at appropriate moments. Transition control also allows us to recognise the meaning of such behaviour in others.
- *Sequence Control:* At this level, we control the sequence, flow, intensity, and content of our communications. The ability to synchronise and relate our responses appropriately to those with whom we are interacting, and to the situational context, is handled at this level. Thus, judgements of the extent to which someone is socially skilled can begin to be made at the sequence control level.
- *Relationship Control:* Here the individual judges and makes decisions about larger sets of relationships (cause–effect, chronological, etc.), so that appropriate strategies can be implemented to attain higher-order goals. For example, the ability to encode and decode deceptive messages is controlled at this level. Likewise, longer-term tactics for wooing a partner, negotiating a successful business deal, or securing promotion at work all involve relational control.
- *Programme Control:* At this level, programmes are developed to predict, direct, and interpret communication in a variety of contexts. Skill acquisition involves a process of knowledge compilation. Two types of knowledge are important here:

- Knowing what is important in social encounters. This type of content or declarative knowledge includes an awareness of the rules of social encounters, the behaviour associated with the roles that people play, and so on. In the early stages of skill learning, this knowledge predominates.
- Knowing how to perform in a skilled fashion. When the individual becomes skilled, declarative knowledge is 'compiled' into procedural knowledge. Here, the person has developed a large repertoire of procedures directly related to the implementation of interpersonal skills.

There has been increasing interest in the role of 'mental representations' in social behaviour. Highly skilled people have a huge store of such representations relating to a wide range of situations.

These representations, or conceptual schemas, allow existing circumstances to be compared with previous knowledge and experience, and so facilitate the process of decision making. For the development of skill, 'knowledge must be acquired in such a way that it is highly connected and articulated, so that inference and reasoning are enabled as is access to procedural action.

The resulting organization of knowledge provides a schema for thinking and cognitive activity'. A schema is a cognitive structure that is developed after repeated exposure to the same situation. It provides the person with a store of knowledge and information about how to behave in a particular context. Schemas contain learned 'scripts' that are readily available for enactment as required. By adulthood, we have developed thousands of schemas to deal with a wide variety of people across a range of situations, such as checking-in at an airport, shopping at the supermarket, or giving directions to a stranger on the street.

New situations can be difficult to navigate, since we have not developed relevant schemas to enable us to operate smoothly and effectively therein. In any profession, learning the relevant schemas and scripts is an important part of professional development. In their analysis of skill acquisition, it was demonstrated how as skill is acquired cognitive demands are reduced (the person no longer has to think so much about how to handle the situation), and this in turn frees up cognitive resources for other activities.

An experienced teacher has a number of classroom-specific schemas, such as 'class getting bored' and 'noise level too high', each with accompanying action plans – 'introduce a new activity' or 'call for order'. These schemas are used both to evaluate situations and to enable appropriate and immediate responses to be made.

Experienced teachers build up a large store of such schemas, and so are able to cope more successfully than novices. The same is true in other professions. Veteran doctors, nurses, social workers, and salespeople develop a range of work-specific schemas to enable them to respond quickly and confidently in the professional context.

This ability to respond rapidly and appropriately is, in turn, a feature of skilled performance. In fact, speed of response is a notable aspect of skilled interaction. Thus, in free-flowing interpersonal encounters, less than 200 milliseconds typically elapses between the responses of speakers. This flexibility to change plans, so as to adapt to the needs of the situation, is another feature of skill.

- *Principle Control:* Programmes must be related directly to our guiding principles or goals, and these, in turn, control their implementation. In this sense, we have to create programmes that are compatible with our goals. However, as Parks pointed out, 'unsuccessful behaviour often occurs because individuals lack the necessary programming to actualize their principles'. This is particularly true when one is confronted by unexpected events, for which programmes have not been fully developed.
- *System concept control:* At the very top of this hierarchy is our system of idealised self-concepts. These drive and control our principles, which in turn

determine programmes, and so on. Someone whose idealised self-concept included being a 'trustworthy person' would then develop principles such as 'always tell the truth' and 'fulfil one's obligations'. Further down the hierarchy, at the programme-control level, schemas would be formulated to enable these principles to be operationalised across various contexts.

SOCIAL SKILLS AND MOTOR SKILLS

From the above analysis, it is obvious that there are similarities and differences between social and motor skills. The parallels between the two sets of skill are not perfect. However, the analogy between motor and social performance has stimulated considerable debate, and there certainly are considerable areas of overlap. The main similarities are that both sets of skill:

- Are goal-directed and intentional
- Involve high levels of cognitive control
- Encompass behaviour that is synchronised and situation-specific
- Are learned and improved through practice and feedback.

Rapidity is a feature of all skilled action. An ability to respond rapidly means that skilled individuals appear to have more time to perform their actions and as a result their behaviour seems less rushed. The skilled person can 'sum up' situations and respond swiftly, so that performance becomes smoother and more fluid. In one study of chess players, Chase and Simon showed novices and grandmasters chessboards on which were placed pieces from the middle of an actual game. After viewing the board for 5 seconds, they were asked to reconstruct the game on a blank board.

On average, novices correctly replaced 4 out of 20, whereas masters replaced 18 out of 20, pieces. Interestingly, in a second part of this study when the subjects were shown a board on which the pieces were placed in a way that could not have resulted from an actual chess game, masters performed no better than novices. Thus, rapidity was related to actual chess playing. Socially skilled individuals develop a similar ability in relation to specific contexts – for example, interviewers will know how to deal with a vast array of interviewee responses. Again, this is context-related, so that an experienced detective may be highly skilled during an interrogative interview but less skilled in a counseling interview. Automaticity refers to the fact that skilled actions are performed 'without thinking'. We do not think about how to walk or how to talk – we just do it. Yet, in infancy, both skills took considerable time and effort to acquire, and in cases of brain injury in adulthood both may have to be relearned.

Chapter 2

Operational Communicative Performance Model

It examines the central processes involved in the implementation of skilled behaviour, and evaluates the extent to which a motor skill model of performance can be operationalised in the study of interpersonal communication. A model of interaction, based upon the skills paradigm, is presented. This model is designed to account for those features of performance that are peculiar to social encounters.

MOTOR SKILL MODEL

Several models of motor skill, all having central areas in common, have been put forward by different theorists. An early example of this type of model was the one presented by Welford, in the shape of a block diagram representing the operation of perceptual motor skills, in which the need for the coordination of a number of processes in the performance of skilled behaviour is highlighted. It represents the individual as receiving information about the outside world via the sense organs (eyes, ears, nose, hands, etc.).

A range of such perceptions is received, and this incoming information is held in the short-term memory store until sufficient data have been obtained to enable a decision to be made about an appropriate response. As explained by action assembly theory, responses are gradually assembled by the individual, taking into account information stored in long-term memory, in terms of previous responses, outcomes associated with these responses, and impinging situational factors. After all of this data has been sifted, a response is made by the effector system (hands, feet, voice, and so on). In turn, the outcome of this response is monitored by the sense organs and perceived by the individual, thereby providing feedback that can be used to adjust future responses.

To take a practical example, let us consider a golfer on the green about to make a putt. Here, the golfer observes (perception) the position of the ball in relation to the hole, the lie of the land between ball and hole, and the prevailing weather conditions.

All of this information is held in short-term memory store and compared with data from the long-term memory store regarding previous experience of similar putts in the past. As a result, decisions are made about which putter to use and exactly how the ball should be struck (translation from perception to action: choice of response). The putt is then carefully prepared for as the golfer positions hands, body, and feet (control of response). The putt is then executed (effectors), and the outcome monitored (sense organs) to guide future decisions. Argyle applied this model to the analysis of social skill.

The model was a slightly modified version of in which the flow diagram was simplified by: removing the memory store blocks; combining sense organs and perception, control of responses, and effectors; and adding the elements of motivation and goal. An example of how this model can be applied to the analysis of motor performance is as follows. Someone is sitting in a room in which the temperature has become too warm (motivation), and therefore wants to cool down (goal).

This can be achieved by devising a range of alternative plans of action (translation), such as opening a window, removing some clothing, or adjusting the heating system. Eventually, one of these plans is carried out: a window is opened (motor response), and the situation is monitored. Cool air then enters the room, making the temperature more pleasant (changes in outside world).

This change in temperature is available as feedback that

can be perceived by the individual, to enable goal achievement to be evaluated. A simple example of the application of this motor skill model to a social context would be a woman meeting a man whom she finds very attractive (motivation), and wanting to find out his name (goal). To do so, various plans of action are translated (e.g. ask directly, give own name and pause, ask someone to effect an introduction).

One of these is then carried out, such as the direct request: 'What's your name?' (response). This will result in some response from the other person: 'Norris' (changes in the outside world). His response is available as feedback, which she hears while also observing his non-verbal reactions to her (perception).

She can then move on to the next goal (e.g. follow-up response, or terminate discussion). At first sight, then, it would appear that this motor skill model can be applied directly to the analysis of social skill. However, there are several differences between these two sets of skills, which are not really catered for in the basic motor skill model.

In fact, many of these differences were recognised by Argyle in the first edition of The Psychology of Interpersonal Behaviour when he attempted to extend the basic model to take account of the responses of the other person in the social situation, and of the different types of feedback that accrue in interpersonal encounters. However, this extension did not really succeed and was dropped by Argyle in later editions. Subsequently, few attempts were made to expand the basic model to account for the interactive nature of social encounters.

GOALS AND MOTIVATION

As discussed, a key feature of skilled performance is its goal-directed, intentional nature. The starting point in this model of social interaction is therefore the goal being pursued, and the related motivation to achieve it. The link between needs, motivation, and goal is also recognised. As pointed out by Slater, 'The presence of various goals or motivations changes the nature of affect and cognitions generated, and of subsequent behaviors.' In essence, goals shape behaviour, while motivation determines the degree of commitment to pursue a particular goal.

Carlson described motivation as 'a driving force that moves us to a particular action. Motivation can affect the nature of an organism's behaviour, the strength of its behaviour, and the persistence of its behaviour.' The motivation that an individual has to pursue a particular goal is, in turn, influenced by needs.

There are many needs that must be met in order to enable the individual to live life to the fullest. Different psychologists have posited various categorisations, but the best known hierarchy of human needs remains the one put forward by Maslow as shown. At the bottom of this hierarchy, and therefore most important, are those physiological needs essential for the survival of the individual, including the need for water, food, heat, and so on.

Once these have been met, the next most important needs are those connected with the safety and security of the individual, including protection from physical harm and freedom from fear.

These are met in society by various methods, such as the establishment of police forces, putting security chains on doors, or purchasing insurance policies. At the next level are belonging and love needs, such as the desire for a mate, wanting to be accepted by others, and striving to avoid loneliness or rejection.

Getting married, having a family, or joining a club, society, or some form of group, are all means whereby these needs are satisfied. Esteem needs are met in a number of ways: for instance, occupational status, achievement in sports, or success in some other sphere. At a higher level is the need for self-actualisation, by fulfilling one's true potential. People seek new challenges, feeling the need to be 'stretched' and to develop themselves fully. Thus, someone may give up secure salaried employment in order to study at college or set up in business.

The goals are determined in three main ways, in that they can be:

- Assigned. Goals may be decided for us by others (e.g. parents, teachers, managers), who tell us what goals we should (and should not) pursue.
- Self-set. Here, goals are freely chosen by the individual.
- Participative. In this case, goals are openly agreed in interaction with others.

Goal conflict may occur where goals being pursued by both sides do not concur, or where there is internal inconsistency in goals. Informing a good friend of an annoying habit, while maintaining the same level of friendship, would be one example of the latter. Encounters such as this obviously require skill and tact. Yet we know little about how to ensure success in such situations. We have goals and those with whom we interact also have goals, and these may not concur. However, for relationships to develop, ways must be found of successfully negotiating mutual goal achievement. Despite a great deal of interest in the subject of goal-directed action, relatively little work has been carried out to investigate the process whereby communicators negotiate intentions. What is clear is that goals, needs, and our motivation to satisfy these, all play a vital role in skilled performance. Once appropriate goals have been decided upon, they have an important bearing on our perceptions, behaviour, and the intervening mediating factors.

MEDIATING FACTORS

The term 'mediating factors' refers to those internal states, activities, or processes within the individual that mediate between the feedback perceived, the goal being pursued, and the responses that are made. What has been termed the 'mediated mind' is therefore an important feature of interpersonal communication. Mediating factors influence the way in which people and events are perceived, and determine the capacity of the individual to assimilate, process, and respond to the social information received during interpersonal encounters. It is at this stage that the person makes decisions about appropriate courses of action for goal achievement.

This is part of the process of feedforward, whereby the individual estimates the likely outcome of particular responses in any given context. There are two core mediating factors, cognition and emotion.

COGNITION

As discussed, cognition plays a very important role in skilled communication, in terms of control of responses. This is because 'it is in the mind that intentions are formulated, potential courses of action considered, and efferent commands generated. Cognition has been defined as 'all the processes by which the sensory input is transformed, reduced, elaborated, stored, recovered and used'. This definition emphasises the following aspects:

- Cognition involves transforming, or decoding and making use of the sensory information received.
- To do so, it is often necessary to reduce the amount of information attended to, in order to avoid overloading the system.
- Conversely, at times, we have to elaborate upon minimal information by making interpretations, judgements, or evaluations.
- Information is stored either in short-term or long-term memory. While there is debate about the exact nature and operation of memory, there is considerable evidence to support the existence of these two systems. Short-term memory has a limited capacity for storage, allowing for the retention of information over a brief interval of time (no more than a few minutes), while long-term memory has an enormous capacity for storage of data that can be retained over many years. Thus, information stored in short-term memory is quickly lost unless it is transferred to the long-term memory store. For instance, we can usually still remember the name of

our first teacher at primary school, yet a few minutes after being introduced to someone for the first time we may have forgotten the name. The process of context-dependent coding is important. Remembering occurs by recalling the context of the original event. When we meet someone we recognise but cannot place, we try to think where or when we met that person before – in other words, we try to put the individual in a particular context. A similar process occurs in social situations, whereby we evaluate people and situations in terms of our experience of previous similar encounters. Short-term memory is important in skilled performance in terms of listening and retaining information about the responses of others so as to respond appropriately.

- Information that is stored is recovered or retrieved to facilitate the process of decision making and problem solving. As expressed, 'Prior to addressing a communication goal, speakers retrieve from long-term memory knowledge about how that goal has been addressed in the past.' While some thoughts are purposeful and goal-oriented, other cognitive activity may be disordered, less controlled, and more automatic, or involuntary, in nature. The extent to which these erratic thoughts determine the main direction of mental activity varies from one person to another, but is highest in certain pathological states, such as schizophrenia, where a large number of unrelated thoughts may 'flood through' the mind. Socially skilled individuals have greater control over cognitive processes and use these to facilitate social interaction. Snyder demonstrated how those high in social skill have a capacity for monitoring and regulating their own behaviour in relation to the responses of others – a system he termed self-monitoring. This process of regulation necessitates an awareness of the ability level of the person with whom one is interacting and of the 'way they think', since, as Wessler pointed out, 'In order to interact successfully and repeatedly with the same persons, one must have the capacity to form cognitive conceptions of the others' cognitive conceptions.' Such metacognition is very important in forming judgements about the reasons for behaviour. However, as with many of the processes in skilled performance, there is an optimum level of metacognition, since, if overdone 'all of this thinking about thinking could become so cumbersome that it actually interferes with communication'. In other words, it is possible to 'think oneself out of' actions. However, highly skilled individuals have the ability to 'size up' people and situations rapidly, and respond in an appropriate fashion. Such ability is dependent upon the capacity to process cognitively the information received during social interaction.

EMOTION

The importance of mood and emotional state in the communication process and the part they play in shaping our relationships with others has been clearly demonstrated. The effective control of emotion is a central aspect of socially skilled performance. For this reason, measures of the emotional domain figure prominently in interpersonal skill inventories. Skilled individuals are adept both at encoding their own emotions, and at accurately decoding and responding appropriately to the emotional state of others. Being responsive to the emotional needs of others is a key aspect of effective relational communication. Indeed, one of the characteristics of dysfunctions of personality, such as psychopathy, is emotional malfunction.

RESPONSES

Once a goal and related action plan have been formulated, the next step in the sequence of skilled performance is to implement this plan in terms of social responses. It is the function of the response system (voice, hands, face, etc.) to carry out the plan in terms of overt behaviours, and it is at this stage that skill becomes manifest. Social behaviour can be categorised as shown.

Thus, an initial distinction is made between linguistic and non-linguistic behaviour. Linguistic behaviour refers to all aspects of speech, including the actual verbal content (the words used), and the paralinguistic message associated with it. Paralanguage refers to the way in which something is said (pitch, tone, speed, volume of voice, accent, pauses, speech dysfluencies, etc.).

Non-linguistic behaviour involves all of our bodily communication and is concerned with the study of what we do rather than what we say. While there are many approaches to the analysis of non-verbal behaviour, this domain encompasses the following three main categories.

- Tacesics is the study of bodily contact – in other words, with what parts of the body we touch one another, how often, with what intensity, in which contexts, and to what effect.
- Proxemics is the analysis of the spatial features of social presentation – that is, the social distances we adopt in different settings, how we mark and protect
- Kinesics is the systematic study of body motion – the meanings associated with movements of the hands, head, and legs, the postures we adopt, and our gaze and facial expressions.

One important element of individual behaviour is the concept of style, defined by Norton as 'the relatively enduring pattern of human interaction associated with the individual', involving 'an accumulation of "microbehaviors"... that add up to a "macrojudgment" about a person's style of communicating'. Norton identified the following nine main communicative styles, each of which can be interpreted as a continuum:

- *Dominant/submissive*: Dominant people like to control social interactions, give orders, and be the centre of attention; they use behaviours such as loud volume of voice, interruptions, prolonged eye contact, and fewer pauses to achieve dominance. At the opposite end of this continuum, submissive people prefer to keep quiet, stay out of the limelight, and take orders.

- *Dramatic/reserved*: Exaggeration, storytelling, and non-verbal communication are techniques used by dramatic individuals who tend to overstate their messages. At the other end of the continuum is the reserved type of person, who is quieter, modest, and prone to understatement.
- *Contentious/affiliative*: The contentious person is argumentative, provocative, or contrary, as opposed to the agreeable, peace-loving, affiliative individual.
- *Animated/inexpressive*: An animated style involves making use of hands, arms, eyes, facial expressions, posture, and overall body movement to gain attention or convey enthusiasm. The converse here is the dull, slow-moving, inexpressive person.
- *Relaxed/frenetic*: This continuum ranges from people who do not get overexcited, always seem in control, and are never flustered, to those who are tense, quickly lose self-control, get excited easily, and behave frenetically.
- *Attentive/inattentive*: Attentive individuals listen carefully to others and display overt signs of listening such as eye contact, appropriate facial expression, and posture. Inattentive individuals, on the other hand, are poor listeners who do not make any attempt to express interest in what others are saying.
- *Impression-leaving/insignificant*: The impression-leaving style is characterized by flamboyant individuals who display a visible or memorable style of communicating and leave an impression on those whom they meet. They are people who, for example, wear loud clothes, have unusual hairstyles, or exhibit a controversial interactive manner. The opposite of this is the insignificant individual who 'fades into the fabric' of buildings, is non-controversial, and dresses conservatively.

- *Open/closed*: Open people talk about themselves freely, and are approachable, unreserved, candid, and conversational. At the opposite end of this continuum are very closed individuals who disclose no personal information, are guarded, secretive, and loath to express opinions, and 'keep themselves to themselves'.
- *Friendly/hostile*: This style continuum ranges from the friendly person who smiles frequently, and is happy, very rewarding, and generally non-competitive, to the hostile person who is overtly aggressive, highly competitive, and very unrewarding.

Most people can be evaluated overall in terms of these continua, although style of communication can also be affected by situations. A dominant teacher in the classroom may be submissive during staff meetings, while a normally friendly individual may become hostile when engaging in team sports. Nevertheless, there are elements of style that endure across situations, and these have a bearing on a number of facets of the individual. For example, someone who tends to be dominant, frenetic, inattentive, or hostile will probably not make a good counsellor. Similarly, a very dominant person is unlikely to marry someone equally dominant.

As discussed, behaviour is the acid test of skill. If someone always fails miserably at actual negotiation we would not call that person a skilled negotiator. For this reason, much of this text is devoted to an analysis of a wide array of responses in terms of skills, styles, and strategies. However, in order to respond appropriately, it is also necessary to be aware of available feedback during communication.

PERSONALITY

The concept of personality and the role it plays in determining behaviour has long occupied the minds of social scientists. While recognising that there are many differing perspectives on personality, and hence varying definitions, as defined it as 'those characteristics of the person that account for consistent patterns of feeling, thinking and behaving'. One common unit of analysis in the study of personality has been that of traits. It is argued by trait theorists that whether we are cooperative or competitive, extraverted or introverted, dominant or submissive, dependent or independent, and so on, influences both how we interpret and how we respond to situations.

Although many inventories have been developed to measure a plethora of such characteristics, there is considerable debate regarding the exact number of traits, or factors, which can reliably be charted. Most agree on the validity of what have been termed the 'big five' traits of extraversion, neuroticism (or anxiety), tough-mindedness, conscientiousness, and open-mindedness.

Traits can be viewed as representing naturally occurring goal tensions within individuals. For example, extraversion–introversion represents the tension between wanting to meet and socialise with others, on the one hand, and the desire to have peace and quiet and be alone, on the other hand. It would seem that while traits are not universally reliable in predicting behaviour, they are most useful in predicting individual responses across similar situations.

However, there is no clear agreement about the exact determinants of personality. Although a combination of hereditary and prenatal factors is contributory, experiences in infancy and early childhood seem to play a vital shaping role.

Furthermore, while personality is relatively stable, it can and does change as a result of experiences throughout the lifespan. There is also some evidence that differences in personality may differentially affect skill acquisition, though research in this field is at a very early stage. In addition, skills need to be adapted to meet the specific requirements of different types of people.

GENDER

During social interaction, we tend to respond differently to, and have differing expectations of, others depending upon whether they are male or female. All cultures recognize male/female as a fundamental divide and accord different sets of characteristics and behavioural expectations according to which side of the divide an individual is on. The first question asked after the birth of a baby is usually whether it is a girl or a boy.

Sexual differences are then perpetuated by the ways in which infants are dressed and responded to by adults. Not surprisingly, therefore, by the age of 2 years, children can readily distinguish males from females on the basis of purely cultural cues such as hairstyle and clothing. Gender stereotypes proliferate in child rearing, with children being reminded of gender role expectations in phrases such as 'big boys don't cry' or 'that's not very lady-like'. Such practices inevitably contribute to later differences in behaviour and expectations thereof.

However, the extent to which gender-specific patterns of behaviour are innate or learned remains unclear. For example, 'social constructionist' theorists view gender as being constructed through everyday discourse and relational communication.

However, this perspective, which purports that masculinity and femininity exist only in relation to one another, is rejected by evolutionary theorists. The latter argue that gender variations in behaviour can be understood from an evolutionary perspective, as these arise from biological differences. Each side cites evidence to substantiate its claims. It seems likely, however, that both nature and nurture play a part in shaping gender response patterns, although the precise manner in which this occurs remains a matter of considerable debate.

Differences have been reported in studies of non-verbal behaviour, some of the trends being that women tend to require less interpersonal space, touch and are touched more, gesture less, look and are looked at more, and smile more frequently, than males. In addition, social skills inventories have revealed consistent gender differences on various dimensions, females scoring higher on measures of emotional expressivity and sensitivity. Likewise, gender variations have been reported in several aspects of language. The male-preferred style involves being more directive, self-opinionated, and explicit, whereas females tend to be more indirect, use a greater number of 'hedges' and expressed uncertainties ('kind of', 'it could be'), speak for longer periods, and refer more to emotions.

However, Jones highlighted the fact that there are many inconsistencies in the findings of studies into gender differences, concluding that gender is something that we 'do' rather than something that we 'are'.

In other words, some females choose to behave in what is regarded within their particular culture as a feminine style. This is probably because males or females who deviate markedly from their expected sex role behaviour are likely to encounter problems during social interaction. In this sense, the study of gender needs to take account of not only biological features but also psychological make-up. As a personality factor, gender can be divided into the following four categories:

- High femininity
- Low femininity
- High masculinity
  - Androgynous
  - Masculine
- Low masculinity
  - Feminine
  - Indeterminate

In this way, for instance, a feminine female is likely, in various situations, to behave differently from a masculine female. Research bearing such psychological gender characteristics in mind is likely to be more fruitful in charting actual behavioural variants of performance.

AGE

There has been increasing research into the field of social gerontology. One reason for this is that 'social aging – how we behave, as social actors, towards others, and even how we align ourselves with or come to understand the signs of difference or change as we age – are phenomena achieved primarily through communication experiences'.

Likewise, communication processes are directly affected by maturational phenomena at each stage of our lives. It is also clear that our own age, and the age of those with whom we interact, shape our behaviour and expectations. Skilled individuals therefore take the age of the target (and of course their own age) into consideration when framing their responses. For example, different forms of reward are appropriate for 3-year-olds, 12-year-olds, and 25-year-olds; statements such as 'You're a clever little person'.

Reaction time, speech discrimination, and the capacity for information processing tend to decrease with age. However, there are wide differences across individuals, with some more adversely affected than others. Furthermore, older people have accumulated a larger vocabulary, coupled with a wealth of experience of handling a wide variety of types of people across varying situations. Thus, there can be advantages and disadvantages in terms of the effects of age upon skilled performance. There has been considerable research into patterns of intergenerational communication.

APPEARANCE

The physical appearance of others, in terms of body size, shape, and attractiveness, also affects our behaviour and expectations. People are judged upon their appearance from a very early age, so that nursery school children have been shown to exhibit an aversion to chubby individuals and a greater liking for physically attractive peers. Attractiveness is a very important feature in social encounters. A range of research studies has shown that being rated as attractive has positive benefits.

These include being seen as more popular, intelligent, friendly, and interesting to talk to; receiving higher grades in school; dating more frequently; securing employment more readily; earning more; and being less likely to be found guilty in court.

While they are also seen as more vain, materialistic, and likely to have extramarital affairs, it remains the case that 'on the whole, we seem to equate beauty with goodness'. Ratings of physical attractiveness are fairly consistent across variations in age, gender, socio-economic status, and geographical location. Aronson argued that cross-cultural agreement about ratings of attractiveness has been influenced by popular culture.

It is not surprising therefore that research has shown cross-cultural agreement that attractive facial features in young women include large eyes relative to size of face, high cheek bones, and thin jaw, as well as short distance between nose and mouth and between mouth and chin. The male physique rated as attractive by females includes being tall and slim, with medium-thin lower trunk and medium-wide upper trunk, small buttocks, thin legs, and a flat stomach.

However, research and theory into the study of attraction have also emphasized how initial judgments of attractiveness can be tempered by psychological, sociological, contextual, and relational influences.

Thus, attractiveness involves more than physical features and is not just 'skin deep'. For instance, a physically unattractive professional may be successful and popular with clients by developing an empathic interactive style coupled with a competent professional approach.

Although one of the prime functions of clothes is to protect the wearer from cold or injury, dress also serves a number of social functions. The importance of social signals conveyed by apparel is evidenced by the amount of money spent on fashion wear in Western society. This is because, in many situations, it is very important to 'look the part'. Socially skilled people devote time and effort to the selection of appropriate apparel for interpersonal encounters in order to project a suitable image.

Thus, we 'dress up' for important occasions such as selection interviews or first dates. In addition, we also carefully select other embellishments, including 'body furniture' (rings, bangles, necklaces, brooches, earrings, watches, and hair ribbons or bands), spectacles, and make-up, to enhance our overall personal image. Since so much attention is devoted to the choice of dress, it is hardly surprising that we make judgements about others based upon this feature. In terms of impression management, it is patently advisable to dress with care.

THE SITUATION

As explained, skilled performance is shaped by situational factors. There is ample evidence that social situations have a powerful impact on behaviour. This impact can be understood by examining the core features of social situations.

Goal Structure

As noted earlier, goals represent a central aspect of skill. The goals we seek are influenced by the situation in which we are interacting, while, conversely, the goals we pursue are central determinants of situation selection. Thus, in the surgery, the doctor will have goals directly related to dealing with patients. However, if the doctor has the social goal of finding a mate, social situations in which available members of the opposite sex are likely to be encountered will be sought. In this way, goals and situations are intertwined. Thus, knowledge of the goal structure for any situation is an important aspect of skilled performance.

Roles

In any given situation, people play, and are expected to play, different roles, which carry with them sets of expectations about behaviour, attitudes, feelings, and values. Thus, a doctor is expected to behave in a thorough, caring fashion, to be concerned about patients' health, and to treat their problems in confidence.

The roles of those involved affect both the goals and behaviour of participants. For example, a teacher will behave differently, and have different goals, when teaching pupils in the classroom, attending a staff meeting at lunchtime, or having an interview with the principal about possible promotion.

Rules

Social interaction has been likened to a game, involving rules that must be followed if a successful outcome is to be achieved. Professionals must be aware not only of the rules of the situations they encounter, but also how to deal with clients who break them.

Repertoire of Elements

Different types of behaviour are more or less appropriate in different situations; therefore it is important for professionals to develop a range of behavioural repertoires. Thus, in one situation, fact finding may be crucial and the skill of questioning central, while in another context it may be necessary to explain carefully certain facts to a client. These behavioural repertoires are usually sequential in nature.

Concepts

A certain amount of conceptual information is necessary for effective participation in any given situation. In order to play the game of poker, one must be aware of the specific meaning of concepts such as 'flush' and 'run'. Similarly, a patient visiting the dentist may need to be aware of the particular relevance of concepts such as 'crown' or 'bridge'. One common error is to assume that others are familiar with concepts when in fact they are not. Most professionals have developed a jargon of specific terminology for various concepts, and must ensure that it is avoided, or fully explained, when dealing with clients.

Language and Speech

There are linguistic variations associated with social situations, with some requiring a higher degree of language formality. Giving a lecture, being interviewed for a managerial position, or chairing a board meeting all involve a more formal, deliberate, elaborated use of language than having a chat with a friend over coffee. Equally, changes in tone, pitch, and volume of voice change across situations: there are vocal patterns associated with, inter alia, evangelical clergymen addressing religious gatherings, barristers summing up in court, and sports commentators describing ball games. Professionals need to develop and refine their language and speech to suit a particular context.

Physical Environment

The nature of the environment influences behaviour. Humans, like all animals, feel more secure on 'home territory' than in unfamiliar environs. Thus, a social worker will tend to find clients more comfortable in their own homes than in the office, whereas the social worker will be more relaxed in the latter situation. People usually feel more at ease, and therefore talk more freely, in 'warm' environments (soft seats, concealed lights, carpets, curtains, and pot plants). The physical lay-out of furniture is also important in either encouraging or discouraging interaction.

Culture

Few aspects of the communication process have attracted as much attention in recent years as the study of culture. Culture can be defined as 'the sets of behaviors, beliefs, values, and linguistic patterns that are relatively enduring over time and generation within a group'. It is passed from one generation to another and, while not static, is a stable system within which people negotiate identity and relationships. Furthermore, any group that is significantly different from the rest of society forms a subculture, and the actions of individuals are more readily understood in the light of subcultural influences.

Culture has been shown to have a definite influence on how interpersonal skills are enacted. This is because, 'Based on the beliefs and values of our culture, we learn not only what are appropriate interaction scripts within our culture, but also the meanings that should be assigned to these interactions'.

Cultural expertise refers to the ability to adapt one's responses appropriately across differing cultural settings. An example is contained in the old adage, 'When in Rome, do as the Romans do.' It necessitates the development of a knowledge and understanding of the cultural and subcultural norms, beliefs, values, and responses of those with whom we are interacting.

Being a skilled person includes the possession of a high level of such cultural expertise. While culture is a multifaceted concept, a common broad distinction is made between collectivist and individualistic cultures. Eastern cultures communicative meaning is implicit and attached to relationships and situations rather than to what is said. The style of communication is more indirect and self-concealing, with the result that verbal messages can be ambiguous.

These cultures foster an interdependent self with high value placed upon external features such as roles, status, relationships, 'fitting in', being accorded one's proper place, being aware of what others are thinking and feeling, not hurting others' feelings, and minimizing imposition when presenting requests. Time is conceived as being subservient to duties, relationships, and responsibilities.

Western cultures are low context, with an emphasis upon open, direct communication with explicit meaning, so that verbal messages tend to be clearer, more complete, specific, and pointed. There is a discomfort with ambiguity, and anxiety when meaning depends upon something other than the words uttered.

These cultures encourage the development of an independent self that is bounded, unitary, stable, and detached from social context, with a consequent focus upon internal abilities, thoughts and feelings, expressing oneself and one's uniqueness, and being 'up front'. Goals tend to be more personal and instrumental, and time is seen as paramount – being viewed as akin to a commodity, which can be 'spent', 'saved', 'invested', or 'wasted'.

Collectivist cultures therefore inculcate a 'we' identity as opposed to the 'I' identity in individualist cultures. This directly affects interpersonal skills. For example, cultural differences have been found in style of request, between direct forms ('Close that window'), indirect forms ('It's getting cold') and those in between ('Would it be OK to have the window closed?'). Kim and Wilson found that US undergraduates considered the direct style as the most skilful way of making a request whereas Korean undergraduates rated it as the least effective strategy.

Furthermore, the US sample saw clarity as a key dimension of successful requests, while Koreans viewed clarity as counterproductive to effectiveness. However, it has also been found that there are individual as well as cultural differences in individualism and collectivism. As noted by Ivey, 'individuals differ as much as or more than do cultures.

You will want to attune your responses to the unique human being before you.' Furthermore, at different times, in varying situations, and with different people, we may adopt either a more individualistic or a more collectivist style of communicating. Skilled individuals therefore consider both the nature of the specific individual and prevailing cultural norms when deciding how to respond.

Chapter 3

Non-verbal Communication Approaches

NON-VERBAL BEHAVIOUR IN PERSPECTIVE

In recent years, it has become increasingly recognized that investigators in a field of enquiry – any field – bring personal perspectives and figurative comparisons to bear on their work. Such perspectives have been called paradigms, metaphors, or fundamental analogies, and their influence has been thought to be pervasive. Indeed, both philosophers and working scientists acknowledge the value and necessity of such processes in the realm of creative thought.

At least in earliest, gesture as a medium of communication coordinate with vocal and written language was recognized by Francis Bacon. He suggested that 'as the tongue specked to the ear, so the hand specked to the eye. Subsequent analyses, inspired by Bacon's proposal, were undertaken to examine chirologia (manual language) as both a rhetorical and natural language form. During the eighteenth and nineteenth centuries, scholars argued that emotional expression and gesture, the so-called 'natural languages', surely provided the foundation for the more refined and artificial verbal symbolic communication.

Tthe boundaries of the particular variations in the 'behaviour as communication' analogies which have been identified are fuzzy, and the explicit categories of the metaphors as employed by particular investigators are difficult to articulate fully. Yet the three variations of the communication analogy seem valid as the history and current investigation in non-verbal behaviour as communication is examined. In this spirit, a fourth general communication metaphor can also be identified – non-verbal behaviour as dramatic presentation.

NON-VERBAL BEHAVIOUR AS STYLE

Although the 'non-verbal behaviour as communication' analogies hold historical precedence in the area, two additional analogies can be identified: non-verbal behaviour as personal idiom and non-verbal behaviour as skill. Allport introduced the important distinction between the instrumental aspects of action and the expressive aspects, the latter being personalised and stylistic ways of accomplishing the tasks of life. Comparisons with one's signature, voice, or thumb print are offered.

This perspective emphasises holism, consistency, and configural uniqueness, while de-emphasising complexity, skill, and authenticity. Demonstrations of the application of the analogy have been offered (certainly among the ranks of the stage impressionists, if not scientific workers), but the richness and fruitfulness of the metaphor have not yet been fully exploited. Perhaps the most inviting metaphor of non-verbal behaviour has been the emphasis on skilled performance.

The fruitfulness of the analogy of acquired skills as a way of thinking about non-verbal behaviour has been recognised for some time. However, its extension to non-verbal behaviour has been rather recent; Rosenthal, The analogy has directed attention to the expressive or sending (encoding) and interpretive or receiving (decoding) aspects of non-verbal exchange, and has begun to highlight aspects of face-to-face interaction not investigated hitherto.

SCIENTIFIC STUDY OF NON-VERBAL BEHAVIOUR

Literature dealing with non-verbal behaviour as communication has increased dramatically in volume and complexity, particularly during the last several decades.

Wolfgang and Bhardway listed 170 book-length volumes published during the previous 100 years that contained non-verbal communication materials, the vast majority of which had appeared within the last 15 years. Today's electronic databases attest to the health and continued development of the field. A search of the area, covering the time period, yielded over 300 books and chapters on the subject of non-verbal behaviour as communication.

The results of the search listed over 700 entries that had the descriptor term 'non-verbal behaviour' or 'non-verbal communication'. Over 500 of these entries were journal articles, the vast majority of which were empirically based. The topic is usually presented with two different emphases: (1) a theoretical-research orientation and (2) an application-demonstration orientation.

Because of its relation to the subtle and interpretative aspects of communication, there is a tendency on the part of popular lay texts to emphasise application without a balanced presentation of the theory and research which examines the validity and reliability aspects necessary for proper understanding of non-verbal behaviour as one form of communication. Indeed, an interesting piece in this vein appeared on the Internet recently, providing an extended discourse on the psychological meaning of the handshake.

While fascinating, and probably face valid, no recognizable empirical data accompanied the analysis.The challenge of the present chapter is to discuss non-verbal behaviour as a communication skill, while maintaining the scientific integrity needed to evaluate critically the degree to which application is appropriate for any particular reader. It is hoped that the reader will assume a critical, scientific perspective in treating non-verbal behaviour as a meaningful yet complex topic for research and application.

BEHAVIOURAL DIMENSIONS

The first category is kinesics, commonly referred to as 'body language', and includes movements of the hand, arm, head, foot, and leg, postural shifts, gestures, eye movements, and facial expressions. A second category is paralanguage and is defined as content-free vocalisations and patterns associated with speech such as voice pitch, volume, frequency, stuttering, filled pauses (for example, 'ah'), silent pauses, interruptions, and measures of speech rate and number of words spoken in a given unit of time. A third category involves physical contact in the form of touching. Another category is proxemics, which involves interpersonal spacing and norms of territoriality.

A fifth category concerns the physical characteristics of people such as skin colour, body shape, body odour, and attractiveness. Related to physical characteristics is the category of artefacts or adornments such as perfume, clothes, jewellery, and wigs. Environmental factors make up the last category and deal with the influences of the physical setting in which the behaviour occurs: a classroom, an office, a hallway, or a street corner. Knapp's seven dimensions help depict the breadth of non-verbal communication. It is interesting to note that the physical characteristic, adornment, and environmental factor categories do not involve an assessment of overt non-verbal expressions, but rather information about the actor that is communicated non-verbally.

There are numerous examples in the literature that detail these categories, either individually or in combinations and the reader is referred to these for detailed discussion. This chapter will present these categories in various combinations as they pertain to non-verbal behaviour as a communication skill. It is important to stress that non-verbal behaviour is dependent upon all of these factors for meaningful communication to take place. Some of these categories are covered in the theoretical and empirical presentation; others are not, but are nevertheless important and should always be considered as part of the 'universe' comprising non-verbal communication.

SETTING AND ROLE INFLUENCES ON NON-VERBAL BEHAVIOUR

One of the major problems in focusing on the

interpretation of non-verbal behaviour is to treat it as a separate, independent, and absolute form of communication. This view of the topic is much too simplistic. The meaning of non-verbal behaviour must be considered in the context in which it occurs.

Several types of contextual factors will be used to guide this discussion of non-verbal communication and the behaviours associated with it. One involves the environmental setting of the behaviour. Both the physical and social aspects of the environment must be described in sufficient detail to assess possible contributing factors to non-verbal behaviour as meaningful communication. For example, the furniture arrangement in an office can be a major factor influencing the non-verbal behaviours exhibited therein.

Body movements differ depending upon whether the person is sitting behind a desk or openly in a chair. The proximity and angle of seating arrangements have been shown to serve different functions during interaction and to affect such behaviour as eye contact, gazing, and head rotation Non-verbal behaviour may have very different meanings when exhibited on the street rather than, say, in a classroom. Background noise level in a work setting may produce exaggerated non-verbal communication patterns that would have very different meaning in a more quiet setting such as a library.

The influence of ecological factors on behaviour has become an increasingly important focus in the study of human behaviour. Most research in nonverbal communication dealing with physical-environmental factors focused on interpersonal spacing, proxemics, and cultural differences in interaction patterns.

The social climate of the environment is also an important factor in the consideration of non-verbal behaviour. Research has demonstrated that different behaviours are produced in stressful versus unstressful situations. The formality of a setting will determine the degree to which many non-verbal behaviours are suppressed or performed. Competitive versus cooperative interaction settings will also produce different types, levels, and frequencies of nonverbal behaviours. These are just several examples of factors affecting the communicative meaning of non-verbal behaviour. The reader is encouraged systematically to survey factors that may be of importance in more personally familiar settings.

Requiring communicative behaviour to be explicitly goal-directed, with an immediate adjustment on the part of the encoder depending upon the decoder's response, limits the number of behaviours that can be considered communicative. In typical conversations, many non-verbal behaviours become automatic responses and are performed at low levels of awareness or involve no awareness at all.

What was once a specifically defined, goal-directed behaviour becomes habitual and is no longer a product of conscious intention. The degree to which non-verbal behaviours involve varying levels of awareness then becomes difficult to determine. Another consideration for the understanding of non-verbal communication is whether or not the encoder and decoder share a common, socially defined signal system.

APPROACHES TO NON-VERBAL BEHAVIOUR AS COMMUNICATION

Perhaps the most useful model of non-verbal communication that encompasses these issues (but does not resolve them) is one which is originally presented. They began by distinguishing between three characteristics of non-verbal behaviour: (1) usage, (2) origin, and (3) coding. Usage refers to the circumstances that exist at the time of the non-verbal act. It includes consideration of the external condition that affects the act, such as the physical setting, role relationship, and emotional tone of the interaction.

For example, the encoder and decoder may be communicating in an office, a home, a car, or a street. The role relationship may involve that of interviewer–interviewee, therapist–client, supervisor–employee, husband–wife, or teacher–student. The emotional tone may be formal or informal, stressful or relaxed, friendly or hostile, warm or cold, and competitive or cooperative. Usage also involves the relationship between verbal and non-verbal behaviour. For instance, non-verbal acts may serve to accent, duplicate, support, or substitute for – or they may be unrelated to – verbal behaviours.

Usage is the characteristic Ekman and Friesen chose to employ in dealing with awareness and intentionality on the part of the encoder, as discussed previously. In addition, usage involves external feedback, which is defined as the receiver's verbal or non-verbal reactions to the encoder's non-verbal behaviours as interpreted by the encoder.

This does not involve the receiver's actual interpretations of the sender's behaviour, but is only information to the sender that his or her non-verbal behaviours have been received and evaluated.

Finally, usage also refers to the type of information conveyed in terms of being informative, communicative, or interactive. Informative and communicative acts have been discussed. Interactive acts are those that detectably influence or modify the behaviour of the other participants in an interaction. Thus, these three information types involve the degree to which nonverbal messages are understood, provide information, and influence the behaviour of other people.

Some non-verbal behaviours are rooted in the nervous system, such as reflex actions; other non-verbal behaviours are commonly learned and used in dealing with the environment: for example, human beings use their feet for transportation in one form or another.

A third source of non-verbal behaviour refers to culture, family, or any other instrumental or socially distinguishable form of behaviour. Thus, we adopt idiosyncratic behaviours when driving a car; we eat in a certain manner and groom ourselves in various ways. Social customs dictate nonverbal patterns of greeting one another, expressing approval or disapproval, and apportioning appropriate distances from one another depending upon the type of interaction involved.

The third characteristic of non-verbal behaviour is coding, that is, the meaning attached to a non-verbal act. The primary distinction is between extrinsic and intrinsic codes. Extrinsically coded acts signify something else and may be either arbitrarily or iconically coded.

Arbitrarily coded acts bear no visual resemblance to what they represent. A thumbs-up sign to signal that everything is OK would be an arbitrarily coded act since it conveys no meaning 'by itself'. An iconically coded act tends to resemble what it signifies, as in the example of a throat-cutting movement with a finger. Intrinsically coded movements are what they signify. Playfully hitting a person, say on the upper arm, is an intrinsically coded act in that it is actually a form of aggression.

EMBLEMS

These are non-verbal acts that have direct verbal translation and can substitute for words, the meaning of which is well understood by a particular group, class, or culture. Emblems originate through learning, most of which is culture-specific, and may be shown in any area of the body. Examples include waving the hands in a greeting or frowning to indicate disapproval.

Ekman found substantial regional, national, and intranational variation in these displays, leading them to suggest compiling an international dictionary of emblems. Differences have also been found in the way cultures interpret emblems: cultures studied include the Catalans in Spain, Dutch interpretations of Chinese and Kurdish gestures and Hebrew speakers in Israel.The culture-specific nature of emblems can come into sharp focus when unintentional communication occurs as a function of an encoder and decoder having learned different meanings for identical emblematic displays.

ILLUSTRATORS

These are movements that are tied directly to speech and serve to illustrate what is verbalised. Illustrators are socially learned, usually through imitation by a child of a person he or she wishes to resemble. An example of an illustrator is holding the hands a certain distance apart to indicate the length of an object.

REGULATORS

These non-verbal acts serve to regulate conversation flow between people. Regulators are often culture-specific and may be subtle indicators to direct verbal interaction such as head nods, body position shifts, and eye contact. Because of their subtle nature, regulators are often involved in miscommunication and inappropriate responses among people of different cultures or ethnic backgrounds. This will be examined later in greater detail when the authors' police–citizen research is described.

ADAPTORS

These are object or self-manipulations. The specific behaviours are first learned as efforts to satisfy bodily needs, usually during childhood. In adult expression, only a fragment of the original adaptive behaviour is exhibited.

Adaptors are behavioural habits and are triggered by some feature of the setting that relates to the original need. There are three types of adaptors: (1) self-adaptors such as scratching the head or clasping the hands; (2) alter-adaptors, which may include protective hand movements and arm-folding intended to protect oneself from attack or to represent intimacy, withdrawal, or flight; and (3) object adaptors, which are originally learned to perform instrumental tasks and may include tapping a pencil on the table or smoking behaviours.

AFFECT DISPLAYS

These consist primarily of facial expressions of emotions. There is evidence that people from different cultures agree on their judgements of expressions for the primary emotions (happiness, sadness, anger, surprise, fear, disgust, and interest) but disagree on their ratings of the intensity of these expressions). However, these expressions are usually modified and often hidden by cultural display rules learned as 'appropriate' behaviour. Thus, affect displays may be masked in social settings in order to show socially acceptable behaviour.

Recent findings related to this issue have led to the development of an interactionist perspective that integrates findings supportive of both cultural specificity and universality. Extended use of the system has focused on a number of significant topic areas, among which could be cited many investigations into the relationships between genuine and recalled emotion and facial expression and the utility of the system in distinguishing honest and authentic expressions from the deceptive and dissembling. Perhaps one of the most promising findings to emerge from this literature is the recognition of a particular smile, 'the Duchenne smile', which seems to be a reliable indicator of genuine enjoyment and happiness.

Moreover, this facial profile seems to be quite resistant to staging and dissimulation. Results from current investigations of the Duchenne smile suggest that there may exist a universal cross-cultural response to these displays that might have evolved due to the important communicative role of such smiles.

DITTMANN

Another way of organising non-verbal acts in terms of their communicative nature is by focusing on the 'communication specificity' and channel capability of message transmission. These concepts have been presented by Dittmann as part of a larger model of the communication of emotions and are an important aspect of using non-verbal behaviour as a communication skill. Dittmann focused primarily on four major channels of communication: (1) language, (2) facial expression, (3) vocalisations, and (4) body movements. These four channels can be discussed in terms of their 'capacity', defined as the amount of information each may transmit at any given moment. Channel capacity can be described along two dimensions: (1) communication specificity (communicative-expressive) and (2) information value (discrete-continuous).

The closer a channel is to the communicative end of the continuum, the more discrete its information value will be in terms of containing distinguishable units with identifiable meanings (for instance, words).

The more discrete a communication is, the greater the communication specificity it will usually have. These channels have the greatest capacity for conveying the largest number of messages with a wide variety of emotional meaning. Channels at the other end of the capacity dimension are described as being relatively more expressive and continuous. For example, foot movements or changes in posture are more continuous behaviours than are spoken words, and are more expressive than specifically communicative in their emotional content.

These channels have a lower capacity for conveying information regarding how a person is feeling. Facial expressions and vocalisations (paralanguage) may vary in their capacity to convey emotional expression depending on their delivery, the role the person is playing, the setting of the behaviour, and whether the decoders are family, friends, or strangers.

NON-VERBAL COMMUNICATION IN CONTEXT

This chapter has stressed that non-verbal behaviour, as a communication skill, is most usefully understood when discussed in role- and setting-defined contexts. With the possible exception of facial expressions subject to display rules, non-verbal communication cannot be discussed adequately by presenting principles that have universal application.

Perhaps a useful way of presenting research results as applied to communication skills is to provide a sampling of findings in selected contexts. At present, research on non-verbal communication is incomplete and asks more questions than it provides answers, yet it is hoped that the reader will better appreciate scientific attempts to study this communication skill meaningfully.

In the review, the relevance of non-verbal behaviour to

communication in general and suggested several assumptions from which the research can be viewed. Among these are that human communication consists primarily of combinations of channel signals such as spatial, facial, and vocal signals operating together.

Another assumption is that communication is composed of 'multilevel signals' and deals with broader interpretations of interactions such as general labelling (for example, a social or professional encounter) and inferences about longer-term relationships among the interactants. His last assumption is most crucial for the present discussion, since it points out the critical importance of context for generating meanings from human communication encounters.

SETTING AND ROLE APPLICATIONS

A major limitation of much non-verbal behaviour research is that it is conducted in a laboratory setting devoid of many of the contextually relevant environmental and social features present in real-life interactions. This is a serious problem in attempts to generalise techniques of impression management and processes of impression formation to specific role-defined settings, health professional–patient interactions, the employment interview, and police–citizen encounters.

Professionals in these areas have a special interest in non-verbal behaviour. Accurate and effective communication is crucial to accomplishing the purposes of the interaction.

One series of studies conducted over a number of years is illustrative of setting- and role-defined research and reveals the importance of the interplay among the categories of kinesics, paralanguage, proxemics, physical characteristics, adornments, and environmental factors mentioned earlier as describing major categories of non-verbal behaviour. The specific role-defined setting was that of a standing, face-to-face, police citizen interaction.

In the initial study, police officers were asked to indicate the 'characteristics and features they look for when interacting with a citizen while in the role of a 'police officer'. They were also asked to indicate cues they used in forming these impressions of the citizen.

These cues or information items were classified as either behavioural (that is, the other person's verbal and non-verbal behaviour) or situational (that is, aspects of the environment, such as number of other people present, whether inside a room or on the street, and lighting conditions). The officers were asked to compare a 'dangerous' and a 'non-dangerous' situation.

Under conditions of danger, the officers indicated a broadened perceptual scan and were more likely to utilise behavioural (mainly non-verbal) and situation environmental cues (for instance, area of town, size of room, activities on the street) in forming an impression of the citizen. Under the non-dangerous conditions, the officers concentrated almost exclusively on specific facial and vocal cues, eye contact, arm and hand movements, and dress and behavioural sequences such as body orientation and postural positions. Under these less stressful conditions, police officers indicated an impression formed that described the citizen primarily in terms of dispositional characteristics.

Dispositional causes of observed behaviour are contrasted with situational causes such as attributing one's behaviour to momentary discomfort or confusion, crowding, response to another's actions, or other events in the immediate environment.

Thus, in the more typical police–citizen interaction, which is non-stressful for the police officer (for instance, obtaining information from a witness to an accident or crime), the officer focused predominantly on the citizen's non-verbal behaviours and dispositional attributions, rather than situational attributions, to explain the citizen's behaviour (for example, guilty or innocent).

Some Research Implications

Building on the idea of cultural display rules, investigations designed to discover the situations which produce guilt for members of different cultural groups would be helpful. Situations that produce guilt are likely to vary with an individual's cultural background and experience. When identified, these situations could then be used as settings for enacting scripts that involve either deception or truth telling by subjects from those cultures. The enactments should reveal the non-verbal behaviours that distinguish deceivers and truth tellers within the cultural groups. These behaviours would be culturally specific 'leaked' cues.

Following this approach, such studies could be implemented in stages. First, interviews would be conducted to learn about a culture's 'folk psychology' of deception. Respondents would be asked about the kinds of lies and lying situations that are permissible and those that are taboo within their culture. econd, experimental deception vignettes would be presented for respondents' reactions in terms of feelings of guilt, shame, and stress. The vignettes could be designed to vary in terms of such dimensions as whether the person represents a group or her/ himself, the presence of an audience during the interview, and the extent to which he or she prepared for the questions being asked.

Analyses would then suggest the dimensions that influence feelings of guilt or shame for each cultural group. Preliminary findings on subcultural groups, obtained by the authors of this chapter, showed differences in stress for members of different cultural groups and less guilt felt by respondents in all cultural groups when they were in the role of group representative rather than non-representative. Third, the information gathered from the interviews could provide the bases for more structured experimental studies designed to discover those non-verbal behaviours that distinguish between liars and truth tellers (the leakage cues) for each of several cultural groups. These cues could then be used for diagnostic purposes as well as for the development of training modules along the lines of work.

EXAMPLE

In this, a programme of research will be briefly presented that illustrates an attempt to identify systematically certain non-verbal behaviours associated with specific intentions of the communicator (encoder), and then to apply these findings to develop better skills in interpreting (decoding) observed behaviour of others.

The context selected for this research is international politics. This is an area that encompasses a broad range of situational, cultural, personal, and social factors and thus attempts to deal with the complexity of non-verbal expression and interpretation. It is also an area that contains elements similar to a variety of everyday experiences encountered by a broad range of people in professional and social interactions.

LABORATORY RESEARCH

The initial research project involved a role-playing study in which upper-level university students were instructed to play the role of a foreign ambassador being interviewed at a press conference. A set of pertinent issues was derived from United Nations transcripts and presented to the subjects in detail. After studying the issues, subjects were randomly assigned to one of three intention conditions, which directed them to express their country's position on the issues in either an honest, deceptive, or evasive fashion.

Examples of honest, deceptive, and evasive arguments and discussion points were presented to the subjects to help prepare them for the interview. A formal, 15-minute, videotaped interview was conducted between the 'ambassador' and a trained actor playing the role of a press interviewer. An informal, 7-minute, post-interview discussion was also videotaped in which the subject was asked to be 'him/herself' and discuss his or her activities at the university. It is important to note that the subject ambassadors were not aware that the purpose of the study was to assess non-verbal behaviour exhibited by them during the interview.

Thus, the study dealt with 'informative' rather than consciously controlled 'communication' acts as described. Moreover, the interviewer was unaware of whether the subject was in the honest, deceptive, or evasive intention condition. Ten subjects served in each of the conditions. An elaborate process involving 200 coded the videotaped interviews student volunteers carefully trained reliably to observe specific channels of nonverbal behaviour patterns produced by subjects in the honest, deceptive, and evasive conditions.

Themes for Analysis

Moving pictures shown on video or film are panoramas of quickly changing actions, sounds, and expressions. Just where to focus one's attention is a basic analytic problem. Frameworks constructed suggest several leads to guide the research cited above. Providing a structure for analysis, the frameworks emphasize two general themes, namely, focusing on combinations of non-verbal behaviours and taking contextual features into account.

While coded separately, the non-verbal behaviours can be combined for analysis of total displays. Patterns of behaviours then provide a basis for inferences about feelings or intentions. The patterns may take several forms: one consists of linear combinations of constituent behaviours, as when gaze time, leg movements, and object fidgeting are used in equations to identify probable intentions; a second form is correlated indicators or clusters, such as the pattern of trunk swivels, rocking movements, head-shaking, and head nodding shown by subjects attempting to withhold information about their 'nation's' policy; another form is behaviours that occur within the same time period as was observed for deceivers in the study presented above – for example, a rocking/nodding/shaking cluster was observed during interviews with deceptive 'ambassadors'.

Patterned movements are an important part of the total situation. By anchoring the movements to feelings and intentions, one can get an idea of their meaning. But there are other sources of explanation for what is observed. These sources may be referred to as context. Included as context are the semi-fixed objects in the setting (for instance, furniture), the other people with whom the subject interacts, and the nature of the discourse that transpires. The proposition that context greatly influences social interaction/

behaviour. Highlighted here is a structure for interpreting material on the tapes. It is obvious that the particular intention–interpretation relationships of interest vary with particular circumstances. Several issues are particularly salient within the area of international politics. Of interest might be questions such as: What is the state of health of the leader? To what degree are statements honestly expressive of true beliefs? How committed is the person to the position expressed? How fully consolidated and secure is the person's political position?

Knowing where to focus attention is a first step in assessment. A particular theme is emphasised in each of the political issues mentioned above. Signs of failing health are suggested by incongruities or inconsistencies in verbal and non-verbal behaviours, as well as between different non-verbal channels.

Deception is suggested by excessive body activity, as well as deviations from baseline data. Strong commitment to policy is revealed in increased intensity of behaviours expressed in a variety of channels.

The careful recording of proxemic activity or spatial relationships provides clues to political status. Biographical profiles summarise co-varying clusters of facial expressions and body movements.

Each of these themes serves to direct an analyst's attention to relationships (for health indicators and profiles), to particular non-verbal channels (for deception and status indicators), or to amount (as in the case of commitment). Knowing specifically what to look at is the second step in assessment. Results of a number of experiments suggest particular behaviours.

Systematic Comparisons

Non-verbal indicators can be used to build profiles of individual foreign leaders. It is evident that such an approach emphasises Allport's concept of morphogenic analysis and stresses the analogy of expressive behaviour as personal idiom. This strategy of systematic comparison is designed to increase an analyst's understanding of his 'subject'. This is done by tracking the displays exhibited by selected individuals across situations and in conjunction with verbal statements.

Comparisons would be made in several ways: (1) examine deviations from baseline data established for each person (for instance, speech errors); (2) compare nonverbal displays for the same person in different situations (for example, within or outside home country; formal or informal settings); and (3) compare displays for different types of verbal statements (for example, defence of position, policy commitment). These analyses highlight consistencies and inconsistencies at several levels between situations, between verbal and non-verbal channels, and within different non-verbal channels. They also alert the analyst to changes in non-verbal activity:

Being aware of changes from a baseline period would give one a better understanding of relatively unique expressive behaviour. Further analysis consists of comparing different persons in similar situations or dealing with similar subject matter. The value of these comparisons is that they contribute to the development of a system of movement representation similar to the notation and animation systems. Extracted from the data are sets of coordinated movements which may change over time and situations.

The coordinated movements can be represented in animated graphic displays. Illuminated by such displays are 'postural' differences within actors across time and between actors. When associated with events and context, the observations turn on the issue of how the feelings and intentions which are evoked by different situations are represented in body movement. When compared to displays by actors in other cultural settings, the observations are relevant to the question:

Chapter 4

Reinforcement

As a concept within fields such Tas human social communication, learning theory, educational psychology, and applied behaviour therapy, has a lengthy history and very deep research base. Particularly prominent in the twentieth century in the psychological and educational literature, the concept has had less prominence in recent years, particularly in this postmodern era of thinking.

Nevertheless, the significance of reinforcement as a theoretical and practical aspect of human communication, and as a key feature of skilled performance, remains today. This chapter will examine the concept of reinforcement and its place within a social skills model of communication. The relevance of an understanding of how reinforcement plays a number of significant roles in learning to communicate effectively, and in the skilled use of communication in most of the modern forms we use, will be outlined and supported by international research findings from across the decades.

CLARIFYING THE CONCEPT

Simply put, reinforcement is a concept which has arisen as the centre piece of what is called operant psychology theory, which is most associated with the writing and philosophy of the American academic, Skinner was an idealistic and inventive scholar of the twentieth century who may have changed the way we think about behaviour and life, but never quite succeeded in his professed aim to change the world in which people. His work was both revered and reviled by different sectors of the academic and scholarly community throughout his life and beyond into this century. Fred Skinner (as he preferred to be addressed) was, and remains, a controversial theorist.

For many, he was the father of modern behaviourism and its major theorist of the twentieth century. In operant psychology (as the Skinner-led field became known), the term 'reinforcement' is usually defined in terms such as the following: the effect of a stimulus, when matched with an emitted response (an operant action), increases the likelihood of that action/response being repeated.

REINFORCEMENT IN VERBAL COMMUNICATION

Of course, the majority of human social communication is verbal, with a wide range of spoken languages across the world. In each language, there is a large lexicon of words and terms that are imbued with praise and reward connotations. These are clearly meant to be used as responses to other speakers and hence figure strongly as social reinforcement in their application within communication.

Thus, whether we agree or not with the behaviourist's analysis in which the concept of reinforcement is theorised and researched, it is still patently apparent that our languages have many instances of terminology that assume words of praise and encouragement, and that these have some positive and linked effect to repetition of the behaviours to which they are responding.

As mentioned earlier, much of the research work on the place and effect of reinforcement in human communication took place in the mid- to late twentieth century. A good deal of research was also situated within the education field in two spheres: teacher education and special education. More recent work has centred on aspects such as behaviour therapy and modification of atypical behaviours in children and those with personality or communication disorders.

Some interesting recent research has highlighted the culture specificity of some aspects of reinforcement applicability. Weirzbicka presented research to show that the terms 'good boy' and 'good girl', as 'widely used in Anglo parental speech directed to children to praise them for their action', have 'no equivalents in other European languages'. In her interpretation of this assertion, she argued that the terms and their purported effects are culture specific and rooted in the English and American puritan past.

Of course, many previous studies in the education sector have highlighted the considerations, as specified above in the three criteria for reinforcement, that validity and valence are related to the individualisation of reinforcement as well s the specific contingency. General praise is not always reinforcing under these considerations, and terms such as 'good boy/girl' are general and may interplay with different attributional ideas and motivation in the hearer.

Parental use of reinforcement in the development of conversation and social skill has always been a strong feature in most cultures, and current 'good-parenting' volumes attest to the use of selective praise and encouragement linked to child behaviour as evidence of best practice.

Again, specific praise related to the individual child and the actions/behaviours being responded to results in better take-up and repetition of the behaviours.Current theory of language teaching heavily emphasises the need for young students beginning school and in their early literacy and oracy years to be 'scaffolded' (that is supported and encouraged by a more skilled language user, be it parent, caregiver, or teacher) within the theoretically conceived 'zone of proximal development'.

Such terminology and its implications for a social construction emphasis on all language development has been pervasive in most language-teaching texts and research in the past two decades, The implications of these theories do not necessarily support reinforcement ideology, and in some instances their advocates would take some offence at any such links, but the examples often cited include parental and teacher praise and encouragement in language that is clearly interpretable as contingent reinforcement-type feedback, rather than some neutral conversational interaction.

In business, the use and understanding of the impact of

verbal reinforcers in communication and management, as well as human resource management, has a well-established background.

Even a brief perusal, for example, of websites advertising workplace and management courses in such areas as 'interpersonal communication skills in the workplace' will demonstrate the centrality of elements of reinforcement theory and application in handling effective communication practices across such diverse areas from 'difficult staff at work' to 'effective productive employees'. Any reliable search engine on the World Wide Web will give results on each of the aforementioned terms as search words that will open up a myriad of websites.

As stated above, the applicability of the concept of reinforcement in understanding how we, as human communicators in social interaction, behave and develop is important within the overall communication field. Most analyses of the skills we utilize to develop conversation and language will frequently bring the communication theory and research reader to the topic of reinforcement.

Whether the current literature tends to offer alternative terms, such as praise and encouragement or response, is not the issue, as the underlying theory and conceptualization remain cogent. The specificity of the concept and its roots in operant psychology are not currently mainstream in the literature, but strong elements of research and application of the ideas and principles are still evident with applicable results.

REINFORCEMENT IN THE NEW COMMUNICATION MEDIA

In the second half of the twentieth century and into this millennium, the 'new media' have become essential and central to communication patterns in most modern and postmodern nations.

The new media are heavily visual (even the cellular telephone is moving into a medium for more visual content), although multimedia elements are becoming more prevalent as time goes by. Included in this general category for the purposes of this discussion are email, Web pages, interactive Internet chat rooms, blogs, and the ubiquitous text message, photo, and other image services of the modern cellular telephone networks.

Many of these media are used more by the younger generations and have a linguistic edge which is starting to emerge as almost a new dialect, or even a new language with standardised English short cuts and symbolic elements at times reminiscent of rebus symbols in early twentieth-century reading instruction in schools. Research into aspects of how these media are changing communication patterns and interactivity is emerging, and there will be much more to come in the near future.

What is interesting for the purposes of this chapter is that the skill and use of reinforcement are easily identified when these modern-use media are investigated. Most of the symbols which are so heavily used in cellular telephone messaging, for example, include various ways of praising or rewarding, or positively reinforcing comments and messages. These symbols include emotions, such as smiling faces and hearts, which may be attached to messages. Similar symbols in various keystrokes combinations also are found in many emails, particularly between close friends who share the dialect.

It is important in this set of considerations, however, to differentiate the use of some of the media from among the remainder, in terms of the extent of interaction with a device that is a mediator of communication between two people, as compared to the situation where the computer or device is programmed in a way that appears to be non-mediating and has some apparent stand-alone qualities.

Arguments for thinking computers, chaos theory, memetics, and the emergence of nanotechnology and devices with inbuilt elements of 'fuzzy logic' are starting to make the science fiction computer with a mind of its own a closer possibility than previous generations would have imagined.

Direct synchronous communication in which both parties

are device connected in real time is one clear case of mediation, and the communication device is just a filter or medium between normal face-to-face encounters with all the attendant issues that may generate. There has been a long history of this type of communication through the development and use of the telephone, and many of the modern devices have merely extended this into a range of social and time and distance dimensions as a development of that paradigm.

The advent of telephone etiquette, and specific language patterns of greeting, answering and conversation punctuation, enhancers, and inhibitors, has been the subject of considerable work over many decades. Asynchronous communication (where the parties are operating in different time spheres or zones but still communicating) is something which used to be only in the domain of letter writing but now also happens through email and various discussion forums and other interactive patterns.

Different from both of these situations is the computer as a programmed teaching or interactive device. Here the communication may have a range of interactive elements that allow different responses and 'conversations' or interactions to happen, depending on an algorithm or sequence which has been built into a programme within the device. Some of the modern versions of such communication packages at their crudest level are the telephone-answering systems in which the caller punches in a number for a specific submenu service. The rigidity of this simplest 'voice-mail jail' version has become a modern social curse, and it is the subject of many a complaint.

The latter may often have built-in tests and progress checks with planned reinforcement schedules and social reinforcement comments in voice or text. Early research in this area seems to indicate that computer text criticism, for example, is quite powerful in its effects on motivation and recall. This field is ripe for additional detailed research and development. At this stage of the chapter, it is important to consider that these modern media and their implications for communication theory and research are where the leading edge will be for the first half of this millennium. Whether reinforcement, as a conceptual framework, has a large place in this development and in the study of how and why and in what ways people interact with machines, and how the human communications are or are not mediated by devices, will be a fascinating aspect to watch.

There is no doubt that early work in programmed instruction and computer-mediated instruction, for example, suffered from a too heavy dose of behaviourist-dominated approaches emphasising small sequenced parts as the basic learning paradigm, and that this has led to a vigorous search for alternative theories and approaches.

CONCEPT OF COMMUNICATION REINFORCEMENT

This chapter now moves to suggest that, in order to understand clearly the way reinforcement figures in human social communication, the concept of communication reinforcement may be a useful way to discuss and analyse the application of operant theory and models of communication. For the purposes of this chapter, communication reinforcement refers to the consequences of a communication from one person to others which increases the likelihood of further communication happening.

The consequences of the emitted communication may be positive reinforcement in the form of social reinforcers, such as praise and other positive responses, and may be verbal or non-verbal, as with nods, facial expressions, or other gestures of approval or support.

MANIPULATION OF COMMUNICATION REINFORCEMENT IN RESEARCH AND THERAPY

Early research into the place and application of reinforcement theory in human communication emphasised the way positive reinforcement could be used in a deliberate sense to alter language behaviours and usage. Such research began in areas such as using reinforcement in increasing conversation skills and frequency, as, for example, in 'delinquent girls' or socially isolated elderly men in an institutional setting.

In addition, work employing negative reinforcement was conducted in the 1960s with a therapy group to stimulate conversation. Likewise, there has always been considerable discussion of the linked (contingent) use of praise and reward by parents in assisting their children to develop language and social skills. Basically, such materials emphasise a set curriculum sequence of behaviours that are presented with repetition and lots of positive contingent reinforcement to small groups of school-age children, and introduce small, carefully arranged elements at a time.

Another programme, aimed at language development in disabled children, that has similar reinforcement patterns as its basis is the TALK Language Development Programme. As originally described, this programme used positive reinforcement in a behaviourally oriented approach to teach language-disabled children to talk. In more recent years, these two authors have continued to work with language development in both disabled and non-disabled children, and have developed a model for the understanding and treatment of autistic children. While their model has attracted considerable interest, it has not gone without criticism from other autism researchers.

At the same time, the field of reinforcement application and behaviour modification has maintained a strong base in dealing with children with special educational and behavioural needs, as well as work in aberrant adult and child communication disorders. Speech-delayed, aphasic, and autistic children have been assisted by these techniques, based on the operant theories of language and reinforcement connections in the UK, where autistic children are taught by applied behaviour analysis (ABA) techniques featuring reinforcement).

In various places and writing across the broad field of operant psychology and its many variants, terms such as 'applied behaviour analysis', 'behaviour therapy', and other variations distinguish the many approaches to utilising reinforcement concepts and practices to affect human behaviour and communication patterns.

While these may have differing elements and emphases, they all have the concept of reinforcement as central and the application of it as the major means to change or adapt behaviour and language. Within this field, a recent development is functional communication training (FCT), and a number of studies have utilised this set of techniques, which use reinforcement to improve communication in children and some adults who demonstrate severe dysfunctional behaviour.

The basic approach of FCT involves an initial functional analysis of the behaviour that is seen as at issue (be it a misbehaviour or a lack of communication). The reinforcers that apparently currently support that behaviour are also noted in this stage.

The next step is to organise for the child a new or different behaviour (it may be a simple oral statement or use of some communication cards if the child cannot yet verbalise). The significant interactors with the child (or adult) concerned then actively reinforce the new behaviour/ communication each time the child exhibits it. The latter behaviour/communication is termed a replacement behaviour for the previously unacceptable behaviour.

APPLICATIONS OF COMMUNICATION REINFORCEMENT IN VARIOUS FIELDS

In addition to the above specific application of reinforcement and the operant model of psychology to learning and language aspects, there have been a number of related and derivative developments which have emerged over the past two decades, and which are currently bringing some new light to the applicability of reinforcement ideas and their relationship to human communication and behaviour. Two aspects which have developed in this vein are cognitive behaviour therapy and, more recently, relational frame theory.

Cognitive behaviour therapy is an approach with direct

roots in Skinnerian thinking and operant psychology. This approach blends both cognitive therapy, which was pioneered by the psychologists The use of language and reinforcement is involved in such aspects of treatment of behavioural problems as the use of 'self-talk' and reinforcement of appropriate thinking about the behaviours.

Cognitive behaviour therapy does not, like other therapies, seek to delve into the unconscious mind, as in more psychodynamic models, and tries to treat the faulty individual schemas and behaviours with specific reinforcement approaches common in behaviour-modification approaches. Cognitive behaviour therapy seeks to treat people with communication and social behaviour disorders and maladaptive behaviour, and, as such, is an attempt to bring the reinforcement concept into a modern approach whereby better human communication and behaviour can be assisted in such contexts.

There is a good deal of research and writing on this therapy concept and its applicability to language and behavioural disorders.The second major recent development that has been developed from the Skinnerian operant basis, in what is termed a post-Skinnerian approach, is relational frame theory; This is a recent and potentially powerful approach that argues for a new and different perspective on the way human language is discussed from a behaviourist point of view.

Relational frame theory maintains that there is a place for contingencies of reinforcement in the traditional operant sense, but the basic book and theory exposition is set up as a critique of Skinner's original book, Verbal Behaviour, and as such attempts to take the field beyond the Skinnerian views. The field of relational frame theory is emerging as one that has inspired a good deal of recent research and controversy as well. Two different reviewers of the basic book, edited by Hayes, Barnes-Holmes, and Roche, have taken the group to task for a number of reasons, including that the text is difficult to read and complex, that the theory promises much but is less convincing to those who hold Skinnerian views and that there is some doubt as to the merit of seeing relational frame theory as a basic new theory.

As Palmer states in the abstract of his lengthy review of the work, The authors dismiss Skinner's interpretation of verbal behaviour as unproductive and conceptually flawed and suggest a new definition and a new paradigm for the investigation of verbal phenomena. I found the empirical phenomena important but the conceptual discussion incomplete. A new principle of behaviour is promised, but critical features of this principle are not offered. In the absence of an explicit principle, the theory itself is difficult to evaluate.

The emergence of relational frame theory as a new paradigm with some promise is not doubted so much by writers such as Salzinger of the American Psychological Association, who concedes that the work is thought provoking and worthy of additional notice, research, and follow-up. Relational frame theory may offer a more useful approach to the place of reinforcement in human communication.

Chapter 5

Reflecting

Eflecting, as a feature of skilled interpersonal communication, is closely associated with active listening: with responding to the other in such a way as to convey interest, understanding, and engagement. The topic of listening, though, is taken up in another chapter of this book, so little more, as such, will be said about it here. Rather, the focus in this chapter is more specifically on both functional and structural aspects of the process called reflecting. Its various functions are outlined and contrasting theoretical perspectives brought to bear.

A review of research into reflecting is also presented and conclusions drawn as to the interpersonal effects of this way of relating. Before setting off in this direction, though, time spent reminding ourselves of some of the key features of interpersonal communication may be worthwhile. One of the commonly agreed characteristics of this transactional process is its multidimensionality.

Messages exchanged between interactors are seldom unitary or discrete. In a seminal work, the attention was drawn to two separate, but nevertheless interrelated levels at which people engage. One has to do with substantive content, and the other with relational matters which help determine how participants define their association in terms of, for instance, extent of affiliation, balance of power, and degree of intimacy and trust.

Content is probably the more immediately recognisable dimension of interpersonal communication, dealing as it does with the subject matter of talk – the topic of conversation.

Through relational communication, on the other hand, interactors work at establishing where they stand with each other vis-à-vis, for instance, closeness and liking. Dominance and control are also important aspects of relational communication that have to be managed, and some sort of implicit or explicit working agreement reached.

While the issue of who should control the conversation may be a topic for discussion (content), such matters are more often handled in indirect and subtle ways. It is typically in how interactors talk about what they talk about that relational work is carried on. Dominance and control may be manifested in a plethora of verbal and nonverbal actions such as initiating topic changes, interrupting, maintaining eye contact, and speaking loudly.

INTERACTIONAL STYLE AND DIRECTNESS

An important consideration in the exercise of control is that of interpersonal style, a construct discussed extensively by Norton. Style can be thought of as how what is done is done, with the characteristic manner in which someone handles an interactive episode. Cameron emphasised its expressive function in creating a particular 'aesthetic' presence for the other. Conversational style includes the degree of formality, elaboration, or directness adopted. We will dwell upon the latter characteristic, directness, which has been commented upon in various domains of professional practice, including teaching, social work, medicine and counselling and psychotherapy.

REFLECTING

Reflections are accordingly a type of response. They involve the interviewer striving to capture the significant message in the respondent's previous contribution and re-presenting this understanding. This has been described as mirroring back to the interviewee what the interviewee has just said, as grasped by the interviewer.

Reflections can be contrasted with questions, for example, which often serve to lead in this sense. Reflecting, as a topic of scholarly enquiry, is bedevilled by conceptual confusion, terminological inconsistency, and definitional imprecision, some of which has been alluded to by Hill and O'Brien. An attempt is made here to disentangle the central themes.

At a broad level, reflecting is operationally concerned with person A in some way grasping the significance of person B's preceding contribution and, in the form of a statement that re-presents this key message, making person B aware of A's understanding. Rogers who is commonly credited with coining the term although he later came to disparage it, regarded reflecting as a method of communicating an understanding of the other and the concerns expressed, from the other's point of view, and of 'being with' that person.

Wilkins also highlighted a role in checking accuracy of understanding. Attempts to introduce greater precision and, in particular, to specify how these effects can be achieved by the interviewer have, however, led to some of the semantic difficulties mentioned above. These inconsistencies and indeed contradictions can be illustrated by considering several definitions of the term.

Returning to the term 'reflecting', we should recall that one line of thought suggests that reflections are essentially repetitions. Similarly, Nicholson and Bayne wrote that, when using this technique, 'The interviewer repeats a word or phrase which the client has used'. They contrasted reflections with paraphrases in this respect.

For others, as will be shown shortly, the cognitive-affective dimension is of greater relevance in conceptualising paraphrases. Simple repetitions have alternatively been referred to as verbatim playbacks, as reflections of content, but perhaps more frequently as restatements. In its most extreme form, according to Benjamin, the restatement is an exact duplication of the original statement, including the pronoun used, although more frequently this is changed; indeed, the restatement may repeat in a more selective fashion.

Those who talk about restatements as repetitions tend to

set them apart from reflections on the basis of not only form but also function.

For some, restatements are of limited utility and, at best, have more to do with indicating attempts at rudimentary hearing than with understanding. Adler, Rosenfeld, and Proctor cautioned that consistent use runs the risk of making the interviewer seem foolish or even hard of hearing. Indeed, depending upon circumstances, restatements may even convey incredulity, disapproval. or sarcasm.

REFLECTING: THEORETICAL PERSPECTIVES

The process of reflecting can be interpreted from at least three fundamentally different disciplinary positions. These are humanistic psychology, behaviourist psychology, and linguistics (more specifically, pragmatics). In keeping with the former, it is, in part, the communication of those attitudes and conditions promoting psychological growth and maturity. To the behaviourist, it is a means of influencing and modifying what people do and how they respond to their social environment. Finally, in keeping with pragmatics, reflecting can be thought of as part of the elaborate business of managing talk in the course of interaction.

The Humanistic Approach

Were the actualizing tendency permitted to operate unimpaired, the outcome would be a person in the process of becoming self-actualized. Such individuals show an openness to experience, self-trust, the adoption of an internal locus of evaluation, and a willingness to continue the self-actualizing process.

They are not dependent upon others as a source of evaluation but are confidently self-reliant in this respect. Few, unfortunately, live self-actualizing lives. The personally experienced world of the individual is called the phenomenological field and consists of everything that is, at least potentially, available to awareness. Part of this totality relates to the self; the child develops a particular self-concept. This can be thought of as a view of self together with an evaluation of it. Significant others, such as parents, have a key role to play in this process due to the individual's need for positive regard. This need to gain the love, respect, and esteem of others important to the person is deep felt.

Such positive regard, however, is generally not provided unconditionally. Instead, certain conditions of worth are attached – the child knows that behaviour of a certain type must be displayed in order to win approval. Therefore, it becomes imperative for the child to behave not only in keeping with the actualizing tendency but to ensure that conditions of worth are not violated.

Such dual standards invariably lead to conflicts and attempted compromises. Within the individual is held in tension, as it were, a self-concept at odds with the organism self. The outcome is incongruence; the self-concept becomes divorced from the actual experiences of the organism. As observed by Butt, 'Rogers' theory proposes a split between the natural and the social: an organism process that is good and true, and a social world that impedes and hinders.' Incongruence is associated with feelings of threat and anxiety and, consequently, the falsification or indeed denial of experiences leading to the distortion of the self-concept. This is the antithesis of becoming self-actualized.

Reflecting, as a way of listening and a method of responding that imposes no external evaluative comment on client disclosures, thereby satisfies these requirements. Reflecting is, however, more commonly associated with another characteristic of the effective relationship – accurate empathic understanding. In his earlier writings, Rogers proposed that the empathic counselor assumes, in so far as he is able, the internal frame of reference of the client, to perceive the world as the client sees it, to perceive the client himself as he is seen by himself, to lay aside all perceptions from the external frame of reference while doing so and to communicate something of this empathic understanding to the client.

It was considered that accurate reflecting is the most effective means of communicating this understanding to the client although, as will be outlined, subsequent views on this issue changed somewhat. Developments have taken place in person-centered thinking over the years.

Three distinct phases in the ongoing evolutionary process labelled, chronologically, non-directive, reflective, and experiential, can be identified, each characterized by a particular outlook on counselor function and style. The non-directive counselor strove to create a permissive, non-judgemental climate by unintrusively displaying acceptance. Clarification of client contributions in order to promote increased insight gradually was also provided.

With the advent of the reflective era, greater stress was placed upon effecting a more integrated self-concept and putting the client more completely in touch with his phenomenological world.

As far as technique is concerned, reflecting was employed extensively during both of these phases, but particularly in the latter. However, it would seem that subtle differences in use are detectable, which go some way to shedding light on the reasons for the various nuances of definition disentangled in the previous section. Thus, a gradual switch in emphasis took place from reflecting, largely at a fairly superficial level, the factual content of the client's verbalized message (and frequently doing so by simply repeating what was said) to dealing with the affective dimension through mirroring back, in fresh words, feelings expressed. Reflection of feeling became the most widely used technique.

Reflecting is still a legitimate activity, nevertheless, but its effectiveness is dependent upon relating directly to clients' current experiencing and encouraging them to focus more intensely upon and become more fully aware of it. Reflecting should also assist in the process of converting implicit (or universalized) meaning into a communicable form without misrepresentation.

Rogers came to see checking on accuracy of understanding as the important task being achieved. According to Wilkins, he consequently preferred the labels 'checking perceptions' and 'testing understanding' to 'reflecting feeling'. Regardless of label, the therapeutic effect of responding in this way is to promote the individual's experiencing and consequently produce change toward greater congruence. Since such responses must be directed at the felt meanings experienced by the client, there is no longer the stipulation that reflections must deal with only affective issues.

Memories, experiences, thoughts, fantasies, sensations, and such like have equal legitimacy and should be responded to as well. Content in this sense becomes less important. The reflective statement may be cognitive, affective, or perhaps more usefully both.

Brammer introduced the variant reflecting experience to describe this technique. A further development is a greater move away from the explicitly stated and obvious in the client's utterance to inchoate and vaguely expressed concerns. In offering deeper levels of empathic understanding, the reflection should move beyond the familiar to point tentatively toward experiences only faintly hinted at and less clearly grasped by the client.

Although possibilities of inaccuracy are increased, such reflections have the potential to move the client forward in experiencing to greater degrees of realization. Here again can be identified a further source of the conceptual confusion discussed previously.

Empathy has been cast as a multidimensional construct with cognitive, affective, and behavioural aspects. According to the latter, and for empathy to make a difference, it must be actually manifested in some way. As a piece of interpersonal behaviour, reflecting is accordingly one (but only one) of a number of possible ways of making someone aware of the fact that they are being empathically understood.

Indeed, the point has been put that the specific behavioural expression is largely immaterial, provided that it succeeds in communicating a strong sense to the client of being engaged with in this way. (It should also be mentioned that some, from a person centred perspective, express increasing unease at the technique-ridden connotations of any behavioural terms such as 'reflecting', 'paraphrasing', and so forth.) Nevertheless, when used appropriately, reflecting is one possible method consistently mentioned when the communicative dimension of the construct of empathy is discussed Furthermore, analyses of Rogers in videotaped counseling sessions have confirmed that, in fact, he made extensive use of reflective skills.

Changes in person-centred thinking have taken place since first formulated by Carl Rogers. Much of the definitional confusion to do with the term 'reflecting' derives from this evolution. Nevertheless, from the point of view of this branch of humanistic psychology, reflecting can be thought of as facilitative communication with the potential to convey unconditional positive regard and empathic understanding thereby pointing the way to possibilities of personal growth and maturity through enhanced self-actualisation.

THE BEHAVIOURIST APPROACH

Reflecting has also been interpreted and investigated in keeping with behaviourist principles. Beginning with Watson, behaviourists have traditionally regarded psychological enquiry as an extension of the natural sciences. Behaviourism, though, is far from a monolithic system of thought but includes, among others, methodological and (more prominently) radical variants.

Philosophical underpinnings of the perspective are explored by Hocutt will not be pursued here. Behaviourists have historically restricted psychology enquiry to behaviour, environmental happenings associated with it, and the relationship between these two types of 'in the world' happening. The individual's environment is of paramount importance in shaping what individuals do and what they become. The goal of psychology is to describe, explain, predict, and control behaviour by identifying the regularities existing between it and features of the environment in which it occurs.

The early theory placed emphasis upon identifiable environmental stimuli serving to elicit particular responses from the organism according to predictable patterns. While some of these stimulus–response connections may be basic reflexes, others are learned. In either case, the individual was regarded as essentially passive, with responses triggered by stimuli in the form of environmental events. Extending earlier thinking by Thorndike, as enshrined in the Law of Effect, Skinner (1938) drew attention to the fact that the environmental consequences for an organism of those actions that are carried out have a considerable bearing upon what is done subsequently.

This simple but immensely powerful idea formed the basis of his work on operant conditioning. Skinner stressed the operant rather than the respondent nature of behaviour. Instead of merely reacting to happenings as 'triggers', the organism was seen as emitting behaviour that operated on the environment to effect consequences which, in some cases, led to an increased likelihood of that class of behaviour being performed under comparable sets of circumstances. Such consequences are termed reinforcers or reinforcing stimuli, and operant conditioning is the process whereby they act to increase the frequency of occurrence of designated behaviour by being made contingent upon it:

Operant behaviour is behaviour that is sensitive to its consequences. When operant behaviour becomes more likely because of the consequences it has had, we speak of reinforcement.

Some consequences produce increases in the likelihood of operant behaviour, and others do not. Reflecting can be conceived of and researched in terms of operant conditioning procedures. Reflective statements by person B, acting as reinforcing stimuli on the preceding contribution by person A, will make it more likely that person A will persist with this line of talk. The process can be thought of as one of systematic selection: 'Those responses that are selected increase in relative frequency, while most of the remainder decline'. Reinforcement can take a positive or a negative form.

Positive reinforcement is formally defined by Maag as referring 'to any stimulus, when presented after the occurrence of a behaviour, that increases the future occurrence of the behavior'. He goes on to describe it as 'the most powerful and effective method for increasing or maintaining appropriate behavior'.

With negative reinforcement, by contrast, an act is associated with the avoidance, termination, or reduction of an aversive stimulus that would have either occurred or continued at some existing level had the response not taken place. Behaviour resulting in the noxious stimulus being reduced, eliminated, or avoided will become more prevalent, the sine qua non of reinforcement in action.

Examples of negative reinforcement in everyday life are common. We have a headache, take FeelFine analgesic, and the pain disappears, making it more likely that we will take FeelFine the next time a headache strikes.

Positive reinforcing stimuli can take a variety of different forms. Primary reinforcers include such things as food, drink, sex, etc., the reinforcing potential of which does not rely upon a process of prior learning. Secondary, token, or conditioned reinforcers, on the other hand, come to be valued through prior association with primary reinforcers, money being an obvious example in contemporary society.

The implication is that various verbal and non-verbal behaviours associated with attention giving, for instance, have the ability to shape how others act in interpersonal situations through selectively acting as social reinforcers. Lieberman defined social reinforcers, in broad terms, as 'stimuli whose reinforcing properties derive uniquely from the behaviour of other members of the same species'.

Social behaviour, by definition, presupposes the involvement of other people. In the main, those with whom we mix and intermingle and are a powerful, though often subtle, influence on our actions also contribute the types of reinforcers that govern and shape it. Buss suggested that they be thought of as either process or content.

The former are an inherent part of interpersonal contact and include, in order of increasing potency, the mere presence of others, attention from them, and their conversational responsiveness. Too much or too little of these activities can be aversive: it is only at some notional level of intermediacy that they become reinforcing. To switch to the second element of Buss's categorization, the content of interaction can also have reinforcing ramifications. Here, Buss mentions acts such as showing deference, praising, extending sympathy, and expressing affection. Unlike their process counterparts, these are held to operate along unipolar dimensions. In other words, there is a direct linear correlation between amount and reinforcing effect.

For some, reflecting acts as a social reinforcer because it connotes attention, interest, and acceptance, thereby serving to increase selectively verbal output of the type reflected. In an early experiment, Powell examined the effects of reinforcing subjects' self-referenced statements (statements about themselves) by means of reflections. The results showed that when, in an interview-type situation, the interviewer responded by using this technique the frequency of such statements increased significantly. In effect, subjects talked more about themselves. Other research, which is reviewed in a later section of this chapter, has produced largely comparable findings.

Some researchers, while remaining within an operant conditioning framework, see reflections working in a slightly different way. When a certain action succeeds only in eliciting reinforcement in the presence of particular accompanying stimuli, that piece of behaviour is said to be under stimulus control and those stimuli have become discriminating stimuli in respect of it. They signal the availability of a reinforcer for behaving in that way. When the overall context acts in this way, contextual control is in operation.

Reflections may, therefore, function more as discriminative than reinforcing stimuli. Discriminative stimuli are part of the environmental context within which the organism responds. They signal that reinforcing stimuli are available and, as such, are present at the time of responding rather than afterward (and differ from reinforcing stimuli in this respect). They cue the occasion for reinforcement but do not themselves reinforce. By reflecting feeling, for example, the interviewer may actually be signaling to the interviewee that subsequent reinforcement is available for further affective responses. In the sequential stream of verbal interchange, the task of locating sources of influence is, however, fraught with difficulty.

To summarise, reflecting is a method of influencing verbal behaviour by affecting the frequency of occurrence of particular types of response This can be accounted for in terms of the behaviourist principles of operant conditioning and behaviour analysis. As such, reflective statements act as reinforcing (and perhaps discriminative) stimuli and, by implication, promote the class of response represented in the other's preceding line of talk.

THE LINGUISTIC APPROACH

A reflective statement, whatever else it may be, is part of talk and, as such, is subject to the sphere of influence of linguistics, particularly pragmatics, and amenable to techniques of conversational analysis (CA). Pragmatics explores the factors behind our choice of language, from among a range of possibilities in any given situation, and the effects of those choices on others. It therefore concentrates on language put to use by people as they live their lives. CA has its roots in sociology and, as pointed out by Pridham argues that conversation has its own dynamic structure and rules, and looks at the methods used by speakers to structure conversation efficiently'.

People normally succeed in understanding one another in ordinary conversations and manage their intercourse in a well-ordered fashion. But this can never be taken for granted, and the identification of the embedded rules and principles that underpin conversational coherence is of considerable interest to scholars of language.

Conversationalists constantly work at making talk run smoothly. They anticipate possible confusions and misunderstandings and take avoidance action. When problems do arise, they are identified and repair strategies implemented. Stokes and Hewitt referred to these management procedures that keep conversation on track as aligning actions, and, as specific examples, Nofsinger discussed continuers and formulations.

From this background, reflections could be regarded as forming part of the complex and often subtle operation of organising and orchestrating conversation. The process of formulating talk can be thought of as providing comment upon what has been said or what is taking place in the interaction.

It has been outlined as follows: A member may treat some part of the conversation as an occasion to describe. That conversation, to explain it, or characterize it, or explicate, or translate, or summarize, or furnish the gist of it, or take note of its accordance with rules, or Remark on its departure from rules. That is to say, a member may use some part of the conversation as an occasion to formulate the conversation.

Reformulations may relate to something the person providing the formulation has contributed (A-issues or events), something the other participant has mentioned, or, although less frequently, to both (AB-issues or events). A further distinction is that between formulations of gist and upshot.

The former involves extracting and highlighting the central events and issues featured in the immediately preceding utterance. Formulations of upshot go beyond this to frequently draw conclusions based upon assumptions that may or may not meet with the agreement of the other partner. It would seem that from this standpoint reflections could be regarded as essentially B-event or issue formulations of gist. (It should be also noted, though, that, in analysing Carl Rogers' verbal contributions in a counselling session, Lietaer (2004), in a study already cited, developed separate categories for reflections and reformulation.)

It has been noted that formulations of this type are often tentative proposals and require a decision from the other interactor a 'o their acceptability. Likewise, in the helping context, counsellors have been urged to reflect feelings in a tentative way that always leaves open the opportunity of denial or correction by the client. If the other is unwilling to agree to a particular representation of his or her position, one or more modifications are likely to be presented and worked through until agreement is forthcoming. The frequent association between a formulation of this type and confirmation by the other led Heritage and Watson to characterise them as adjacency pairs.

Adjacency pairs are a further feature of conversation that gives it structure and predictability. These are conversation sequences that are 'two turns long, having two parts said by different speakers in adjacent turns at talk'. Furthermore, there is a rule-driven expectation that, in initiating this type of sequence, one positions the other in the role of respondent and places restrictions around what can be offered as an acceptable next speech turn.

For example, questions beget answers; requests invoke refusals/acceptances; greetings initiate greetings, and so on. If reflection-confirmation/elaboration works in this way as an adjacency pair, then an obligation is placed upon the other either to explicitly confirm/deny the reformulation or to continue to elaborate the original pronouncement. According to the two theoretical interpretations previously considered, reflections promote more intense experiencing or reinforce continued discussion of a particular topic.

It is discussed that, continuers as conversational alignment devices that mark a listener's intention to forego making a substantive contribution to the conversation at that precise point. Following early work by Duncan and Fiske and Sacks, Schegloff, and Jefferson, the mechanisms involved in conversational turn taking have been extensively researched. Back-channel communication refers to listener contributions that sustain the listener role.

They seem to signal that the listener is attentive, interested, even comprehending, but does not seek the floor at that point. A further possibility is that reflections operate essentially in this way. Indeed, their role in the interviewing/ counselling literature is often presented as such. If so, reflections can have an additional alignment role as continuers or minimal responses, promoting the continuity of the conversational status quo in respect of topic and speaker/listener arrangement.

The use of 'mm hmm' was operating in this way in at least some of the instances when used by him in counselling. But formulations would also seem on occasion to be a way of engineering a change of topic or even the termination of conversation. It has been reported that conversational lapses are often immediately preceded by an utterance of this sort. Likewise, from their detailed analysis of doctor–patient communication, Stiles and Putnam discovered that reflective statements by doctors often seemed to cut patients off conversationally, rather than encourage deeper exploration. Likewise, Beach and Dixon identified a characteristic three-step sequence in their in-depth analysis of a medical history interview between a physician's assistant and a female patient. Here a reformulation by the medic led directly to a confirmatory response by the patient followed by a shift of topic initiated in the medic's subsequent conversational turn.

For the authors, 'Such actions essentially detoxify topic shift, therefore minimizing the likelihood that movement forward in the interview can be framed as [the interviewer's] heavy-handed pursuit of a medical "agenda" removed from [the patient's] concerns'.

How can reflection act both to stimulate deeper exploration of a topic and to preface a hiatus in the conversation or mark the occasion for a change of topic? One possible explanation has to do with the broader communicative frame within which the reflective statement is delivered.

In the situated interactive context of eliciting facts leading to a valid medical diagnosis, for example, patients may understand formulations as operating essentially to check the accuracy of a sequence of limited pieces of information under characteristic time pressures. At a more obviously micro analytic level, the prosodic accompaniment of the verbal content of the reflection may also be crucially important.

Variations in pitch can make a statement either interrogative or declarative.

Based upon the linguistic analysis of naturally occurring interactions, Schegloff and Sacks reported that words spoken with a downward intonation served to terminate topic discussion. It was conceived of reflections as repetition passes (that is, speech acts which serve to forego the opportunity of making a substantive contribution to the continued exploration of the topic), which can be used to bring about a conversational change.

However, it was emphasised that in order for reflections to function in this fashion, they must be delivered with a downward rather than a sustained or rising vocal intonation. The corollary of this, it could be argued, is that when reflections are used to facilitate further interviewee exploration, they need to be delivered with a sustained or rising intonation pattern. The depth of the intertwining of verbal and non-verbal modes of communication is increasingly being recognised. Additional features of contemporaneous non-verbal behaviour are also likely to be influential in determining the conversational effects of reflective statements.

Three radically different views of reflecting have been outlined in this section. According to the person-centred humanist, reflections are a means of accepting the other without condition, of empathising with the other, and helping that person become more fully self-actualising.

To the behaviourist, reflections act as social reinforcers to influence the verbal performance of the other by increasing the amount of preordained talk. Lastly, reflections have been depicted as techniques, which are used in the organisation and management of conversation not only to maintain or change it but also, under certain circumstances, to bring it to an end.

REFLECTING: FUNCTIONAL PERSPECTIVES

Functional aspects of reflecting have already been mentioned in this chapter to some extent. The present section, however, will cut across perspectives to concentrate more single-mindedly on the various potential effects claimed for the proper use of this technique.

Many are applicable to reflections generally while others are more specific to paraphrasing or reflecting feeling. One of the more basic functions of reflecting is to show respect for conversational partners by indicating that they are being fully attended to and that active listening is taking place. Reflecting is widely discussed within the context of listening actively. Active listening on the part of the therapist, in turn, was reported by Myers to have had a profound effect on the experiences of therapy by clients.

As one client disclosed, 'When a person is not listening I notice that he or she will draw on their interpretation and dismiss my position'.Listening demonstrates to speakers that they are sufficiently valued and accepted for another to be interested in them and prepared to become involved. Reflecting has, therefore, the potential to form the basis upon which to build a positive, facilitative relationship typified by openness, trust, respect, and empathy.

Reflections are also frequently used in order to clarify. An accurate paraphrase,by condensing and crystallising what has been said, can often help interviewees to see more clearly the exigencies of their situation. Mirroring back the core message contained in the interviewee's previous statement enables issues that are vague and confused to be thought through more clearly and objectively.

Since problems and concerns, especially of a personal nature, are things experienced, for the most part at a 'gut' level rather than being intellectualised or even verbalised, it often proves difficult to find the words and indeed thoughts to express them unambiguously. By encapsulating and unobtrusively presenting the most salient features of what has just been said, the exigencies of the helped person's predicament can be made more accessible to them.

In addition to acting as a means of enabling the interviewee to appreciate more clearly experienced concerns, reflecting assists the interviewer to check accuracy of understanding and obtain a clearer realisation of the actualities of circumstances. By reflecting, the interviewer not only conveys a desire to get to know, but also, when it is accurate, demonstrates to the interviewee the level of understanding accomplished, despite the fact that the original message may have been inchoate and vague.

Supported in this way, the interviewee is often motivated to continue to explore particular themes more deeply, concentrating upon facts, feelings, or both depending upon the content of the reflective statement. Commenting more particularly upon reflecting feeling states, It is pointed out that, as a result, interviewees are influenced to devote greater attention to phenomena of this type. They can be assisted to become more completely aware of their feelings by being encouraged to explore and express them in this way.

This can be difficult to accomplish and requires tact but is very worthwhile. Egan noted that while some feelings are quite laudable and easily accepted, many others prompt defensive reactions and, consequently, are either consciously or subconsciously repressed and denied.

As a result, people become estranged from these affective facets of their being. Through the reflection of feeling, such individuals can be put more fully in touch with these realities. By using this technique, the interviewer acknowledges the interviewee's right to feel this way and indicates that it is permissible for those feelings to be expressed and discussed. Another function of reflection of feeling, which is mentioned by Brammer, is to help people to 'own' their feelings – to appreciate that ultimately they are the source, and can take responsibility for their affective states.

Finally, the possibility of reflective statements being employed in order to regulate conversation by perhaps serving to engineer the termination of discussion should not be overlooked. Martin, for instance, referred to reflections being used to regulate the pace of the transaction. The various propositions outlined in this section differ substantially in terms of their epistemological basis. While most are, for the most part, theoretically derived or experientially grounded, others have emerged from systematic empirical enquiry. The final section of this chapter selectively reviews some of the research that has been conducted into reflecting.

REFLECTING: EMPIRICAL PERSPECTIVES

The lack of consistency in the operational definition of reflections and related terms has already been discussed at length. The work of categorising individual investigations and trying to abstract broad and consistent relationships among variables is consequently making that much more difficult. Further disparities in the research conducted relate to the theoretical basis of the enquiry, research design and procedures, number and type of subjects, and dependent variables chosen for investigation.

REFLECTIONS OF FEELING

Studies featuring this skill can be divided into two major categories and one minor. The former encompass: first, experiments, largely laboratory-based, designed to identify effects of reflecting feeling on subjects' verbal behaviour; and, second, studies that have attempted to relate the use of the technique to judgements, by either interviewees or observers, of interviewers in terms of such attributes as empathy, warmth, and respect.

In many instances both types of dependent variable have featured in the same investigation. The minor category includes descriptive studies that have charted the use of reflective statements by counsellors such as Carl Rogers. In an analysis of the counselling session captured on film and entitled the Individual and found that almost 53% of Rogers' contributions took the form of reflections of expressed feeling by the client. A further 5.5% were reflections of underlying feelings.

With respect to the effects of reflecting feeling on judgement of personal/ relational qualities, a significant relationship was found with ratings of empathic understanding in research conducted by Uhlemann, Lea, and Stone. These ratings were provided by external judges and were based upon both written responses and audio recordings of actual interviews. A similar procedure, labelled 'sensing unstated feelings', emerged as a significant predictor of counsellor effectiveness when assessed by surrogate clients after a counselling-type interview. However, not all findings have been positive.

It was failed to reveal any significant differences in clients' perceptions of counselling climate, counsellor comfort, or personal satisfaction between clients allocated to a reflection of feeling and to a probe treatment. It is found that no significant relationships between ratings of counsellors' reflections, on the one hand, and, on the other, separate assessments by counsellors, clients, and judges of empathy, genuineness, and acceptance displayed toward clients. As acknowledged, the small sample size may have been a factor in the outcome of this investigation.

PARAPHRASES

Research studies on the skill of reflecting in general, and paraphrasing in particular, are limited. For the most part, these have been experimental in design, conducted in laboratory settings, and have sought to establish the effects of paraphrasing upon various measures of interviewees' verbal behaviour. In some cases, though, paraphrases are defined in such a way as to include affective material, while, in others, affective content is not explicitly excluded. These definitional inconsistencies have also been noted by Hill and O'Brien in reviewing research in the area and should be kept in mind when interpreting the following findings.

Kennedy reported an increase in subjects' self-referenced statements attributable to paraphrasing, while similar findings featuring self-referenced affective statements were noted. According to Citkowitz, on the other hand, this skill had only limited effect in this respect, although there was a tendency for the association to be more pronounced when initial levels of self-referenced affect statements were relatively high. The subjects in this experiment were chronic schizophrenic in-patients, and the data were collected during clinical interviews. The distinction between the affective and the factual has been more explicitly acknowledged by others who have researched paraphrasing. Waskow, for instance, investigated the outcome of selective interviewer responding on the factual and affective aspects of subjects' communication in a psychotherapy-like interview.

It emerged that a significantly higher percentage of factual responses was given by those subjects who had their contributions paraphrased. In both cases, however, paraphrasing took place on an essentially random basis. Affective responses by subjects were also selected as the dependent variable. The few studies considering the effects of this technique on attitudes toward the interviewer, rather than behavioural changes on the part of the interviewee, have reported largely favourable outcomes.

A positive relationship was detailed by Dickson between the proportion of paraphrases to questions asked by employment advisory personnel and ratings of interviewer competency provided by independent, experienced judges. It would therefore seem that when paraphrases are used contingently and focus upon factual aspects of communication, recipients' verbal performance can be modified accordingly. In addition, paraphrasing seems to promote favourable judgements of the interviewer by both interviewees and external judges. Counselling trainees have also indicated that this is one of the skills they found most useful in conducting interviews.

OVERVIEW

This chapter has been concerned at conceptual, theoretical, practical, and empirical levels with reflecting as an interactive technique. After identifying and attempting to disentangle a number of conceptual confusions, three contrasting theoretical perspectives on the process deriving from humanistic psychology, behavioural psychology, and linguistics were presented. The various functional claims for the skill, based upon theoretical and experiential, as well as empirical, considerations, were discussed. From the research available (although there seems to be little recent work in this field), it would seem that reflections, whether of fact, feeling, or both, are perceived positively by both interviewees and external observers.

Many from a humanistic perspective are at pains, though, to ensure that qualities such as empathy and positive regard are not defined solely in terms of what they refer to as techniques such as reflecting.

There is also evidence that reflections can promote interviewee self-disclosure, but that a range of psychological and demographic characteristics of the interviewee may mediate their effects. Further research should concentrate upon more naturalistic settings than the psychology laboratory. The possible effects of such interviewer and interviewee variables as sex, status, socio-economic class, and cultural/ethnic background deserve further enquiry, as do situational factors, including the nature of the encounter. Meriting further attention is the impact of the location of the reflection in the sequence of exchanges and the effects, which paralinguistic and non-verbal accompaniments may have on the other interactor.

Chapter 6

Explaining

DEFINITION

The etymological root of explaining is explanare, to make plain. This root suggests two powerful metaphors: 'to strip bare' and 'to reveal'. These metaphors hint at different purposes of explaining. The first has connotations of getting down to the essentials.

The second leans toward revelation, to revealing subtleties, intricacies, and perhaps the uniqueness of an object, action, event, or occurrence. The first metaphor resonates with scientific approaches, such as the development of attribution theory, which seeks to identify the dimensions, through statistical analysis, on which people provide explanations of their behaviour. The second metaphor resonates with work in discourse analysis and hermeneutics, which seeks to tease out the patterns and meanings of speech in a specific context such as a courtroom or classroom.

In standard Modern English, the term 'explain' has come to mean 'make known in detail' (OED). It is arguable whether providing more detail improves an explanation.

Equally arguable is whether the standard definition covers the many personal meanings of explanations constructed and used by explainers. It was perhaps for this reason that Antaki offered the general principle that explaining is 'Some stretch of talk hearable as being a resolution of some problematic state of affairs.' However, this broad definition does not cover written explanations, and it deliberately leaves open the question of intentions, meanings, and interpretations of utterances. Its core is that there is a problem to be explained in terms of causes, reasons, excuses, or justifications.

NATURE OF UNDERSTANDING

Given that explaining is an attempt to give understanding, it is necessary to explore the nature of understanding – otherwise, one may be accused of explaining the known in terms of an unknown. Put simply, understanding involves seeing connections which were hitherto not seen. The connections may be between ideas, between facts, or between ideas and facts. This apparently simple definition has strong links with much of cognitive psychology.

As described in five steps in arriving at understanding, which began with 'felt' difficulty and proceeded to the search for corroborative evidence. His approach also describes neatly the process of explaining to oneself. Thyne emphasises the importance of recognising the appropriate cues in the information presented.

EXPLAINING

Importance of anchoring ideas in the learner's cognitive structure, of the use of advanced organisers, and of the learner's meaningful learning set. Pask's conversational theory of understanding and research on how students learn are built on the proposition that understanding is concerned with forming connections. Entwistle's more recent and qualitative work has revealed students'conceptions of understanding. He reports that, for many students, understanding was not merely cognitive but a feeling, including a feeling of satisfaction at creating meaning for themselves.

They stressed, above all, coherence and connectiveness and a sense of wholeness, although many recognised that the 'wholeness' was provisional yet irreversible. Once you understood something you could not 'de-understand' it, although your understanding could increase. The composite of their views captures the essence of understanding.

Understanding? It's the interconnection of lots of disparate things – the feeling that you understand how the whole thing is connected up – you can make sense of it internally.

You're making lots of connections which then make sense and it's logical. It's as though one's mind has finally 'locked in' to the pattern. Concepts seem to fit together in a meaningful way, when before the connections did not seem clear, or appropriate, or complete. If you don't understand, it's just everything floating about and you can't quite get everything into place – like jigsaw pieces, you know, suddenly connect and you can see the whole picture. But there is always the feeling you can add more and more and more: that doesn't necessarily mean that you didn't understand it; just that you only understood it up to a point.

There is always more to be added. But if you really understand something and what the idea is behind it, you can't not understand it afterwards – you can't 'de-understand' it! And you know you have understood something when you can construct an argument from scratch – when you can explain it so that you feel satisfied with the explanation, when you can discuss a topic with someone and explain and clarify your thoughts if the other person doesn't see what you mean.Experts on human information processing have rarely considered understanding.

But from Baddeley's (2004) model of memory, it is possible to deduce a model of understanding which is rich with implications for explaining as well as understanding. For an explanation to be understood, the explainee must first perceive there is a gap in knowledge, a puzzle or a problem to be explained.

This perception activates the working memory to retrieve schemata from the long-term memory. These schemata may have been stored in any of the procedural, semantic (thoughts and facts) or episodic memories (narratives, events). Cues in the explanation being given are matched to the activated schemata. This matching may lead to assimilation of the explanation into the existing schemata or it may modify the existing schemata. In both, it produces new connections of concepts and/or facts. The degree of stability of those new connections depends in part upon the network of existing concepts and facts. The validity of the new connections, that is, of the understanding, can be tested only by reference to corroborative evidence, which may be from an external source or from other evidence and rules stored in the person's cognitive framework.

If the cues are clear and well-ordered, they can be rapidly processed. If they are confusing, they will not link with existing schemata and may be rapidly forgotten. Given the limitations of sensory and working memory, one should not explain too quickly, and one should chunk the information provided into meaningful and relatively brief sentences. Pauses should be used to separate the chunks of information. Too fast or too distracting explanations cannot be processed by the working memory. The use of analogies, metaphors, and similes will create new connections rapidly with the existing schemata of the explainee. The use of frequent summaries, guiding statements, and cognitive maps can help explainees to change their schemata, which they can then elaborate on subsequently.

Personal narratives interwoven with concepts and findings can trigger the procedural, episodic, and semantic memories and so aid storing and retrieval of understanding.This brief exposition of understanding has obvious implications for providing explanations in many professional contexts. The problem must be presented so as to be recognised as a problem, the cues given must take account of the existing cognitive structure of the explainees, the cues must be highlighted so they can readily be matched, and, if possible, there should be a check on whether understanding has occurred.

TYPES OF EXPLAINING

The literature abounds with typologies of explanations. In considering these typologies, It is seen that a robust, simple typology which would be relatively easy to use by researchers and practitioners. The typology consists of three main types of explanation: the interpretive, the descriptive, and the reason-giving. They approximate to the questions, What? How? Why? However, the precise form of words matters less than the intention of the question.

They may be supplemented with the questions, Who? When? Where? Together, these questions can rapidly provide a framework for many explanations. Interpretive explanations address the question, 'What?'

They interpret or clarify an issue or specify the central meaning of a term or statement. Examples are answers to the questions: What is 'added value'? What is a novel? What does impact mean in physics? What does it mean in management? Descriptive explanations address the question, 'How?' These explanations describe processes, structures, and procedures, as in: How did the chairperson lead the meeting? How do cats differ anatomically from dogs? How should a chairperson lead a meeting? How do you measure sustainability?

Reason-giving explanations address the question, 'Why?' They involve reasons based on principles or generalisations, motives, obligations, or values. Included in reason-giving explanations are those based on causes and functions, although some philosophers prefer to distinguish causes and reasons. Examples of reason-giving explanations are answers to the questions: Why do camels have big feet? Why did this fuse blow? Why do heavy smokers run the risk of getting cancer? Why are some people cleverer than others? Why is there more crime in inner-city areas? Why am I reading this chapter? Why should I keep to deadlines? Of course, a particular explanation may involve all three types of explanation. Thus, in explaining how a bill becomes a law, one may want to describe the process, give reasons for the law, define certain key terms, and consider its implications for legal practice.

FUNCTIONS OF EXPLAINING

The primary function of giving an explanation is to give understanding to others, but in giving understanding, one can also fulfil a wide range of other functions. These include ensuring learning, clarifying ambiguities, helping someone learn a procedure, reducing anxiety, changing attitudes and behaviour, enablement, personal autonomy, and, last but not least, improving one's own understanding. These functions imply that explaining and understanding are not merely cognitive activities but also involve a gamut of motivations, emotions, and conation. Clearly, one needs to take account of the specific function of an explanation when considering the tasks and processes of explaining.

TASKS AND PROCESSES OF EXPLAINING

Explaining is an interaction of the explainer, the problem to be explained, and the explainees. The explainer needs to take account of the problem and the knowledge, attitudes, and other characteristics of the explainees and use appropriate approaches in the process of explaining. To assist in this process, it was suggested that a 'P5' approach as shown in beneficial:

- pre-assessment of the explainees' knowledge
- planning
- preparation
- presentation
- post-mortem.

Their approach was developed from the work and the model is pertinent to formally presented explanations, such as lectures or presentations, and to 'opportunistic explanations' prompted by a question from a client, patient, or student, although in the last, one may have little time to prepare.

Some of suggestions have been incorporated into the approach advocated in this section. It follows the sequence of defining the problem, determining the process, and clarifying and estimating the outcomes. The problem to be explained and the problem of explainees First, the explainer has to identify and specify the problem that requires explanation.

The problem may be posed initially by the explainer or by the explainee. The problem presented by a client may require clarification and refinement. It is well known by medical and legal practitioners that the problem presented by a patient or client is not necessarily the problem. One has to diagnose and communicate clearly the problem in a way that is acceptable to the client.

Herein lies a difficulty of ownership. If patients do not perceive the problem as their own, the proposed solution may not be accepted and acted upon. Even if the problem is accepted, the solution proffered may not be acceptable.

More subtly, the solution may be accepted but not acted upon. This observation is relevant to research using the health belief model. Changes in beliefs do not necessarily lead to changes in behaviour. In teaching and management, a similar difficulty may arise. If pupils, students, or employees do not perceive the problem presented as one worthy of solution, they may reject it and the process of acquiring the solution. Rhetoric, persuasion, principles of pedagogy, and power all have a part to play in the acceptance of a problem, and the solution and its implementation.

But it is not enough merely to identify the problem. To be a skilled explainer, one as also to take account of the explainees, and their social and cultural backgrounds, motivations, linguistic ability, and previous knowledge – and plan accordingly before embarking upon the explanation. An important point here is empathy. To be a good explainer, one needs to empathise with the explainees, see the world through their eyes, and relate one's explanation to their experiences. But empathy per se is not enough.

As an explainer, one has to decide on one's goals in relation to the explainees, identify appropriate content, highlight and lowlight the content appropriately, and select appropriate methods and resources to achieve the goals. Once the problem and its possible solution(s) have been identified, the problem might helpfully be expressed in the form of a central question, and that question may be then subdivided into a series of implicit questions or hidden variables. Thus, the explanation of how local anaesthetics work contains the implicit questions, 'What is a local anaesthetic'?' and 'How are nerve impulses transmitted?' These implicit questions or hidden issues can then provide the structure of an explanation.

Process of Explaining

The task of the explainer is to state the problem to be explained and present or elicit a series of linked statements, each of which is understood by the explainee and which together lead to a solution of the problem.

These linked statements may be labelled 'keys' since they unlock understanding. Each of these keys will contain a key statement. A key statement may be a procedure, a generalisation, a principle, or even an appeal to an ideology or a set of personal values. The key may contain examples, illustrations, metaphors, and perhaps qualifications to the main principle. When the problem to be explained is complex, there might also be a summary of key statements during the explanation as well as a final summary.

The keys are the nub of explaining. But, as emphasised earlier, for an explanation to be understood, it follows that the explainer has to consider not only the problem to be explained but also the characteristics of the explainees. What is appropriate as an explanation of the structure of DNA to postgraduate biochemists is unlikely to be appropriate as an explanation to 11-year-olds.

There is no such thing as the good explanation. What is 'good' for one group may not be good for another. Its quality is contingent upon the degree of understanding it generates in the explainees. For different groups of explainees, the keys of the explanation and the explanation itself will be different, although the use of keys and other strategies may not be.

The essence of the process of explaining is that its goal, understanding, is a function of the existing cognitive structure of the explainee as well as of the new information being provided: hence, the importance of similes, analogies, and metaphors. These devices may, as understanding grows, be seen as crude, perhaps even as false, explanations. Hooks and balls may be a very crude analogy for explaining atoms and molecules, but they may be a useful starting point for explaining molecular structure to young children. 'Rotting garden posts' may be an inadequate metaphor for describing the roots of a patient's teeth, but the metaphor might be a useful device for justifying extraction.

The process of explaining is not only concerned with identifying problems and proffering solutions. Sometimes, the task of the explainer is to explain the problem and sometimes to explain the connection between the problem and the solution.

A problem such as the relationship between truth and meaning may not have any solution, or it may have several unsatisfactory solutions, but at least the problem may be understood. This point is emphasised, since much high-level teaching and counselling is concerned not with explaining the solutions of problems but with explaining the nature of a problem, exploring the possible solutions, and judging their relative merits.

Outcome

The outcome hoped for when explaining is that the explainee understands. The explainer has to check that the explanation is understood. This task is akin to feedback and it is sometimes neglected by doctors, teachers, lawyers, and others. Understanding may be checked on by a variety of methods, including, of course, formal assessments. The most primitive method is to ask, 'Do you understand?' The answer one usually gets is 'Yes'.

The response is more a measure of superficial compliance than of understanding. Other methods are to invite the explainee to recall the explanation, to ask questions of specific points in the explanation, to apply the explanation to another situation or related problem, to provide other examples of where the explanation might hold, or to identify similar sorts of explanations.

All of these may be used to measure the success of an explanation, providing the procedures are appropriate and valid. A check on understanding much favoured by health professionals is a change in behaviour. As a measure of explanatory power, it is weak.

The explanation may be understood, but it may not lead to action. The explanation may not be understood orimperfectly understood yet the patient changes behaviour. However, if the purpose of a particular explanation is to change behaviour, and understanding is a mere mediator, then changes in behaviour may be useful outcome measures. But one should bear in mind that such changes in behaviour are unlikely to be sustained unless they are integrated into the cognitive structure of the student, patient, or client. Aristotle provided a conceptually illuminating start to the study of explaining. His four causes (aition), the material, the formal, the efficient, and the final cause, are the basis of most explanations, although it should be noted that the ancient Greek term for 'cause' includes reasons.

His notions of ethos personality and stance), pathos and logos laid the foundations of rhetoric (persuasive explanation and argument in speech and written texts) and later studies in this field. Locke, the seventeenth-century empiricist, also had an important influence on the study of understanding and explaining.

The following example of his advice is still relevant today: Confound not his understanding with explications or notions that are above it, or with the variety or number of things that are not to his present purpose. Mark what 'tis his mind aims at in the question and not words he expresses it in; and when you have informed and satisfied him in that you shall see how his thoughts will enlarge themselves, and how by fit answers he may be led on farther than perhaps you could imagine.

Since the time of Galileo, there have been debates about measurement and judgement, appeals to experimentation and appeals to authority, qualitative and quantitative methods, and nomothetic and ideographic approaches. Galileo's famous dictum, 'Measure that which is measurable and make measurable that which is not', is at the heart of much scientific and pseudo-scientific research and of the fashionable debate of evidence-based approaches in medicine and education. This approach includes the development of models for explanation, prediction, and control. It has an underlying concern with quantitative measurement, with problems of measuring reliability and validity, and with, as far as possible, identical repetition of experiments. Associated with the mode of scientific explanation is often an interest in the organic, in disease centred models, and in the search for mathematically based generalisations within a closed system of concepts.

In contrast, 'humanistic' or broadly 'phenomenological' approaches are more concerned with personal understanding than with 'scientific' proof; with qualitative methods; with intentions, meanings, and their constructions in different contexts; and with tentative generalisations based on themes. For example, a 'humanistic' researcher might look at how an individual doctor adduces the relevant hypotheses or explanatory principles; how he or she detects regularities, distinguishes differences, and arrives at decisions.

Such a researcher often has an interest in the individual patient's conceptions of illness, in patient-centred models of management, and in a search for interpretations and meanings within the consultation. Not surprisingly, the differences between those who favour scientific explanations and those who favour searches for understanding and meaning spill over into conflicts about research, research funding, and approaches to teaching. They permeate attitudes toward 'hard' and 'soft' human resources management.

The Covering Law Model

At the core of explanation is the triadic principle derived from Aristotle's syllogistic method. There must be:

1. A generalisation or universal law
2. An evidential statement or observation that the situation being considered is an instance of that generalisation
3. A conclusion: At first sight, procedural explanations do not fit the covering law model. Certainly, in giving a procedural explanation, it may not be necessary to

use the covering law model. Indeed, its use could confuse the explainee, but there should be an explanation based upon the covering law model which justifies the procedure. If not, the procedure is likely to be faulty. Put in different terms, a good practice is always underpinned by a good theory, even if the practitioner is unaware of the theory.

The covering law model is used for scientific explanations based on strong scientific laws or in a weaker form for highly probabilistic explanations or for generalisations believed by an individual or group. Values, obligations, ideologies, or beliefs might form the first statement of an explanation. Kruglanski points out that at some point individuals stop generating hypotheses and attain closure on a belief.

This 'frozen' belief becomes the regularity principle which they use to explain their behaviour. Many of the errors in explanations can be identified by recasting the explanation in this form and examining the links between the three statements. The generalisation may not hold, the instance may not be an instance of the generalisation, and the conclusion not validly drawn from the principle and instance. More subtly, the instance may fit more appropriately into another generalisation.

To complicate matters further, an explanation may be incorrect yet believed, or correct and not believed. Examples of both complications abound in the history of medicine and science, and in history itself. One should be wary of overextending the first statement of the model lest the explanation become vacuous.

Appeals to universals such as 'God's will' or the 'misfiring of neurons' do not pick out the reasons for a specific action or event.

Sometimes, one needs to use a counter-factual model to identify the regulatory principle that has the most explanatory potency. To answer the question, 'Why did the car ferry, the Herald of Free Enterprise, sink so quickly?', one looks at the question, 'When does a car ferry sink slowly?', and looks for the regularity principle that accounts for the difference. This may identify a chain of reasons that could lead to the door of the boardroom.

The link between the first and second statements of the covering law model raises questions about the validity of the method used to obtain the evidence and issues concerning 'truth' and 'phenomenological' truth. Professions and academic disciplines vary in their truth criteria and what counts as acceptable evidence. What might be accepted as evidence in a research journal might not be accepted as evidence in a court of law.

The link between the second and third statements raises the question of whether the conclusion is justified by the principle and the evidence (cf. arguments concerning weapons of mass destruction and the war in Iraq). But even if the covering law holds for an explanation, there is the question of whether the explanation provided would be better if it had been derived from a different principle and evidential statement, and the further question of whether the explainer was deliberately attempting to give a false explanation.

There are further difficulties here. Even if an explanation is valid, or believed to be valid, there remains the question of whether it is understood. Now, clearly, it is possible for a scientist or scholar to give an explanation that is not understood in his or her own time, or, as was more frequently the case, the explanation may have been understood but rejected by his or her peers.

However, even in such extreme cases, one can assume that the scientists or scholars intended to give understanding to their audience. But is intention enough? On this issue there are various views. On the one hand, explaining may be seen as a task word such as hunting or fishing; on the other hand, it may be seen as an achievement word such as killing or catching. If explaining is regarded as an achievement word, then the outcome of the explanation takes primacy.

As observed: 'If the teacher really has explained something to his class, they will understand it, and if they do not understand it, despite his efforts, what purported to be an explanation was not an explanation after all.'Our own view is that the intentional position is too weak and the outcome position too strong. We suggest there is usually an intention to explain, an attempt to explain, and a check on understanding. We recognise that some outcomes may not be attained or attainable, and some explanations, not intended, can deepen understanding. A person may carry away from an explanation much more than the intentions of the explainer.

EVIDENCE FROM THE FIELD

Most of the experimental evidence on explaining is based on studies of teaching and the doctor–patient consultation. The evidence provided in some professions, such as law and management, tends to be expertise-based rather than evidence-based. While it is easy to disparage such craft knowledge, 'practical' wisdom in a profession may run alongside the evidence collected by research and might be more influential than the research findings per se.

Indeed, it could be argued that unless the research findings are integrated into craft knowledge they are unlikely to have much effect on practice. The following sections focus primarily upon evidence-based approaches in the different professions. While it may be tempting to read only the sections related to one's own profession, there is much to be gained from exploring findings in other professions, matching these against one's own professional experience, and considering whether the findings provide a springboard for similar explorations in one's own profession.

EXPLAINING IN CLASSROOM

Estimates of the proportion of time spent on explaining by teachers vary from 10% to 30%, according to the definition of explaining adopted. Time spent on a task is but a crude measure of its efficacy. More important is the quality: the way the time is spent. Some people explain aptly, getting to the heart of the matter with just the right terminology, examples, and organisation of ideas. Other explainers, on the contrary, get us and themselves all mixed up, use terms beyond our level of comprehension, draw inept analogies, and even employ concepts and principles that cannot be understood without an understanding of the very thing being explained. The remark is apposite to explanations in other professional contexts.

Studies show that the foremost reasons for liking a teacher are clear explanations of lessons, assignments, and difficulties, helpfulness with school work, and fairness. Reviews of the literature also reveal that good explanations are not only clearly structured, but they are also interesting.

PROCESSES, STRUCTURES, AND OUTCOMES

Presentation techniques have been the subject of most studies, and these have demonstrated that explanations which yield greater pupil or student achievement are based on clarity, fluency, emphasis, interest, the use of examples, summaries, and recall or application questions. Clarity, including the use of definitions, yields greater pupil or student achievement. Fluency, including the notions of emphasis, clear transitions, absence of vagueness, and absence of false starts and verbal tangles, have all been shown to be associated with effective presentation. Studies of expressiveness show that purposeful variations in voice, gesture, manner, and use of teaching aids all contribute to the interest and effectiveness of an explanation.

The pattern, not the frequency, of examples determines the effectiveness of an explanation. The pattern should be associated with both the type of explanation and the pupils' prior knowledge. In teaching an unfamiliar topic, the sequence examples.

Principle should be used; in restructuring pupils' ideas, the sequence principle. examples should be used. The principles should be educed or stated, and positive and negative examples provided. It is indicated that good explanatory lessons have more keys and more types of keys that vary the cognitive demands on the pupils. These lessons contained: more framing statements, which delineate the beginning and ending of subtopics; more focusing statements, which emphasise the key points; more relevant examples; more rhetorical questions; better use of audiovisual aids; and fewer unfinished summaries. The teachers of low-scoring lessons introduced so many ideas that the pupils became confused. The teachers of high scoring lessons used simple language and examples to which the pupils could relate. In psychological terms, the teachers activated and built upon the cognitive schemata of their pupils.

Chapter 7

Strategic Revelation in Personal and Professional Relationships

THE PROCESS

As stated, 'In every sort of interpersonal relationship, from business partnerships to love affairs, the exchange of self disclosure plays an important role. People disclose to friends and spouses, to physicians and hairdressers, to solicitors and pub governors.

The importance of self-disclosure for individuals and their relationships is not always apparent. Revelation of such mundane matters as the events of the day may be a cherished ritual in a marriage, while people sometimes confide personal problems to virtual strangers.

The pervasiveness and importance of self-disclosure accounts for the intense interest in this phenomenon shown by social scientists. Literally thousands of quantitative studies have been conducted over a period extending 40 years. The periodic publication of reviews of this literature has helped provide coherence and helped organise this body of knowledge.

Both reviews of thematic issues and more comprehensive treatments enable readers to cope with a mounting body of knowledge.

The present review offers a strategic perspective on self-disclosure by highlighting the motivations and means by which people manage the disclosure of information in personal and work relationships. We review

SELF-DISCLOSURE IN PERSONAL RELATIONSHIPS

Self-disclosure is one of the defining characteristics of intimate relationships: 'Two people cannot be said to be intimate with each other if they do not share some personal, relatively confidential information with one another'. Self-disclosure serves important functions in relationship development.

We can not initiate, develop, or maintain a relationship without self-disclosure. We terminate relationships, in part, by terminating self-disclosure. Self-disclosure has other important relational consequences, including eliciting liking and reciprocal self-disclosure. Requests for disclosure are common when individuals want information about their partner, including details about the partner's sexual history in order to engage. Self-disclosure performs important relational functions.

Revealing information about self can help people as they attempt to initiate and develop relationships with others. Some authors even suggest that self-disclosure may be a strategy by which people seek to obtain desirable responses from others.

On the other hand, self-disclosing some information creates problems for individuals and relationships. Telling others exactly how we feel can be cruel and destroy trust. Consequently, individuals must learn how to regulate their disclosures. Below we discuss both the role of self-disclosure in different stages of relationship development and the necessity of managing personal information by regulating self-disclosures.

Self-disclosure is used to initiate relationships. In initial interaction, people reveal their names, hometowns, hobbies, and so on.

As stated by Derlega, 'it is hard to imagine how a relationship might get started without such self-disclosure.' Self-disclosure is typically superficial and narrow in breadth in the early stages of a relationship. Although this self-disclosure may not be intimate, it is the prelude to more intimate self-disclosure. Self-disclosure in the initial phases of a relationship functions to promote liking and to help people get to know each other. Self-disclosure provides information that helps us reduce uncertainty about the other person's attitudes, values, personality, and so on, thereby enabling the relationship to develop.

Similarly, through self-disclosure we acquire mutual knowledge, or knowledge that two people share, know they share, and use in interacting with one another. Self-disclosure is also an important component in the development of a relationship; thus, If you like this person, you will want to know more about him or her, and you will, in turn, be willing to share more information about yourself. You will begin to talk about attitudes, feelings, and personal experiences; in brief, you will begin to disclose more personal information. If your new friend likes you, he or she also will disclose personal information.

Research indicates that people strategically use self-disclosure to regulate the development of a relationship. In the study of strategies individuals use to develop and restrict the development of friendships, participants described how they got to know others and how they chose appropriate topics of conversation for interacting with someone they just met and a close friend.

They also indicated strategies they would use to restrict and intensify a relationship's development. Superficial self-disclosure, appropriate for conversing with a stranger, was also used to restrict the development of a relationship. Similarly, intimate self-disclosure, appropriate for conversing with friends, was used to intensify a relationship.

In study of romantic relationships, seriously dating college students reported self-disclosing information about self as a strategy to intensify dating relationships. Another strategy was to disclose things about the relationship, feelings in the relationship, and what is desired for the future of the relationship.

Thus, disclosing information about yourself as well as your thoughts and feelings about the relationship is a strategy to increase the intimacy of a relationship.

RELATIONAL MAINTENANCE

Self-disclosure about the events of the day, referred to as 'catching up' or 'debriefing', is an important relationship maintenance strategy. All relationships involve periods when the partners are away from each other (e.g. while they are at work). One of the behaviours used by partners to maintain the continuity of their relationship across these periods of physical absence is catching up. When couples are reunited at the end of the day, they often talk about what happened during the day: how their day went, who they saw, what they did, and so on. Research indicates that debriefing one another is a relationship maintenance strategy that is positively related to marital satisfaction.

Self-disclosure of intimate information is also important for maintaining a relationship. Once partners feel they know each other, the exchange of objective or factual information about the self probably decreases. As a relationship progresses, the amount of subjective or emotional information that can be exchanged between partners increases; not only how the speaker feels about himself or herself but also how the speaker feels about the partner and the relationship can be revealed.

Thus, self-disclosure in relationships continues to include the disclosure of facts and feelings about the self, but it also includes feelings about the partner and the relationship. Self-disclosure is essential for preventing probiems in relationships and solving problems after they have occurred. Discussing our relationship and the rules in our relationship is important for preventing relational transgressions, and it is also important in repairing relationships after relational transgressions have occurred.

An alternative conclusion is that openness is an effective communication strategy for some types of couples, but not others. As described three types of couples, traditionals, independents, and separates, and argued that there are similarities within and differences among the types of couples in the degree to which they self-disclose and value self-disclosure in their marriage. Fitzpatrick argued that these couple types establish different norms about what is appropriate to reveal in their relationship, and that these norms determine the relationship between communication and satisfaction. Fitzpatrick found that traditionals value self-disclosure in marriage and that they self-disclose to their spouses.

However, their self-disclosure is limited to positive feelings and topics about the partner and the relationship. Independent couples value self-disclosure, disclose substantially more to their spouses than other types of couples, and are willing to disclose both positive and negative feelings to one another. Separates do not value openness and self-disclosure in marriage and also do not self-disclose to their spouses. Thus, self-disclosure is important to maintain a relationship, but full disclosure is not universally prescribed.

Relational Dialectics/Boundary Management Theory

One of the important principles of a strategic perspective on self-disclosure is that individuals have multiple goals in interaction and relationships. Sometimes, the goals are compatible and the pursuit of one goal facilitates the accomplishment of the other. However, sometimes goals are contradictory and the fulfilment of one goal conflicts with the fulfilment of the other. For example, the goal of being open and honest with your partner may conflict with the goal of maintaining the relationship. Recent theories have elaborated the forces working against self-disclosure in relationships. Early theories on personal relationships, such as social penetration theory, argued that there is a linear relationship between self-disclosure and relationship development, self-disclosure gradually and incrementally increasing as the relationship develops.

Many scholars have rejected the idea that the development of relationships always follows a unidirectional and cumulative path, with ever-increasing openness of self-disclosure. As argued by these authors, initial theory and research on self-disclosure were simplistic. Instead, more recent theories recognise the possibility that developing or continuing relationships might exhibit cycles of openness and closedness, or that some relationships might not progress toward increased openness at al. Although some relationships may generally proceed toward greater openness, they probably have cycles or phases of openness or closedness within this overall developmental pattern.

Individuals can respond to the dialectical tension of openness–closedness with a number of strategic responses. Baxter found the predominant strategy reported for the openness–closedness contradiction to be segmentation, which involves a differentiation of topic domains into those for which self-disclosure is appropriate and those regarded as 'taboo topics' (i.e. topics that are 'off limits' in a relationship). Similarly, privacy regulation is a strategic response to the dialectical nature of self-disclosure. It is defined that, privacy as 'an interpersonal boundary process by which a person or group regulates interaction with others. By altering the degree of openness of the self to others, a hypothetical personal boundary is more or less receptive to social interaction with others'. Similarly, communication boundary management theory argues that individuals manage their communication boundaries in balancing the need for disclosure with the need for privacy.

The basic thesis of communication boundary management theory is that revealing private information is risky because one is potentially vulnerable when revealing aspects of the self. To manage disclosing private information, individuals erect a metaphoric boundary as a means of protection and to reduce the possibility of being rejected or getting hurt. Thus, privacy regulation is a strategic response to the dialectical tension of the need to reveal and conceal. By regulating privacy, we engage in a strategy designed to satisfy the oppositional forces of openness and closedness.

The dialectical perspective paints a more complex picture of the skills involved in competent self-disclosure. Competent self-disclosure is responsive to partners' needs for intimacy and privacy. Rawlins' (1983) analysis suggests that it may be just as important for an individual to develop skill at restrained remarks and selective disclosure of intimate information: 'An apt handling of the dialectic means that self limits self's own vulnerability and strives to protect other while still expressing thoughts and feelings'.

FACTORS AFFECTING SELF-DISCLOSURE

Some variables affect self-disclosure, such as gender, requests for self-disclosure, and another person's self-disclosure. In this section, we explore some of the factors facilitating and inhibiting the process of self-disclosure.

Sex Differences

Who discloses more, men or women? Gender stereotypes would have us believe that women are far more disclosive than men. However, a meta-analysis of sex differences in self-disclosure indicates that while women disclose more than men, the difference is small. It is examined over 200 studies on sex differences in self-disclosure. Regardless of whether self-disclosure was observed between strangers or measured by self-report or observational measures between partners in intimate relationships, approximately 85% of men and women overlapped in their self-disclosure.

Reciprocal Disclosures

Perhaps the most enduring generalisation from the literature on self-disclosure is that self-disclosure is reciprocal. The pioneering researcher, Sidney Jourard, noted: 'in ordinary social relationships, disclosure is a reciprocal phenomenon. Participants in dialogue disclose their thoughts, feelings, actions, etc., to the other and are disclosed to in return. I called this reciprocity the "dyadic effect": disclosure begets disclosure'.

A recent meta-analysis of over 60 studies found that self-disclosure is reciprocal, although the degree of matching depends on how reciprocity was measured. But in all cases, whether self-disclosure was measured by self-report or observational measures, whether self-disclosure was to strangers or intimates, self-disclosure was highly reciprocal.

Several theories explain reciprocity of self-disclosure, including trust attraction, social exchange, and modelling. The trust-attraction hypothesis assumes that disclosing intimate information to a recipient indicates that the other is liked and trusted and this then leads the recipient to disclose as a sign of liking and a willingness to trust the original discloser. The social exchange perspective suggests that receiving disclosure is a rewarding experience and that when we receive something of value we feel obligated to return something of similar value, such as a similar disclosure.

The modelling hypothesis posits that one person's self-disclosure serves as a model for the other person's self-disclosure. More recent theoretical explanations attribute reciprocity to more global constraints of conversational norms, that is, rules that indicate the kinds of comments that would be appropriate given previous comments. Reciprocity of self-disclosure is assumed to be a time-bound process in which people mutually regulate their self-disclosure to one another at some agreed-on pace.

But little more is known about the temporal aspects of reciprocity. The rate at which it occurs, how it ebbs and flows, and factors that accelerate or retard reciprocity of exchange have not been discussed in detail. Some people have argued that the need for immediate reciprocity declines as the relationship increases in intimacy and commitment; however, one study indicated that married couples reciprocate self-disclosure within a 10-minute conversation.

Berg and Archer noted that a variety of responses to self-disclosure are appropriate and that a common reaction to receiving intimate self-disclosure is to express concern or support, rather than to reciprocate self-disclosure. In their experimental study, Berg and Archer observed that the most favourable impressions were made by listeners who expressed concern for a discloser rather than listeners who responded with self-disclosures.

Thus, it may be more important to respond to self-disclosure with interest and support than immediately to reciprocate self-disclosure.

Self-Disclosure and Liking

Self-disclosure and liking are thought to be related in at least three ways: self-disclosure to another person causes the other person to like the discloser, liking another person causes an individual to self-disclose, and individuals like another person as a result of having disclosed to them. A meta-analysis of the research on self-disclosure and liking confirmed that we like people who self-disclose to us, we disclose more to people we like, and we like others as a result of having disclosed to them.

The effect of self-disclosure on a recipient's liking for the discloser has been of greatest theoretical interest, and studies examining this effect make up the bulk of the studies on self-disclosure and liking.

This effect is typically referred to as the 'disclosure-liking hypothesis'. Though the research indicates that self-disclosure leads to liking, there are at least two qualifications to the disclosure– liking relationship. First, disclosure that violates normative expectations will not lead to liking. Low-intimacy, descriptive self-disclosures that reflect positively on the self are normative in initial interactions. Revealing information that deviates from this norm may produce negative evaluations.

Even in developed relationships, norms exist specifying appropriate and inappropriate topics for discussion. Research also indicates that the disclosure of negatively valanced information does not lead to liking. As Bochner stated, 'discriminating disclosers are more satisfied and more likely to remain attractive to their partners than are indiscriminating disclosers'. Second, people who disclose a lot to everyone are not liked more than low disclosers. Miller observed that sorority women who generally disclosed more to others were not more popular than other members. However, women who disclosed more to a particular partner than they generally disclosed to others were liked more by that partner.

People make attributions regarding another person's disclosure, and the reasons or motivations we attribute to another person's self-disclosure are an important part of what the self-disclosure will mean to the relationship. People can attribute another person's self-disclosure to the person's disposition or personality ('he disclosed to me because he is an open person') or to their relationship.

When we perceive another person's self-disclosure as personalistic (revealed only to the target) rather than non-personalistic (revealed to many people), research indicates that it leads to increased liking concluded from their meta-analysis of the research on self-disclosure and liking that the relationship between disclosure and liking is stronger if the recipient believes that the disclosure was shared only with the recipient.

Requests for Disclosures

For a variety of reasons, people frequently desire personal information about others. It was suggested that 'when strangers meet, their primary concern is one of uncertainty reduction'. To reduce that uncertainty, initial interactants engage in high levels of information-seeking.

There are several strategies for acquiring information about a partner in interactions, the most obvious being asking questions. However, because norms of social appropriateness restrict the use of information requests, initial interactants are hypothesised to use less direct strategies as well. In particular, participants in initial interaction may use self-disclosure to acquire information about each other. Because of the norm of reciprocity, self-disclosure is a 'potentially powerful way to induce the other to disclose similar information about himself'.

This is especially true in initial interaction, where the need to reciprocate self-disclosure immediately and on a tit-for-tat basis is strong. It is found that self-disclosure occurred more frequently than asking questions during a 6-minute initial conversation between strangers; across the entire conversation, 49% of the utterances were coded as self-disclosures, whereas 18% of the utterances were coded as questions. As the conversation continued, individuals' uncertainty level and question asking decreased, but their self-disclosure increased. Thus, disclosure appears to be a more appropriate strategy than asking questions for acquiring information in initial interaction.

Self-Disclosure on the Internet

In the interpersonal communication researchers began considering how computer-mediated communication (CMC) compares to face-to-face communication. Early views of CMC were that on-line communication is impersonal in comparison to f2f communication due to the lack of non-verbal cues. Social information-processing theory rejected the view that the absence of non-verbal communication restricts communicators' ability to engage in interpersonal communication.

Walther argued that communicators are just as motivated to reduce interpersonal uncertainty, form impressions, and develop affinity in on-line settings as off-line. When denied non-verbal communication, communicators substitute other cues to engage in impression formation and relational messages, such as content, style, and timing of verbal messages. The rate of information exchange is slower on-line but, given enough time, relationships conducted through CMC can be just as personal as f2f communication. Research supports the proposition that CMC can be just as personal as f2f communication.

More recently, a third view has emerged in which on-line relationships, because of the characteristics of CMC, are often hyperpersonal (more personal and involve higher levels of self-disclosure and attraction than f2f). Some have argued that Internet users come to know one another more quickly and intimately than in f2f relationships. They argue that the features of CMC may make it easier to self-disclose on-line versus f2f. Individuals in CMC often are anonymous, and the psychological comfort that comes from such anonymity may lead them to reveal more information about themselves. Walther argued that CMC is hyperpersonal because of sender, receiver, message, and channel effects.

Receivers initially engage in stereotypically positive and idealised attributions of on-line partners. Senders exploit

CMC's absence of non-verbal communication for the purpose of selective self-presentation, presenting a positive and idealised image of self. The channel facilitates goal-enhancing messages by allowing sources greater control over message construction.

The process of feedback creates self-fulfilling prophesies among senders and receivers. Cooper and Sportolari refer to this as the 'boom and bust' phenomenon: When people reveal more about themselves earlier than they would in F2F interactions, relationships get intense very quickly. Such an accelerated process of revelation may increase the chance that the relationship will feel exhilarating at first, and become quickly eroticized, but then not be able to be sustained because the underlying trust and true knowledge of the other are not there to support it.

It was highlighted in the media accounts of people who are certain they have found their 'soulmate' and leave an established relationship, travelling across the country, to meet people who do not turn out to be what they seemed. Others have noted that Internet romantic relationships progress through an inverted developmental sequence. In real life, we meet people, then get to know them; on-line, we get to know people and then choose to meet them. Some, say this makes for an unstable relationship. However, the opposite is plausible.

CMC may be characterised by a higher degree of personal investment of time and self-disclosure than is typical in f2f relationships. This greater investment may result in a stronger relationship. Overall, there is little evidence that on-line communication is more personal than f2f communication. Nor is there empirical evidence to support the boom and bust phenomenon.

Nonetheless, some have cautioned that when developing relationships on-line one should move from virtual to f2f in a short period of time before unrealistic expectations have time to build up. Another dimension along which the nature of self-disclosure in CMC versus f2f communication may differ is that of sex differences in self-disclosure. The issue of gender differences in self-disclosure in CMC has yet to be empirically examined; however, some have speculated that such differences would be less evident. That is, in CMC, the anonymity of the Internet may permit users to step outside constricting gender roles of communication, and may allow men and women to self-disclose equally. However, it should be remembered that technology and the uses of technology (for instance, the relatively recent use of Web cameras) change so quickly that any generalisations regarding self-disclosure on the Internet are problematic.

Revealing Risky Information

Self-disclosure always involves a certain amount of risk, but the risk becomes acute when disclosing highly intimate and negative information about self. Sometimes, not engaging in self-disclosure can result in serious consequences, such as not talking about safer sex. Sometimes, engaging in self-disclosure can result in serious consequences, such as disclosing stigmatised information about self. Though attaining information about past relationships, other present relationships, sexual habits, and sexual experiences is necessary for making informed choices for sexual intimacy, these topics are taboo in developing relationships.

EMPLOYMENT INTERVIEWS

Although performing numerous functions, the initial job interview primarily serves to provide the employer with information allowing the discrimination of applicants and provides the interviewee with information concerning potential employment. Although both the interviewer and interviewee roles require the selective revelation of information, disclosures by the interviewee are much more likely to be personal than are disclosures revealed by and about the employer.

The standard script for employment interviews includes a section where questions are asked about the applicant's personal, educational, and work history. Additionally, some interview research suggests that interviewers should rely less on speculative questions, such as, 'what would you do if...?'and more on questions requiring recollection of specific behaviours, such as, 'what did you do When...?'. Interviews based on these questions have been shown to improve the selection process and result in hiring people who perform better on the job. Additionally, a review of research on interviewing concluded that interviewees infrequently seek information about or opinions of interviewers.

Thus, personal revelations by interviewees are an integral part and may reasonably be said to be the primary focus of employment interviews. What kind of disclosures do interviewees reveal? Given the importance of making a positive impression, it might be expected that the interviewee will reveal largely attributes and experiences that portray the speaker favourably.

As one guide suggests, interviewees 'try to demonstrate the characteristics of the interviewers' ideal employee through answers and references to their education and experience'. Research predictably indicates that interviewers rate more highly interviewees who present favourable information, elaborate answers, and talk fluently.

Gilmore and Ferris stated: Most job seekers try to present their positive qualities in an interview, with self-enhancing statements intending to create a good impression. Statements that suggest positive qualities or traits, if credible, should positively influence the interviewer. This somewhat obvious ingratiation technique is employed frequently by applicants seeking to bolster their image in an interview. Moreover, interviewers ask more questions designed to elicit positive information than ones to get negative information. Thus, the interview may be thought of as 'a search for confirmation of a positive hypothesis'.

The preference for positive disclosure should not result in a standardisation of interviews such that everyone professes honesty, dependability, helpfulness, and so on. Rather, interviewees would be best advised to reveal experiences indicating personal traits consistent with job characteristics. For example, a person interviewing for a job as a counsellor might describe incidents of helping others, while a candidate for a job writing advertising copy might disclose experiences that reveal independence and creativity. Disclosures are, however, so commonly self-flattering that interviewers may discount as exaggeration some of the information revealed. One study suggested that 25% of interviewees falsified information, while polygraph study of 400 job applicants concluded that 20% of interviewees falsified or concealed information that might jeopardise their employment.

Trinkaus's survey reported that most respondents would not disclose information that would potentially adversely and unfairly affect their employer's evaluation. Thus, self-revelations may be viewed sceptically by interviewers. One professional publication even offered suggestions for detecting deception in employment interviews. Interviewees can deflect such scepticism by providing supporting evidence, such as curricula vitae, letters of references, and portfolios, when appropriate. Interviewers might also take steps to improve the accuracy or honesty of disclosures made by interviewees.

Ordinarily, people who reveal too much positive information may be perceived as bragging or overly aggressive. However, interviewers expect a positive bias in information revealed, and the general tendency of interviewees is to reveal only favourable information. Consequently, the thresholds will probably be very high for making these negative assessments and attributions. Moreover, aggressiveness may even be seen as a desirable trait in some occupations.

Because the failure to reveal relevant qualifications or attributes may put the interviewee in a relatively unfavourable position relative to other interviewees, and negative attributions are unlikely to be made because of overly positive disclosures, people should reveal information in the employment interview that otherwise might appear self-serving. Because of the bias toward positive information in the interview, negative information about the interviewee significantly and adversely affects interviewer perceptions and selection decisions. These circumstances make it difficult for people to reveal past failures, shortcomings, or problems.

For example, several studies suggest that voluntary disclosures about a disability may jeopardise an individual's prospects of being hired and reduce opportunities for advancement. One study indicated that 80% of a sample of individuals with learning disabilities did not discuss their condition with their employer while seeking their current job.

For individuals with disabling illnesses or conditions, such as rheumatoid arthritis, the issue of concealment or disclosure is a recurring one. However, a person who does not disclose this information in the employment interview may be subsequently perceived as devious or untruthful for withholding the information. These alternatives clearly present a dilemma. One strategy for managing this no-win situation is to reveal the negative after the positive information has been disclosed.

Chapter 8

Process of Listening

OVERVIEW

The importance of listening would seem to be obvious. Whenever individuals are asked about the nature of their organisational activities, listening is cited as one of the most central. For example, in a recent survey of the School, listening activities were described as central to the practice of law and success in law school.

Nor is the concern for listening confined to organisational settings. Paul Krugman, describing the stresses of modern politics, notes that neoconservatives today actually seem to have an aversion to listening to others. Given some of this concern, it seems that knowing more about the nature of listening would be of great benefit. Most early research in listening grew out of the cognitive tradition. This research was importantly influenced by an assumption that listening and reading were simply different aspects of a single process – the acquisition and retention of information.

(It should be noted that most early research was conducted in university settings, and the universal assumption was that college students learned by reading textbooks and listening to lectures). If listening and reading produce the same outcomes, it is easy to assume that they are similar (if not exactly the same) skills. Success or failure of listening activity was therefore couched in cognitive (linguistic) terms. This assumption has been the dominant paradigm in listening and other communication research for the last 50 years. In other words, we have believed that linguistic events are central to the educational experience, and that relational and affective issues are less important. This paradigm is firmly rooted in Western philosophical thought. The emphasis on symbols and the universal acceptance of philosophy has been the dominant paradigm in Western intellectual life ever since.

The study of philosophy has been intermingled with the study of language ever since its inception. We use language according to certain well-established principles, and even though a strong case can be made that this usage is 'hard-wired', or determined by the physiological nature of the human brain, the principles seem to be 'inherently' true – so much so that philosophers were led to contend that they indicate 'reality'. More recently, 'social' reality has been invoked as the aim of research in social interactions, especially communication. Language is primary in 'constructing' this reality.

The nature of language is so intermingled with the 'proofs' of the reality hypotheses that it is impossible to approach them separately. From the point of view of the cognitive/linguistic paradigm, communication (or symbolic behaviour) was an early evolutionary step in the development of human beings, leading to social behaviour and the beginning of civilisation.

This explanation asserts that human beings somehow acquired the ability to communicate and subsequently were able to engage in social behaviour. This paradigm, then, tells us that to improve our abilities in communication we should improve our facility with language. Words (cognitions) are either generated by internal processing or received from others, and then behaviour follows the words.

A popular example of this paradigm is 'symbolic interactionism', which takes as its basic assumption that our social life is constructed of words. Some organisational communication theorists have taken the position that a symbolic interactionist perspective is the most productive way in which to study organisations, and they draw on symbolic interactionism as a basic conceptual framework for organisational study. Symbolic interactionism begins with the assumption that all life is a search for 'meaning', which, according to symbolic interactionists, is found in the way that each of us interacts with other persons, our institutions, and our culture.

These interactions are symbolic, in that they take place primarily through language and symbols. This is in contrast to the well-known 'hierarchy of needs', which proposes that 'self-actualisation' (meaningful) needs are addressed only when the more basic needs of food and shelter are satisfied. This approach relies both on interpretation and the acceptance of principles derived from linguistic frameworks. The recipe for social change, therefore, involves a change in the symbol system, and behaviour is assumed to follow. Whether the changes are political, social, or organisational, the communicator must only 'manage meaning' to have significant effect.

THE PROCESS OF LISTENING

We are to increase the numbers of women and minorities in our organisational systems, we should concentrate on building symbol systems that will facilitate changes in hiring and promotional practices. There is no doubt that changes in behaviour sometimes do follow changes in symbol systems. But at the same time, there is abundant evidence that changes in behaviour more often occur through coercion, social pressure, physiological and chemical changes, and sometimes random events. These changes, often termed 'mindless' ones, are then 'justified' by subsequent explanations by the participant. An individual who bows to social pressure in making a group decision then 'rationalises' the event by constructing evidence and logical processes. When this occurs, it is the case that language follows behaviour, rather than the other way around.

While communicative outcomes have traditionally been described as symbolic or behavioural, there are other communicative activities that may be as important, or even more important than these. The development and maintenance of relationships may be far more important than any other aspect of our daily life. Concerns with relationships are clearly facilitated through interactive activity. We communicate in order to maintain and develop relationships with others, and the 'content' of the interaction may be only secondary to the process. Whether we use terms like 'affinity-seeking' or 'homophily', interpersonal relationships are a fundamental human characteristic, and are a significant outcome of communicative activity. In summary, researchers in communication have placed an inordinate amount of emphasis on the linguistic, or cognitive, aspects of the communicative process.This focus on language led to ideas of 'reality' as dominant paradigms governing communicative activity.

The rationale for this emphasis on language assumes that social change and behavioural alteration follow from changes in language and linguistic systems. The opposite view – that language follows behavioural change – is just as defensible but has not received as much attention. Recently, researchers in interpersonal communication have pointed out the importance of interactive behaviour, as well as the central role that relationships play in interpersonal communication. While these more recent trends would seem to lead to questioning the dominance of the language-centredness of traditional 'reality-based' research, we still see linguistic assumptions as pervasive ones. Since these assumptions have affected most thinking in communication, it is not surprising to see that this tradition has also affected examination of the process of listening.

RESEARCH IN LISTENING

Research in listening, like most communication research, has focused on symbolic rather than behavioural or relational outcomes, and, as a result, has had some of the same conceptual problems that have afflicted communication in general. Symbol-oriented definitions of information acquisition assume that since reading, writing, listening, and speaking are all communicative activities, they should share the same methods and outlook, and aim for the same end product – the processing of information. Larger differentiation of communicative outcomes has not traditionally been a part of the research in listening. Instead, we have focused on the inherent differences in persons, looking to research to help us understand why people differ in communicative skill. Individuals vary widely in their ability to receive information that is presented symbolically, and the causes of this variation are poorly understood. Clearly, contexts and media affect the reception of messages. But individual differences are probably the most important source of variability in communication activities.

The most logical explanation for differences in receiving ability would seem to be the possession of a generalised facility to manipulate and remember symbols. To this end, individual variations in reading, both in speed and comprehension, have been extensively studied. A 'general ability' explanation, however, is elusive. For example, reading and writing skills are not closely associated. The lack of a strong association between reading and writing skills leads us to expect that listening and speaking abilities are similarly unrelated to reading skill. But these individual differences in listening ability, if any, have attracted much less attention. This seems anomalous, since listening is probably the most common communication activity.

EARLY ATTEMPTS AT MEASUREMENT

Whether or not listening is a distinct skill – that is, different from reading and writing skills – is a different question. Academic interest in listening is a relatively recent phenomenon, probably beginning with discussions by Wesley Wiksell and Ralph Nichols in the Quarterly Journal of Speech. Nichols' approach to studying listening was to assume that the methods used in studying reading could be used to examine listening, and Nichols' early research attempted to discover what, if anything, could help us predict good listening. In this pioneering study, Nichols adopted an information-based, cognitive definition of good listening.

He constructed lectures with factual content in them, read them to respondents, and then measured subsequent retention in tests. 'Listening', in other words, was defined as what students do in a classroom. Nichols examined the participants' retention and its relationship to many different factors, such as distance from the speaker, previous training in subject matter, hearing loss (!), size of family, and parental occupation. He concluded that retention was 'related to' intelligence, ability to discern organisational elements, size of vocabulary, and very little else.

In other words, he found that intelligent persons retained more information than did unintelligent ones, those who understood organizational. The assumption that the ability to listen is a separate and unitary skill was sharply attacked in the middle of the 1960s by Charles Kelly. He reasoned that if listening tests did indeed measure a separate ability, the Brown–Carlsen and the STEP tests of listening would be more highly correlated with each other than with other measures of cognitive ability.

He found that the tests of listening were not highly correlated with each other; in fact, they were more highly correlated with tests of intelligence. These data led Kelly, reasonably enough, to the conclusion that the ability that had previously been termed 'listening ability' was in fact only an aspect of intelligence, and that the Brown–Carlsen and the STEP tests were only different kinds of intelligence tests. A clue to Kelly's findings was already present in Nichols' data, in that the single best predictor was cognitive ability, with a correlation of 0.54.

While 'intelligence' is clearly not a unitary factor, defining listening as the remembering of facts from a lecture is definitely isomorphic with at least one of them. In his theory of multiple intelligences, Gardner clearly indicates that verbal processing is one of the many intelligences, and listening as defined as efficient word processing would fit well into this definition.

If we take Sternberg's definition of intelligence as the ability to manipulate the environment, we probably would not see the same strong relationship exhibited by the data. The relationship of lecture-defined listening and intelligence is certainly not clear-cut. Cognitive ability interacts with difficulty of material and rate of presentation in predicting retention. Kelly's discovery that 'listening'(as defined by the retention model) is probably not a separate and distinguishable mental ability complicates the problem. Almost everyone involved in the practical study of communication has had experience of persons who are obviously intelligent but could never be called 'good listeners'.

ATTITUDES AND LISTENING

One method of reconciling Kelly's findings with everyday experience is to redefine listening so that it includes something other than intelligence. Many invoked an 'attitude' about listening to explain why some persons listen better than others. This attitude could also be termed a 'willingness' to listen – a basic interest in others' ideas.

Often when we say that someone is a 'good listener', we mean that they have a good attitude about the process, rather than retentive ability. The first researchers incorporate the attitudinal dimension into a formal definition of listening. It was referred to research in perception showing that attitudinal predispositions affect both selection and perception of incoming stimuli.

Listening, to Weaver, was 'the selection and retention of aurally received data'. Weaver went on to discuss 'selective exposure', an attitudinally and culturally determined activity. Weaver also included information seeking as an important component. Weaver's approach, while popular, still avoided the basic question of whether or not listening 'ability' is a separate and distinct psychological characteristic.

Normally attitudes, even social attitudes, are not considered to be permanent traits or abilities. Kelly had pointed out that good listeners were intelligent, and now Weaver asserted that good listeners were those who had respect and interest in others. 'Other orientation' was a popular theme in academic life in the early 1970s, and the 'humanistic psychology' movement seemed to be in tune with concern for other people expressed in the goal of being 'good listeners'. But more sceptical theorists looked at listening as simply a redescription of other, better-known psychological processes, notably selective perception and intelligence.

'Interpersonal' attitudes form the basis of much popular writing about listening today. This writing assumes that a good listener is one that is 'other oriented', in that respect, and that concern for others is the foundation for effective listening. The process of becoming a better listener is akin to the process of becoming a better spouse or work partner, in that the relational elements are deemed to be paramount. It is, of course, possible to call this respect a 'skill' of a kind, and it is also possible to encourage these attitudes in workshops and seminars. But at the same time, it is hard to see how any careful definition of listening can ignore the processes involved in human memory.

LISTENING AND MEMORY

When one listens, one captures, however briefly, the message in memory. One of the most interesting results of recent memory research was the discovery that memory is of various types and is used in different ways. Some researchers, noting that the information in messages is almost always words, have called this process 'semantic memory'. Squire, for example, distinguished semantic memory from episodic memory. When we remember episodes, we remember what someone did, and when we remember words, we remember what they said. Semantic memory and episodic memory affect one another, even though one uses percepts and the other uses language.

So 'memory' research offers a distinct alternative to primarily symbolic approaches to listening. Semantic memory is definitely related to the probabilistic nature of information. It has been studied from the point of view of 'category sizes', 'relatedness', and 'familiarity'. Monsel, for example, speculated that it is the job of the 'input register' to hold the words or phonemes long enough for semantic encoding processes to be brought into play. If so, persons who cannot activate the input register would either encode immediately or lose everything. If they conduct the kind of grammatical processing suggested by data, material presented in a grammatically coherent structure would be easily processed, while material not having structure would be more difficult.

The standard description of how items are processed into long-term storage is highly linear. If this linear description is accurate, then a deficiency at one point of the process would clearly result in deficiencies at later temporal stages.

A good way to identify such deficiencies would be to compare persons with different aptitudes at each stage in the process and see how the end product is affected. But the most important finding, and one that affects conceptions of listening most directly, is that memory has several stages, most probably best described as short term, intermediate term, and long term. The use of this memory model led to the hypothesis that verbal decoding can be divided into several components: short-term listening, short-term listening with rehearsal, and lecture listening. When investigated, these three 'types' (aspects) of listening were initially shown to differentiate among one another; furthermore, short-term listening seemed to have little relationship to cognitive abilities, as shown in intelligence tests.

ALTERNATIVE APPROACHES TO LISTENING

If the linguistic/symbolic view is an acceptable one, and if listening is primarily a cognitive process, then the research reported above, including the memory-based models, would suffice for productive investigations into listening behaviour. The principal research tasks would be the development of reliable and valid tests of the process, and investigation into some of the varying relationships involved in the communicative process.

However, many aspects of listening are not easily subsumed under a typical linguistic/symbolic framework. To begin with, the process of communication is a much more broadly defined activity than a linguistic/symbolic process alone. Defensible distinctions can be made among typical communicative functions such as relaying, stimulating, activating, and linguistic functions.

On a more global level, communication often aims at both instrumental and relational goals. The discovery that short-term listening (STL) was different from other aspects of listening and that individuals differ systematically in this ability was hardly earthshaking. But what was more interesting was that the linear model proposed by Loftus and Loftus could not be maintained for listening, because long-term retention did not depend on short-term retention.

Further, a curious finding appeared in a large-scale investigation of public-speaking 'performance' – good short-term listeners apparently performed better in oral presentations. Another interesting study of 'managerial effectiveness' demonstrated that STL is the best discriminator between good and poor branch managers in banks. Another, even more interesting finding appeared in a long-term study of organisational success.

Short-term listening was the best single predictor of upward mobility in the organisation. Bussey found that those respondents with good short-term skills asked more questions in an interview than those with poor short-term skills. The discovery that short-term listening skill is qualitatively different from long-term listening skill was an important step in separating listening research from the more traditional, symbol-oriented frameworks, but did not go very far.

More recently, the two fundamental questions were raised about the memory model of listening: (1) What is the relationship between the memory for symbols and the listening process? (2) How can relational factors be introduced into the model? Thomas and Levine pointed out that there is no real basis for assuming a connection between short-term listening and interactive skill.

Further, contending that a conversation based on short-term memory alone would be 'nearly incoherent', offered an alternative definition of listening that is primarily relational. In their study, they examined relational cues – eye gaze, head nods, short 'backchat', and long 'backchat'. Short backchat consists of utterances such as 'yes' or 'hmm' during speech, and long backchat comprises typically restatements of the speaker's utterances. Long backchat is identical to the 'statements and questions' aspect of the NTE listening test, but the other three are traditionally defined as 'non-verbal' factors. Nods and gaze are clearly visual stimuli. In short, while some research indicates that STL is closely implicated in interpersonal activities, apparently much more than long-term skills (or ability), just how these abilities relate to one another is not known. These and other studies led to the conclusion that perhaps short-term listening is not a cognitive skill, but an interpersonal skill and should not be confused with other forms of listening.

'Lecture' listening, on the other hand, seems to be very closely related to common definitions of intelligence. In other words, listening was originally modelled on memory models, which contain a minimum of short- and long-term components. Dividing listening into those two kinds of abilities produced the serendipitous finding that short-term listening is apparently closely connected with interpersonal skills in a variety of settings. But clearly (as Thomas and Levine pointed out), no good theoretical explanation exists for this finding. On the other hand, several other aspects of listening are much more important in communication. Prominent among these is the expression and understanding of affective messages. Typically, this has been termed 'interpretive listening'.

INTERPRETIVE LISTENING

Interpretive listening is identical to vocalic decoding. This is usually understood to mean the processing of emotional or affective content from a message, primarily from 'tone' of voice, inflection, and other variations of voice. Most persons feel that they are skilled in vocalic listening, but generally do poorly when called on to decode affect. For example, in one study using a standardised vocalic listening task, a very large sample of college students and adults identified correct answers only 55% of the time. In other words, more than half of the time, people misinterpret vocalic signals. And while accessing this kind of information is universally considered to be of great importance, no one seems to have a clear idea as to how it should be improved.

One factor here is that individuals vary in their 'affect orientation'.Research indicates that improvements in interpretive listening can be accomplished with training procedures, such as sensitivity training, role playing. Interpreting the underlying affect implied in spoken messages may involve personal schemas, constructs, or 'cultural literacy'.

These changes, however, are changes in attitude, awareness, or knowledge, not changes in basic ability. Changes in basic ability are much more difficult. A substantive body of research clearly indicates that interpretive listening is also strongly affected by an individual's ability to decode the non-verbal cues present in the exchange.

Often when non-verbal signals contradict the verbal ones, individuals typically accept the non-verbal as a more valid expression of the true feelings of the interactant. Most investigations of non-verbal cues centre on visual displays, such as facial expression, posture, and so on. Others have investigated 'vocalic' messages, such as pitch, intonation, and inflection. Visual cues have typically been shown to be of greater influence than the vocalic ones in most situations. However, some studies show that vocalic cues are of more use in detecting deception than visual ones.

They compared the ability of respondents to decode visual cues with their ability to decode vocal cues, and found that visual cues are more accurately perceived than vocal ones.

Some gender differences were also observed. In short, the division of messages into 'verbal' and 'non-verbal' categories may be too simple. Visual and vocal cues, both of which have been categorised as non-verbal messages, would seem to differ in important ways. Comparisons of decoding abilities are rare. What the relationships might be among visual/non-verbal decoding ability, vocal/ non-verbal decoding ability, and verbal decoding ability is not known.

SCHEMATIC LISTENING

Another way of examining the acquisition of information in spoken messages may involve the use of schemas.When at the field, they began their infamous Maori wardance. The Sydney team was forced to wait an inordinately long time for this dance to conclude, and at that time, were not mentally ready. As a consequence, and as a result of the emotionality of the ceremony, the Kiwis won easily. If you did not know that the event described was taking place in Australia, and involved Australian football, and that the Kiwis were distinctly the underdogs (and a host of other details), the passage would mean little to you.

A good name for all the interlocking knowledge represented here would be an 'Australian football schema'. Richard Mayer noted that schemas underlie almost all important cognitive activities, and sometimes have been investigated using terms like 'frames' and 'scripts'. Nonetheless, it is clear that quite often interpreting a prose passage is impossible without knowledge of the 'big picture' in the situation. The schema concept was extended to general educational outcomes, calling for colleges and universities to teach a core of cultural knowledge that could serve as common schemas to assist in understanding one another.

Thain used aspects of schema theory in formulating his definition of 'authentic' listening. Thain reasoned that many aspects of listening skill are 'pure traits', such as memory and vocabulary, but an integrative act is vital to put the entire message into meaningful relationships. He presented an example of a situation in which decoding cannot take place without a larger understanding of the situation involved, similar to the 'Kiwi' example above. Further evidence for the distinctiveness of schematic listening is furnished by the ETS.

Chapter 9

Persuasion

IDENTIFYING OBSTACLES TO COMPLIANCE

One common obstacle to the audience's embracing the persuader's advocated action or viewpoint is the audience's current attitudes, that is, the audience's general evaluations (of the advocated action, policy, product, and so on). For instance, low participation in recycling programmes might be the result of negative attitudes about recycling; in that case, a persuader who wants to encourage recycling would obviously be well advised to try to change those negative attitudes. However, skilful persuaders will realise that it is a mistake to assume that what lies behind a person not performing a given action is a negative attitude.

To be sure, sometimes current attitudes are indeed the obstacle, and in such circumstances (as will be discussed) attitude change is needed. But sometimes the basis of the audience's resistance lies somewhere other than attitude. Thus, it is useful to distinguish two broad persuasion circumstances – one in which the audience already has the desired attitudes (but for some reason is not acting consistently with them) and the other in which the audience lacks the desired attitudes. When the audience has the desired attitudes When the audience already has the desired attitudes in place, the persuader's challenge is that of encouraging people to act consistently with those attitudes.

This circumstance is actually not uncommon. For example, people almost certainly already have favourable attitudes toward good health; what is needed is to persuade people to make attitude-consistent behavioural choices about exercise, diet, medical care, and the like. Similarly, persons who have positive attitudes toward energy conservation and environmental protection might not act consistently with those views – might not choose appropriate thermostat settings, engage in recycling, and so on.

Two broad (not mutually exclusive) approaches are available to persuaders here. One is to attempt to connect more closely the existing attitudes with the desired behaviour; the other is to focus on non-attitudinal influences on behaviour. Connecting the existing attitude with the desired behaviour When a persuader seeks to have persons connect their existing attitudes more closely to a. behavioural choice (so as to shape that choice), three general strategies recommend themselves: enhancing the perceived relevance of the attitude to the behaviour, inducing feelings of guilt or hypocrisy, and enhancing the salience of the current attitude.

One strategy for enhancing attitude-consistent behaviour is to encourage people to see their attitudes as relevant to their behavioural choices. The general principle here is that persons are more likely to act consistently with their attitudes if they see the attitudes as relevant to the behaviour in question; hence, increasing perceived attitudinal relevance will increase the likelihood of attitude-consistent behaviour. For example, in a study the measures of their attitudes toward affirmative action, read arguments in an affirmative-action court case, and rendered individual verdicts in the case.

Some participants received instructions from the judge emphasising that the case dealt with a contemporary issue (affirmative action) and thus that decisions in this case could have implications not only for the involved parties, but also for affirmative-action programmes generally (because of the precedent-setting nature of judicial decisions); these instructions underscored the relevance of participants' attitudes to their decision.

Participants who did not receive these instructions displayed little consistency between their affirmative-action attitudes and their decisions, but those who received the instructions exhibited substantial attitude-behaviour consistency. In short, emphasising the relevance of an existing attitude to a current behavioural choice can be one means of inducing attitude-consistent conduct. Indeed, one need think only of the computers, computer programs, tutoring sessions, academic camps, and similar products or services that have been purchased by parents who had been led to see that various of their current attitudes were relevant to the purchase decision.

A second strategy for encouraging attitude-consistent behaviour is that of inducing feelings of hypocrisy or guilt. When people have previously acted inconsistently with their attitudes, drawing their attention to the hypocrisy can lead them to act more consistently with their attitudes. Specifically, the research evidence suggests that when both the existing attitude and the previous inconsistent behaviour are made salient, persons are likely subsequently to act more consistently with their attitudes.

For example, the salience of participants' positive attitudes about safe-sex practices (by having some participants write and deliver a speech about the importance of safe sex) and varied the salience of previous behaviour that was inconsistent with such attitudes. The combination of salient attitudes and salient inconsistency induced greater subsequent attitude-behaviour consistency (reflected in greater likelihood of buying condoms at the end of the experiment) than either one alone.

Similarly, reported that households given feedback about their water consumption, combined with a reminder of their previously expressed belief in their responsibility to conserve water, significantly reduced their subsequent consumption. Feedback alone did reduce consumption, but was not as effective as the combination of feedback and the reminder.Plainly, then, one means of inducing attitude-behaviour consistency may be to lead people to recognise their hypocrisy (which may involve making them feel guilty about their past inconsistency).

But this strategy can easily backfire if not deployed

carefully. For instance, persons made to feel hypocritical about apparent attitudebehaviour inconsistency might resolve that inconsistency not by changing their behaviour so as to align it with their attitudes, but by changing their attitudes so as to justify (be consistent with) their previous behaviour (for an example of such a backfire effect, see Fried, 1998). Similarly, several studies have found that although more explicit guilt appeals do arouse greater guilt than less-explicit appeals, those more-explicit appeals are significantly less persuasive than less-explicit appeals, perhaps because the strategy generates anger or resentment.

A third means of encouraging attitude-consistent behaviour is simply to ensure that the relevant attitudes are sufficiently salient. In the right circumstances, persuasion can be effected through relatively straightforward prompts or reminders.

For example, Conn, Burks, Minor, and Mehr found that mail and telephone prompts led to significant increases in the exercise behaviour of older women compared to conditions without such reminders; Andersen, Franckowiak, Snyder, Bartlett, and Fontaine (1998) reported that stair use in a shopping mall was significantly increased by placing signs (mentioning the benefits of stair use) next to escalators that had adjacent stairs; Austin, Alvero, and Olson found that when a restaurant hostess prompted departing patrons by adding 'don't forget to buckle up' to her usual parting comments, seat belt use increased by over a third; Alemi et al found that computerised reminder telephone calls to parents significantly increased the likelihood that children would be immunised on schedule; Ferrari, Barone, Jason, and Rose reported that persons who had signed a pledge card to donate blood were significantly more likely to fulfil that pledge (more likely to report to give blood) if they received a reminder telephone call a day or two before the blood drive began.

As these findings illustrate, when the relevant attitudes are already in place, effective persuasion can simply be a matter of making those attitudes salient.

FOCUS ON NON-ATTITUDINAL FACTORS

However, even if the audience has the appropriate attitudes and is prepared to act consistently with them (e.g. even if the attitude is seen as relevant to the desired action), attitude-consistent behaviour may nevertheless not occur, because other (nonattitudinal) factors can outweigh any influence of attitude on behaviour. Two such additional factors deserve special mention: normative considerations and the person's perceived ability to perform the behaviour. Concerning normative considerations, a number of generalised models of intentional behaviour recognise that both attitudinal (personal) and normative (social) factors can influence conduct. Thus, even when an individual has the desired attitudes, perceived normative pressures might prevent the person from engaging in the desired action.

CONSTRUCTING EFFECTIVE MESSAGES

Given a diagnosis of the bases of the audience's current resistance to the persuader's advocated action or viewpoint, the persuader can turn to the task of constructing effective messages that are targeted at those obstacles. Some aspects of this task have already been implicitly discussed in the course of indicating how various specific obstacles to compliance might be overcome (e.g. the use of modelling as a means of enhancing perceived behavioural control). But the research literature on persuasion also offers a number of general recommendations concerning effective message construction; here attention is drawn to three particularly important guidelines.

Meeting Objections

Sometimes receivers will have objections (stated or unstated) to the advocate's viewpoint. The question that arises is how a persuader should handle such objections. There are three broad alternative courses of action for a persuader: ignoring the opposing arguments (commonly termed a 'one-sided' message), attempting to refute the opposing arguments (a 'refutational two-sided' message), and mentioning the opposing arguments without undermining them (a 'non-refutational two-sided' message). A considerable body of research evidence bears on the question of the relative persuasiveness of these alternatives.

The evidence suggests that refutational two-sided messages are significantly more persuasive than their one-sided counterparts; non-refutational two-sided messages, on the other hand, are significantly less persuasive than one-sided messages. That is to say, persuaders are well advised to meet counter-arguments head-on by attempting to refute them (a refutational two-sided message) rather than ignoring them (a one-sided message) or – even worse – mentioning them without undermining them (a non-refutational two-sided message).

Being Clear and Specific

For various reasons, persuaders will sometimes be tempted not to be especially clear about exactly what position they are advocating. This might be motivated by concerns about possible resistance or by a belief that leaving the message's point implicit will be more persuasive than making it explicit (because with the conclusion implicit, the audience will need actively to reason its way to the desired point).

But two lines of research evidence suggest that persuasiveness is commonly enhanced by clarity and specificity. The first compares the relative persuasiveness of messages in which the conclusion is stated explicitly or is omitted from the message. For example, Struckman-Johnson and Struckman-Johnson (1996) compared two versions of public service announcements, one with and one without an explicit recommendation to use condoms. Across a number of such studies, the predominant finding is that messages with explicit conclusions are more persuasive than those with implicit conclusions.

The second line of work concerns the specificity with which the communicator's recommended action is described. The contrast is between messages that provide only a general description of the advocated action and messages that provide a more detailed, specific description. For instance, the messages giving relatively general, unelaborated recommendations concerning dental care and messages providing more specific, detailed recommendations. These studies have commonly found messages to be more persuasive when the message contained a more specific description of the advocated behaviour for a review. In sum, persuaders would do well to ensure that their advocated position is made clear to the audience, including being specific about the particulars of any advocated action.

Following-up

Persuaders sometimes seem not to realise that an initially successful persuasive effort may not be sufficient to ensure sustained results. But, for two reasons, follow-up persuasive efforts may be crucial. First, after making a decision, people often immediately experience feelings of regret. (For some readers, this may be familiar as what is sometimes called 'buyer's remorse'.) Such feelings are not entirely irrational. Any given choice inevitably involves choosing between two imperfect options (not one perfectly good option versus some completely terrible option); hence, no matter which option is chosen, there will inevitably be some desirable aspects of the unchosen alternative and some undesirable aspects of the chosen option. In the course of trying to rationalise one's choice, one might quite naturally come to think about those various elements that are inconsistent with one's choice (e.g. drawbacks of the product that was just purchased) on the way to eventually concluding that those inconsistent aspects are in fact trivial (hence, one did indeed make the correct choice).

But before that process reaches its conclusion, people will quite naturally experience feelings of regret, given that their attention has been drawn to all the considerations that argued against the choice that was made. Indeed, these feelings of regret can be so great as to induce people to want to change (back out of) their initial decision. Obviously, persuaders might find it useful to engage in follow-up efforts aimed at minimising such feelings of regret. The potential value of such efforts has been nicely illustrated in a study of automobile purchases. During the period between the time the purchase decision is made and the time the vehicle is delivered, some automobile buyers back out of their initial decision (a reversal that can be induced by regret). But when two follow-up telephone calls were made to the buyer – calls that emphasised the desirable aspects of the chosen automobile and that reassured the buyer of the wisdom of the decision – the number of buyers who reversed their initial decisions was significantly reduced. Second, quite apart from any immediate regret-based reversals of persuasive effects, there is good reason to suppose that, in general, persuasive effects are likely to decay over time (for some general reviews and discussion.

Old habits can return, competing persuasive messages can be received, new obstacles and constraints can emerge – and all these can serve to diminish any previous persuasive effects. For example, in consulting with teachers, school psychologists often seek to convince teachers to adopt some new teaching method or approach. But 'ideas that sound simple during the course of consultation may, in fact, require skills that the consultee [teacher] does not possess to an adequate degree.' Unfortunately, this may not become apparent until the teacher is 'actually attempting to implement the strategy in question'. Of course, when this obstacle arises, the teacher's enthusiasm for the new approach may well fade. Only close attention to the necessity for follow-up efforts will permit the identification and resolution of such problems.

OVERVIEW

Skilful persuasion requires adaptation to the basis of the audience's resistance to the advocated view. Discerning the current obstacles to compliance is not always easy, and fashioning effective messages aimed at those barriers can be difficult. However, as should be apparent, the research literature on persuasive effects provides a number of useful insights into the diagnosis and management of obstacles to persuasion.

Chapter 10

Asserting and Confronting

DESCRIPTION

The contexts in which assertion has acquired increased importance are now quite varied compared to the clinical settings in which it originated. For instance, its value in the work environment is recognised widely particularly within predominantly female professions, such as nursing and social work, where deference by women can undermine job satisfaction.

The benefits of assertion extend beyond the immediate conflict situation by empowering workers as well as managers. For example, it was found that assertively skilled persons, compared to non-assertive individuals, received fairer performance appraisals and also evidenced more positive attitudes toward the appraisal and more trust in the manager. Assertiveness also contributes to physical wellness as consumers negotiate increasingly complex contemporary health-care systems.

For example, the skill helps low socio-economic status cancer patients access the most appropriate medical care and permits women to respond to stress as a challenge rather than as a threat. Assertiveness training is an integral component of interventions for problems that compromise the quality of life, such as chronic pain and depression.

It also can empower vulnerable individuals, such as the chronic mentally ill, who are at risk of contracting HIV infection women with intellectual disabilities who need to be partners in their health care children at risk of being abused or bullied and adolescents who face decisions about substance use. Furthermore, self-help books continue to be published, including The Complete Guide to Assertiveness which surely marks assertion's full acceptance as a legitimate contemporary skill.

Though the social value of assertion is widely embraced, it does not automatically follow that use of these skills is invariably the preferred option; in many cases, in fact, it is not. The purpose of this chapter, therefore, is to summarise the current understanding of the conditions under which assertive behaviour in conflict situations is both appropriate and effective.

DEFINING ASSERTIVE BEHAVIOUR

The early definitions of assertion emphasised the individual's right to express personal desires while simultaneously respecting the rights of the other person. They were developed by clinicians from the pioneering formulations introduced by Salter and Wolpe, and specified components (be direct, use a firm but respectful tone, and maintain eye contact) derived from face or content validity. However, such conceptualisations were unable to promote systematic theoretical and empirical enquiry, due to their insensitivity to situational, individual, and cultural factors.

This led Rich and Schroeder to propose a functional, contentless operant definition: '[Assertive behaviour is] the skill to seek, maintain, or enhance reinforcement in an interpersonal situation through the expression of feelings or wants when such expression risks loss of reinforcement or even punishment the degree of assertiveness may be measured by the effectiveness of an individual's response in producing, maintaining, or enhancing reinforcement. This definition highlights the core features of assertion:

- It is a learned skill that varies as a function of the situation, not a 'trait' that a person 'has' or 'lacks'
- It occurs only in an interpersonal context
- It is an expressive skill, involving verbal and non-verbal components

- It always involves risk that the recipient may react negatively to and/or fail to comply with the assertion.
- It is frequently measured by outcome, which some consider to be the'ultimate criterion for evaluating performance'.

However, assertion must be evaluated by more than a simple outcome criterion. Because assertion involves risk, even technically proficient behaviour may fail to produce reinforcement in any given instance. This technical criterion assesses response quality. Additionally, assertion may achieve its immediate goals but significantly injure the relationship. Such a response 'works' only in a limited way; the net effect of even a 'self-enhancing' skill must be determined by a cost-benefit criterion. Finally, behaviour must have social validity – legitimacy through social acceptability.

Since unskilled behaviour can still produce reinforcement, a cultural criterion that judges social appropriateness is usually necessary. Thus, the immediate effectiveness of the response is but one way to measure assertiveness, and, in fact, trainers emphasise technical expertise, net benefit, and cultural appropriateness far more than immediate outcome. Indeed, when numerous instances of assertion are aggregated, each of the four standards defines self-enhancing yet socially responsible behaviour. Criteria such as technical expertise and cultural appropriateness reintroduce some content into the functional definition of assertion. Thus, a discussion of ways to approach the concept of assertion is essential.

CLARIFICATION OF THE ASSERTION CONCEPT

Assertive behaviour comprises a number of partially independent response classes. Schoeder, after an extensive review of the literature, identified four 'positive' response classes – admitting personal short-comings (self-disclosure), giving and receiving compliments, initiating and maintaining interactions, and expressing positive feelings – and three 'negative' or 'conflict' response classes – expressing unpopular or different opinions, requesting behaviour changes by other people, and refusing unreasonable requests. The asserter's initiative also has been used to categorise responses. Trower identified active assertive skills (self-disclosure, asking favours, disagreeing, and expressing negative and positive feelings) and reactive assertive skills (refusing requests, responding to disagreement, and responding to negative and positive feelings).

Similarly, it was classified as negative assertion as a response to another's initiative (refusing unwanted and tempting requests, and responding to criticism) or as an initiative response (requesting a behaviour change, disagreeing, apologising, and ending interactions). She categorised positive assertion as an initiative response (asking favours and complimenting others). However, this approach has had a limited impact because it was articulated after the majority of the assertion studies had been published. The conflict response classes have received the bulk of the research and clinical attention, probably due to social and historical factors (such as the dominance of male values) rather than to scientific or clinical ones. While the focus here will remain on conflict assertion, it is important to recognise that assertiveness encompasses interpersonal expressiveness in both positive and negative contexts.

DISTINGUISHING ASSERTION FROM AGGRESSION

Assertion typically has been conceptualised as the midpoint on the continuum between non-assertion and aggression. While research has generally supported this approach, more recent data suggest that assertion may incorporate elements of aggressive and submissive behaviour. Furthermore, though a single continuum highlights the appropriateness of assertiveness training for aggressive as well as timid individuals, it fails to offer a clear differentiation between socially appropriate conflict assertive behaviour and inappropriate aggressive behaviour. This is a critical distinction since laypersons often fail to distinguish the two styles of responding: describe assertion as pushy, rude, and insensitive; and label conflict assertion as aggression. Such confusion compromises the social validity of assertive response alternatives. Most attempts to distinguish between assertion and aggression employ one or more of the four criteria discussed earlier. It was suggested that appropriate conflict assertion, unlike aggression, respects the other person's rights and dignity through the use of non-hostile verbal content and vocal attributes.

Assertion is expected to produce strong relationships and relatively few negative emotions, whereas aggression is predicted to result in a strained emotionally charged relationship. Hollandsworth, however, argued that such formulations fail to establish objective criteria; he proposed instead that aggressive responses are defined by their use of coercive content. It was further contended that the distinction cannot rest on content alone, but must also acknowledge intentions, consequences, and context. Thus, Rakos noted that it might be appropriate to 'escalate' the response by including reasonable threats (e.g. to initiate legal action, appeal to higher authority, refuse to cooperate further, withdraw resources) after repeated non-compliance with an assertion.

ASSERTING AND CONFRONTING

Pure functional definitions also are problematic because they exclude critical context such as social values, behavioural goals, and cultural expectations. For instance, Wilson and Gallois demonstrated that people commonly endorse 'the general goals of avoiding conflict and not straining the relationship'. However, it was suggested that the functional definition can serve as the basis from which other functionally related behaviours with specified but general content can be identified.

Assertion, which is generally viewed as a discrete behaviour and a personal right, should instead be considered as a chain of overt and covert responses encompassing rights (actually, rights behaviours) and their functionally related antecedent and consequent responsibilities (obligation behaviours). Verbalisation of the rights behaviour alone, without the attendant social obligation behaviours, is expressive behaviour and, by itself, aggressive. Conflict assertion, in contrast, requires the emission of specific categories of socially responsible behaviour. There are the following antecedent obligations:

- Engaging in sufficient overt and covert behaviour to determine the rights of all participants
- Developing a verbal and non-verbal response repertoire that is intended to influence the other person's offending behaviour but not the self-evaluation of his or her 'worth'
- Considering the potential negative consequences the other person may experience as a function of expressive behaviour. There are also the following subsequent obligations (emitted after expressive behaviour):
- Providing a brief, honest, but non-apologetic explanation for the expressive behaviour
- Providing clarifying or alternative interpretations of the expressive behaviour and empathic communications concerning its implications, in an attempt to minimise any hurt, anger, or unhappiness experienced by the other person as a consequence of the expressive behaviour
- Protecting the other person's rights if that person is unable to do so
- Seeking a mutually acceptable compromise when legitimate rights of both parties exist and are in conflict. The antecedent obligations are necessary prerequisites to expressive behaviour in all conflict situations, and the subsequent ones are the key socially sanctioned elements that preserve relationships while contentious issues are addressed directly. Because women are inclined to employ interpersonal sensitivity to resolve disagreements, they rely strongly on obligations, in contrast to men, who tend to focus on rights. While the subsequent obligations can be emitted as part of an assertion to

a stranger with whom no further contact is anticipated, they do not improve the social reaction in such situations and are unnecessary – there is no relationship to enhance – and potentially problematic, as they extend the interaction and expand the content that is open for discussion.

Furthermore, when the legitimate rights of strangers conflict, the nature of the situation usually precludes a search for a mutually acceptable compromise. The behaviour chain conceptualisation provides a way to distinguish assertion, which includes the emission of the appropriate obligation behaviours as well as the expressive ones, from aggressive behaviour, which involves only the expression of rights. Expressing rights alone violates the general norm of conflict minimisation and employs dominance and power to achieve an outcome. It is not surprising, therefore, that in conflict situations persons exhibiting the dominating, hostile, type A behaviour pattern are less likely than type Bs to include obligation components within assertive responses.

In a continuing relationship with a supervisor, both antecedent and subsequent responsibilities define assertive behaviour. These obligations encompass general and flexible content, so that variability due to situational, social, and cultural norms and values can be accommodated. The components themselves have little meaning apart from the chain. Nevertheless, sufficient specificity is included so that competent emission of the individual components can be reliably trained and then effectively generalised to the natural environment.

THE SKILL OF CONFLICT ASSERTION

Research in clinical, school, and work contexts convincingly indicates that conflict assertive skills characterise psychologically adaptive, 'healthy' individuals and facilitate personal growth and satisfaction, particularly, but by no means exclusively, in cultural contexts dominated by secular Western norms and values. But exactly what behaviours constitute this valuable skill? Certainly, overt response elements, such as verbalisations and eye contact, are important components. However, because the response must be sensitive to the context, covert behaviours must be integrally involved in selecting the overt responses that best meet the needs of the situation. Fortunately, the extensive research provides a good number of general guidelines for the development of a diverse behavioural repertoire that can be adapted to the specific circumstance. Overt behavioural components of conflict assertion The overt response elements can be categorised as follows:

- *Content:* The verbal behaviour of the asserter, or what the person says to the other person(s)
- *Paralinguistic elements:* The vocal characteristics of the verbal behaviour, or how the asserter sounds
- *Non-verbal behaviours:* The body movements and facial expressions that accompany the verbal behaviour, or how the asserter appears
- *Social interaction skills:* The timing, initiation, persistence, and stimulus control skills that enhance the impact of the verbal behaviour, or how the asserter behaves in the process of the interaction.

RESPONSE DURATION Originally, a short duration was assumed to be characteristic of assertion, since non-assertive persons tend to produce excuses, lies, apologies, and long explanations. However, because appropriate assertion involves verbalising obligations as well as rights, the duration of an assertion may be longer than other responses, especially when (as is the case for latency) the assertion involves conflict and is directed toward a male. The assertion must be sufficiently long to communicate effectively in a given context; mere verbiage in and of itself is neither assertive nor unassertive. In fact, it was found a curvilinear relationship between assertiveness and duration: moderately assertive individuals exhibited much shorter duration than either highly assertive or non-assertive persons. Although excessive verbalisation increases the chances of confusion, diversion, and irrelevancy, response duration must be sufficient to meet the demands of unique circumstances.

Response fluency Fluency is considered to be an important paralinguistic feature of assertion, yet it has been poorly investigated. In fact, the few studies directly to address the issue found a very weak relationship. However, hesitant, choppy speech is associated with anxiety, which is presumed to be detrimental to and perhaps even incompatible with effective assertion. Thus, common sense suggests fluency will contribute to the judgement of skill. Interestingly, speech rate has not attracted the attention of researchers or clinicians. It, too, makes intuitive sense: non-anxious, assertive individuals would be expected to adjust their rate of talking to reflect the particular context.

Voice volume The data on loudness, in contrast to the previous characteristics, are fairly consistent: effective conflict assertion is characterised by an appropriate, moderate volume that is louder than the speech produced in ordinary conversation and by non-assertive persons.

Intonation (inflection) Laypersons consider intonation to be one of the most important features of effective assertion, but, like response duration, both highly assertive and non-assertive people evidence greater inflection than moderately assertive individuals. Inflection is therefore an important attribute of assertion, but not a distinguishing characteristic. As with many of the other paralinguistic components, intermediate levels of intonation are judged to be most appropriate.

Firmness (affect) High levels of firmness are strongly correlated with judgements of assertion and may even contribute more than actual content. Assertive psychiatric patients manifest greater affect than non-assertive ones, particularly in conflict situations. With the exception of a study by Bourque and Ladouceur, the data suggest that the absence of vocal firmness is likely to detract from the impact of a conflict assertion, and that the development of an appropriately firm 'tone' should be a high training priority.

PARALINGUISTIC QUALITIES

Firmness, intermediate levels of volume and intonation,

and moderate response latency and duration appear to characterise effective conflict assertion. Intuitively, a fluent response and a moderate speech rate make sense but lack definitive empirical support. Latency and duration have shown a particular sensitivity to situational variables: they are likely to increase in conflict interactions and when directed toward a male.

In general, appropriate conflict assertion requires flexible paralinguistic abilities that are sensitive to changing environmental conditions. The behaviours convey a great deal of information in an assertive interaction, as they do in interpersonal communication in general. Research has examined the contribution eye contact, facial expression, gestures, and 'body language' make to effective conflict assertion.

BODY LANGUAGE

Experts discount the importance of body language, but laypersons consider it significant. Head, neck, shoulder, and torso positions that are upright, exhibit minimal extraneous movement, squarely face the other person, and involve purposive movement while speaking yet remain quiet while listening are associated with assertive behaviour. Non-assertiveness is associated with excessive nodding and head tilting; stooped, hunched, or shrugging shoulders; and squirming, rotating, or rocking torsos.

These cues are more influential in the evaluation of male asserters, but, overall, are the least important non-verbal responses. Finally, while meaningful posture shifts are appropriate, actually approaching the other person while asserting is perceived by laypersons as aggressive.

These data suggest that body language contributes modestly to perceptions of assertion, and is more important for males. Eye contact, facial expression, gestures, and, to a lesser extent, body language, all influence evaluations of conflict assertion. Facial expression for female asserters and gestures for male asserters may be especially important variables. Overall, steady but not rigid eye contact; a calm, sincere, serious facial expression; flexible use of arm and hand gestures; and a relaxed, involved body posture characterise behaviour judged to be assertive. Body movements should be fluid and purposeful when speaking but quiet and inconspicuous when listening.

PROCESS (INTERACTIVE) SKILLS

The overt skill components are emitted within social interaction. Their impact, therefore, depends on competence in the process skills of response timing, initiation and persistence, and stimulus control. Socially unskilled persons fail to time their statements and gestures accurately and respond inappropriately to situational for example, found that skilled individuals spoke more than unskilled persons, and did so at socially proper moments. This suggests that the effectiveness of an assertion will be related to the appropriateness with which it is introduced into the conflict interaction. It is essential that individuals discriminate among the verbal, non-verbal, and situational cues that indicate when it is appropriate to respond. When these stimuli fail to provide clear guidelines, other communication skills may be required.

INITIATION AND PERSISTENCE

The decision to emit an assertive response in a particular situation involves covert responses to be discussed shortly. On occasion, passivity or compliance may be preferred options, as when the realistic risk of assertion is excessive or the offending person's situation invites extraordinary 'understanding'. However, when assertion is the selected option, the initial verbalisation should be the minimal effective response (MER), defined as 'behaviour that would ordinarily accomplish the client's goal with a minimum of effort and of apparent negative emotion.

The MER operationalises the social rules of minimising conflict and relationship strain. If the MER proves ineffective, and the decision is made to persist, escalation is appropriate. This may involve increasing the intensity of para-linguistic qualities (voice volume, intonation, affect, and response duration) and/or expanding the use of non-verbal behaviours such as gestures and body language. Typically, the verbal content will be modified in some manner. For example, in continuing relationships, further explanation may be provided, empathy increased, or additional potential compromises suggested.

Determination of the MER is critical because an escalated response emitted as an initial assertion (a common error by novices) will likely be evaluated as inappropriate and aggressive, and may result in negative consequences for the asserter and reinforce beliefs that such behaviour is indeed risky. For instance, escalation 2 above would likely be perceived as aggressive if emitted as the initial response. Effective persistence requires that the asserter maintain the conflict focus and resist manipulation.

In non-continuing relationships, the asserter must basically provide a repetitive response that avoids the introduction of new material. If the cosmetic salesperson persists, and begins to describe the 'free' travel bag, umbrella, and perfume that accompany a purchase, and that can be given as extra 'gifts' or used for oneself, the appropriate assertive response remains: 'No, thank you, I am not interested.'

This avoids the manipulative ploy of discussing gifts or uses of products; such a shift in focus allows the interaction to continue and may soon force the asserter into explaining gift giving or cosmetic usage, neither of which is the issue. Maintaining the assertive focus in such a situation usually means simple repetition without qualification.

If you say, 'I am not interested at this time,' you may be asked why not 'now', and then 'when', and if 'cost' is the problem, there is a smaller size, and if no person is available to receive the 'gift' now, it will be good to have a gift handy when that person surely comes upon the scene. Maintaining the focus is particularly difficult when a valued continuing relationship is involved and the asserter is starting to behave less submissively. The new behaviour is not consistent with the expectations of the other person and is likely to arouse negative feelings, such as hurt, anger, rejection, depression, or vengeance.

Therefore, persistence by the novice asserter in relationships is a greater challenge than for experienced asserters, who have taught their social environment to expect self-enhancing behaviour. Escalation must be highly skilful to maintain the focus while simultaneously addressing the issues that affect the long-term integrity of the relationship. The escalations must embed repetitions in diverse syntactic surface structures and in layers of elaborations. For example, suppose a father whose grown daughter comes to his house for dinner every Sunday now learns that she will not be coming this week:

MER: 'Dad, I won't be coming to dinner this Sunday. I've made plans to see some friends – we're going to a party. I hope you won't be too disappointed. I'll see you again next Sunday as usual.' (This MER expresses the unpopular communication along with an explanation, attention to feelings, and a potential mutually acceptable compromise.)

Father: 'But I look forward to your visits so much. I don't get out often any more, and your company is so special. Couldn't you meet your friends after dinner?' (Father at this point is responding with an appropriate assertion of his own – a request for a behaviour change – and includes an explanation and potential compromise.)

Escalation 1: 'Dad, if I come to dinner, I'll miss a good deal of the party. I know how much you enjoy my visits, but this is an exception. It's a special party that I really want to attend. I know you'll miss me, but it's only one time.' (Repeated expression of the unpopular content, with additional explanation and empathy, all offered with a changed surface structure.)

Father: 'Then go with your friends to your party! I'll be fine. I'm sorry they are more important to you. One day you'll see how important it is that your kids care, and show that they care!' Here we are dealing with one of the most complex of continuing relationships, that of an adult child with a parent. The daughter initiates assertive behaviour, resulting in the father experiencing an unexpected loss of reinforcement and the feelings of hurt and anger that frequently accompany disappointment. Protecting the relationship and maintaining the focus in this situation involves an increased attention to underlying feelings, repetition and possible expansion of the explanation, and a wider search for a mutually acceptable compromise. The focus will be maintained best if the asserter can manage the exceptionally difficult task of addressing these verbalisations to the existence of the feelings rather than to the content of the feelings.

Escalation 2: 'Dad, I can see how angry and disappointed you are that I will not be coming for dinner this Sunday. I know how important our dinners together are to you, but as I said, I very much want to go to this party. There will be a lot of new people there, and I've been feeling a bit isolated lately.

I hope you understand my feelings. I'm thinking about how to solve this problem, and I know I'm free Wednesday evening – I can stop by for a few hours after work instead of waiting until next Sunday. How does that sound?' This escalated response repeats the assertion, attends to the feelings the father is experiencing, expands the explanation, offers a new compromise, and changes the surface structure. It does not lose the focus by becoming defensive through a debate on the extent of 'caring' for father or the relative 'importance' of different relationships. Caring, if present, can be demonstrated through the compromise. Sometimes, however, the interaction will continue and the content of the feelings will have to be addressed more directly, resulting in an increased probability of losing the assertive focus.

Escalation 3: 'Dad, I really do understand how much you look forward to our Sunday dinners and the time we spend together. I enjoy our dinners too, but sometimes other important engagements occur on Sundays. I feel very close to you, and care about you very much. My missing dinner this week has nothing to do with how I feel about you. I wish you saw this as I do, but all I can do is try to explain my point to you. Anyway, as I said, I am free Wednesday evening.

I'd like to stop by then how does that sound to you?' Escalation in continuing relationships will always involve expanded content (and hence response duration), but louder volume, greater firmness and inflection, or increased use of non-verbal cues will depend on the context. If the other person continues to experience negative feelings as a consequence of the assertion, and the relationship is a valued one, an assertion directed at the negative feelings may be necessary, either immediately or at a later, planned time. Persistence should be conceptualised as the behaviours required to solve the problem as best as possible. As the interaction continues, issues may shift, and further escalation may become counterproductive. A new, legitimate issue usually indicates the need for a new MER rather than endless escalation:

MER: 'Dad, I want to talk to you about our phone conversation last week. You sounded quite hurt and angry, and seemed to feel that if I cared about you I would always make the Sunday dinner. I would like to talk about that because I think I need some flexibility in my plans.' (This MER includes an orienting verbalisation and the conflict statement component of a behaviour change request.) Persistence increases the chances for a desired outcome but cannot guarantee it. The car mechanic may not reduce unwarranted charges regardless of the extent of escalation. An ineffective assertion that specifies a future contingency ('you will hear from my attorney') will not be very satisfying. Even when a desired outcome is achieved in a continuing relationship, the possibility of arousing negative feelings introduces additional risks. Skilful use of the covert components of assertion (see below) is necessary to assess the situation accurately; avoid rationalisations that justify passivity; and decide, first, whether to assert, and second, the extent of escalation that is desirable given the importance of the conflict, the nature of the relationship, and the realistic probability of potential positive and negative outcomes.

STIMULUS CONTROL SKILLS

Antecedent and consequent stimulus control skills

facilitate effective, socially acceptable assertion by altering the context in which the assertion is emitted. Antecedent stimulus control involves arranging the environment prior to asserting so that the likelihood of a favourable outcome is maximised. These skills are assertive behaviours themselves: requests to move to a private room prior to a confrontation, requests for a delay prior to making a decision (which provides time to identify and rehearse appropriate responses), or enquiries to the other person regarding convenient times to set aside for the discussion of concerns.

They may also involve self-management skills that inhibit assertions judged to be inappropriate or counter-productive. Conflicts that are discussed in private, at the right time, without time pressures, and with prior deliberation are more likely to be resolved satisfactorily. Consequent stimulus control refers to reinforcing the other person for listening to and/or complying with the assertion. Providing contingent verbal reinforcement for desired behaviour in response to an assertion is likely to encourage similar behaviour in the future and may also minimise negative perceptions of the conflict interaction.

Cognitive skills are central elements in contemporary conceptualisations of social skill. They categorise and manipulate information and are essential for the self-monitoring, self-evaluation, and self-reinforcement that comprise behavioural self-regulation. For example, socially skilled and unskilled persons differ in the standards they employ to evaluate their actions.

Skilled persons utilise objective criteria based on situational and interpersonal cues that generate social roles, norms, and rules, as well as empirically grounded expectations generated by personal experience. Unskilled individuals, on the other hand, rely on subjective standards that focus on idiosyncratic, non-empirical beliefs, perceptions, and expectations. An illustration of this is provided by Hung et al. who found that non-assertive persons performed more assertively after exposure to a severely passive model than to a moderately or minimally submissive model, presumably because their subjective performance standards were modified. The ability to use empirically based, objective criteria requires conceptual complexity, through which individuals

- Make increasingly precise discriminations among situational cues, allowing consideration of broader and more varied viewpoints
- increase the use of internally but rationally developed standards for problem solving
- integrate more information and increase tolerance for conflict. The importance of CC for assertive performance is clear: assertive individuals demonstrate greater CC than non-assertive persons; furthermore, high-CC people, compared to low-CC ones, manifest a better knowledge of assertive content, superior delivery skills, and more effective use of adaptive cognitions. Moreover, high-CC individuals behave more assertively and include more obligations in conflicts involving continuing relationships. Such relationships demand the greatest ability to utilise multiple perspectives and internal rational standards to resolve conflict and enhance the relationship. Conflicts involving non-continuing relationships require less CC, since social norms provide fairly straightforward behavioural guidelines. The specific cognitive abilities necessary to produce a sophisticated, rational, empirical analysis of, and response to, a conflict include knowledge, self-statements, expectancies, philosophical beliefs, problem-solving skills, social perception skills, and self-monitoring skills.

KNOWLEDGE

Both non-assertive and assertive individuals can accurately categorise and differentiate passive, assertive, and aggressive responses. In addition, non-assertive individuals can describe or enact appropriate assertive responses, reflecting clinical observations that deficiencies in response content knowledge account for some but by no means all instances of non-assertive performance. A second category of essential knowledge concerns the social rules, norms, and expectations that are likely to operate in particular contexts or circumstances, so that an array of appropriate response options can be generated. Unskilled persons, as noted above, are likely to lack accurate social cue knowledge.

SELF-STATEMENTS

A 'negative internal dialogue' interferes with competent social responding. Negative self-statements are exemplified by 'I will be embarrassed if I speak up,' or 'He won't like me unless I agree'. Positive versions might be 'My opinions are valuable' and 'I have the right to express myself '.

In fact, assertive persons emit approximately twice as many positive as negative self-statements when confronted with social conflict, while non-assertive individuals produce approximately equal numbers of each. Further, the 'mix' of positive and negative self-statements may be as important as the absolute frequency of each. For example, assertive persons often use negative self-statements as cues to verbalise positive coping ones. Wine noted that the self-verbalisations that are labelled as 'negative' or 'dysfunctional' typically focus on the needs of others and fear of rejection, and stem from the 'feminine' emphasis on relationships.

An implicit masculine bias can be avoided if such self-statements are conceptualised as conciliatory, nurturant, and communal.

This would remove a biased ('positive/ negative') continuum from the analysis and replace it with two orthogonal dimensions, autonomy and affiliation, each of which makes important but incomplete contributions to adjustment.

Nevertheless, it is important to recognise that effective conflict assertion clearly entails significant use of autonomous self-statements. In fact, direct training in these self-instructions, apart from any other intervention, has resulted in significant gains in assertiveness.

EXPECTANCIES

An expectancy is a cognitive behaviour that makes a specific prediction about performance in a particular situation. Outcome expectancies predict the probability that specific consequences will be produced by a particular response. Assertive and non-assertive persons expect standard assertion, and to a lesser extent empathic assertion, to have greater negative long-term effects on a relationship than non-assertion. However, assertive individuals expect conflict assertion to produce more positive short-term consequences and fewer negative ones than do non-assertive persons. Non-assertive and assertive persons do not differ in their identification of the possible consequences but in the probability that the potential outcomes will actually occur.

Further, the possible outcomes are evaluated differently: assertive individuals perceive the potential positive consequences of assertion as more desirable and the potential negative ones as more unpalatable.

Non-assertive persons may rationalise to reduce the perceived demand for engaging in a conflict interaction. Self-efficacy expectations refer to a person's belief that he or she can emit a specific response in a particular circumstance. Assertive individuals evidence much stronger self-efficacy in conflict situations than do non-assertive persons. Finally, assertive individuals demonstrate greater situational efficacy expectancies, which describe the confidence a person has of being able to generate any successful response to deal with a specific situation. Thus, assertive persons approach conflict situations with an adaptive appraisal of the context and a realistic self-confidence in their ability to emit appropriate behaviours.

PHILOSOPHICAL BELIEFS

It is identified that there are at least a dozen 'irrational' beliefs, of which six are directly related to assertion:

- Demands for perfection in self and others in important situations
- Blaming self or others for fallible behaviour

- Demands for universal and unwavering approval from significant others
- Defining personal rights and self-worth by external achievement in subjectively important areas
- Catastrophising, or exaggerating the meaning of an undesired outcome
- Viewing passivity as preferable to active intervention, in the belief that things will 'work out' eventually without 'rocking the boat'. These irrational thoughts are generally produced only in response to subjectively important issues: the person fails to accept that events in the world occur without regard to the personal value ascribed to a particular situation. Thus, someone may very rationally tolerate incompetence in a meaningless hobby (e.g. failure to perform well in a volleyball game), yet react with extraordinary emotion to an objectively similar event of subjective import (e.g. failure to get a leading role in a community play).

Underlying all irrational thinking is a basic logical error: things, people, or events should be a certain way. Ellis argues that the use of 'should' elevates desires into demands and prevents rational analysis of the situation. Unmet demands lead to upset, which does not facilitate effective problem resolution. If, on the other hand, unfulfilled desires are viewed as unfortunate events that one wished were otherwise ('it would be better if.' rather than 'it should not have happened '), the person will exhibit concern that can contribute to resolution of the problem.

Ellis' theory has been investigated in terms of assertive skills. Non-assertive individuals endorse more irrational ideas than do assertive individuals. In conflict situations, non-assertive persons entertain the possibility of many more negative 'overwhelming consequences' than positive ones, while assertive persons consider similar frequencies of each. As with self-statements, the 'mix' of extreme outcome expectancies may be more important than their intensity or frequency. Thus, rational alternatives to the irrational beliefs are likely to facilitate assertive responding. The typical non-assertive person might engage in the following thought process: 'I must assert myself without any mistakes or the assertion will fail [self-perfection], the other person will think I'm weird or will be hurt or angry [universal approval], and that would be absolutely terrible.

It would be my fault [self-blame] and confirm that I am no good [self-denigration]. It will work out better if I let it pass and see what happens [inaction].' These belief statements might be prefaced by additional irrational ideas: 'I don't have the right to infringe or make demands on this other person [self-denigration]' and/or 'I should not even have to deal with this situation because the other person should not be acting this way [other-perfection/ other-blame].'

Rational alternatives to the irrational beliefs can be taught fairly directly. The initial step requires the identification of the specific irrational thought(s) produced in the particular context. Non-assertive people frequently are so practiced in irrational thinking that they do not actually verbalise the irrational thoughts, but behave 'as if' they did. After specification of the actual or implicit thought, the individual is taught to challenge it and actively substitute a rational alternative, first in safe and structured rehearsal and later in the actual situation. The general content of the rational alternatives would include the following principles.

ACCEPTANCE OF IMPERFECTION

I am human and the world is very complicated; therefore, I will make mistakes even when the situation is important to me and I very much want to behave competently. The importance of an issue to me does not increase its objective status: there is no reason I should behave competently simply because it is important that I do so, although it would be nice if I were able to respond competently. The other person is also human, lives in the same complex world, and will also make mistakes in situations that are important to me. There is no reason that others should act in a desirable fashion, just because it is important to me, although it would be nice if they were able to do so. (These thoughts avoid self- or other-blaming and accept the inevitable frailty and imperfection of the human condition.)

ACCEPTANCE OF DISAPPROVAL

I cannot always satisfy everyone who is important to me, even if I always place their needs ahead of my own, because the world is too complicated and its operation too capricious. It would be nice if I could, but I must recognise that there is no reason why I should do so. (These beliefs recognise that some rejection or disapproval from others is unavoidable.)

NON-CATASTROPHISING

Negative outcomes are unfortunate, inconvenient, unpleasant, perhaps even bad – but not terrible, horrible, awful, or unbearable. I will try to resolve the problem when possible and adapt to the situation when change is not feasible. I must do this even when the undesired outcome involves a personally important issue, because the world does not know or care what is important to me. Things are as they should be, and demanding that they should be different ignores the complexity of the world – although it would be nice if they indeed were different. (These cognitions clarify the nature of the world and foster a realistic understanding and acceptance of one's place in it.)

ACTION

Since the world is not oriented toward fulfilling my desires, active attempts to influence it will increase the probability that my wishes will be achieved. Without action on my part, it is unlikely that events in the complex world will fortuitously meet my desires. (These thoughts promote personal responsibility for change, though they do not demand that such efforts be successful.)

SELF-WORTH

I am worthy, and have the same basic human rights as anyone else, regardless of how much or how little I or others have achieved. I have the basic right to assert myself, if I so choose, in an effort to influence the situation and maximize my rewards. (These ideas accept one's unconditional self-worth and human rights.) The direct modification of irrational thinking has been an important component of assertiveness-training programmes since the early 1970s.

While 'rational relabelling' or 'cognitive restructuring' alone improves conflict assertive performance, it contributes only minimally to a comprehensive training package. This supports Bandura's contention that though performance may be cognitively mediated, those cognitions are most efficaciously changed when the behaviours upon which they are based are first changed. Rational relabelling procedures may prove to be more important in promoting generalisation of assertive responses to novel people and situations than in facilitating initial acquisition of the response.

SOCIAL PERCEPTION SKILLS

Accurate perception and empathic role-taking are two distinct cognitive skills involved in interpersonal perception. These skills are now conceptualised as components of 'emotional intelligence'. Accurate perception has been investigated more thoroughly and the evidence strongly suggests that non-assertive individuals are deficient in this skill. They are less sensitive to external cues, misjudge the amount of anger communicated by assertive and aggressive responses, and place exaggerated emphasis on the status of the other person and the extent of social norm transgression when analysing conflict situations.

A realistic assessment of social norms provides an important guideline for judging behaviour; for example, the reasonableness of a request influences compliance and emotional responses to the asserter. However, non-assertive persons perceive 'reasonableness', and therefore social norms and the legitimate rights of the other person, differently from assertive individuals, especially when requests are consensually evaluated to be of low or moderate legitimacy. Conflict situations of moderate legitimacy pose a particular challenge to accurate perception: in such situations, assertive as well as non-assertive persons produce more thoughts but fewer objective ones and report a decreased intention to assert and weakened self-efficacy beliefs. The legitimate rights of all participants are most difficult to determine in ambiguous contexts, requiring refined conceptual skills that can assess situational considerations, make appropriate reasonableness determinations, and synthesise the resulting increase in positive and negative thoughts into adaptive, accurate discriminations. Distorted judgements of circumstances may be a prime contributor to a decision to behave non-assertively.

A second important perceptual skill is the ability to understand the viewpoint of the other person, termed 'role-taking' or 'metaperception'. It provides the basis for determining the impact of an assertion on the recipient (an antecedent obligation), and it is the foundation upon which the asserter develops an empathic statement (a subsequent obligation). The superior social evaluation of the empathic assertion relative to the standard one highlights the importance of this skill in conflict resolution.

A key element of this skill is the discrimination of the cues that indicate an empathic response will facilitate the interaction. For example, Fischetti et al. found that heterosocially skilled and unskilled persons differed in their ability to recognise when a vocal or gestural response from them would help a speaker continue to talk. The ability to discriminate such cues may explain why skilled and unskilled persons differ in the timing or placement of vocalisations and gestures, but not in the frequency.

INTERPERSONAL PROBLEM-SOLVING SKILLS

The systematic problem-solving skills necessary for social competence are deficient in a variety of clinical populations. The problem-solving sequence involves problem recognition and acceptance, problem definition and goal setting, generation of potential response alternatives, decision making (assessment of alternatives in terms of likely outcomes), and solution implementation and evaluation. Chiauzzi and

Heimberg found that non-assertive persons manifested deficits in problem recognition and assessment (a social perception skill) and in their ability to select an appropriate response. No inadequacies were observed in their capacity to generate response alternatives, in terms of either number or quality.

However, therapist-generated alternatives produce higher outcome expectancies than client-generated ones, suggesting that unskilled individuals lack confidence in their own alternatives.

Robinson and Calhoun (1984) also found a situational effect: more complex and assertive alternatives were produced in response to an angry than to a pleasant male.

Finally, Deluty found that assertive, aggressive, and submissive children generated equal numbers of alternatives in conflict situations, but that the assertive children's possibilities included assertive options to a proportionately greater extent.

Problem-solving skills assume a central role in assertion when it is conceptualised as a sequence of overt and covert responses.

The antecedent obligations are involved in problem definition and assessment (determining the rights of all participants and whether assertion is the preferred option). The subsequent obligation to seek a mutually acceptable compromise is largely dependent on the ability to generate alternative solutions. Because these features contribute to conceptual complexity, problem-solving skills may provide the means through which the former attribute can be operationalised and trained.

SELF-MONITORING SKILLS

Responsible assertion is based on an accurate perception that the situation appropriately calls for such action; in other words, an assertion situation must be distinguished from other social ones and acquire the properties of a discriminative stimulus.

This learned cue, which will prompt the early behaviours

in the assertion chain (the antecedent obligations), will comprise the person's own reactions. Thus, the assertive person must learn to attend to his or her own behaviours and discriminate those reactions that indicate assertion should be considered.

The self-monitored discriminative stimuli can be behaviours, emotions, and/or cognitions. Behavioural cues include coping strategies that are indirect, hostile, or avoidant (e.g. hinting at desires, using phoney excuses or excessive apologies; engaging in withdrawal, aggression, passive-aggression, or submission).

Emotional cues include frustration, resentment, shame, guilt, anger, depression, and upset. Cognitive cues are present when the person engages in excessive ruminations and self-statements that blame or denigrate the self and others, rationalise the unimportance of the concern, and are generally affiliative ('negative') or irrational. When these behavioural, emotional, and cognitive reactions are produced in response to a social conflict, they are the primary signals that assertion should be considered.

SOCIAL VALIDITY OF CONFLICT ASSERTION

Technical proficiency, immediate outcome, overall net cost-benefit, and social validity were discussed earlier as four distinct and partially independent measurements of the assertive response.

For instance, a skilled assertion that meets social and cultural norms may still fail to produce desired short-term outcomes or enhance the long-term stability of a relationship. But because the functional value of an assertion will provide the tangible benefits, the social reaction to assertion assumes critical importance.

GENERAL FINDINGS

The social validity of standard assertion (expression of the assertive right without the inclusion of obligations) was discussed earlier. Briefly, it is judged to be more socially competent, but less likeable, than non-assertive behaviour, and to be at least as potent as, and more favourably evaluated than, aggressive behaviour. Empathic assertions, which express rights and obligations, are judged more favourably than standard assertions and comparably to non-assertion. The obligations are consistent with social expectations and thereby enhance the potency of the assertion.

The evaluation is less positive when the assertion requires a significant sacrifice on the part of the recipient or is in response to a relatively reasonable request. Adults judge assertion to be most appropriate when directed toward strangers rather than toward friends or intimates, but college students perceive it to be the preferred option for resolving conflicts with friends and relatives.

These studies demonstrate that empathic and standard conflict assertions are judged by observers to be socially appropriate and competent, if not always exceptionally likeable. However, the person whose reaction is most important is the real-life recipient, not an observer.

Although an observer may appreciate the abstract value of an assertion, the natural social environment may react differently. Not surprisingly, the appraisal may be relative to the alternatives.

Evaluations by recipients of assertion delivered by confederates in staged encounters confirm that non-assertive behaviour is judged to be more likeable than standard or empathic assertion. Furthermore, in vivo and abstract comparisons between standard assertion and aggression suggest that the superior observer evaluation of assertion is magnified in the in vivo situation.

The social acceptance of a standard assertion can be increased by use of the empathic assertion's obligations, as noted above, and also by more extensive interaction with the asserter that includes experience with non-conflict as well as conflict behaviours, as will occur in most continuing relationships. Thus, individuals who emit positive assertions (such as requesting or offering help, or expressing compliments or thanks), general conversational comments, and task-oriented interactions are viewed as more likeable and competent than persons exhibiting standard assertion alone.

Thus, empathic elaborations and contextual experience can moderate the evaluation of assertion. Nevertheless, concerns regarding social evaluation remain highly relevant in continuing relationships, unlike transient interactions in which instrumental utility is usually the primary consideration.

GENDER

Conflict assertion has been seen as a powerful tool through which pervasive societal sexism can be challenged including its failure to include assertion as a component of healthy or appropriate female behaviour.

Some feminists, however, contend that the assertion construct is 'androcentric' and blames women rather than challenging societal prejudice. Further, women writers have long contended that behaving assertively entails significantly greater risks for females than for males, even though 30-plus studies published in the 1970s and 1980s failed to confirm such a bias. However, this body of research on gender was conducted primarily with US college students in contexts that established arbitrary social interactions and at a time when the notion of assertiveness was trendy and the conservative social and political Zeitgeist that was to suffuse the West was still nascent.

The handful of studies that appeared in the 1990s strongly indicate that conflict assertion is riskier for women than for men. This may be why the social rules governing conflict assertion by women – but not by men – emphasise obligation behaviours and even submission. Even so, women still expect empathic assertion to result in more problematic long-term consequences than do men. In the work environment, for example, women who promote themselves in a direct and confident manner decrease their social attractiveness and are perceived as less socially skilled than males who engage in similar behaviour.

These devaluations are in response to socially dominant behaviours (e.g. competitiveness) rather than to demonstrations of competence, such as autonomy and ambition. Women can, however, temper the unfavourable judgements by meeting expectations of communality, such as by exhibiting warmth, sensitivity, and caring.

In addition, assertive women are valued by business people who are outcome oriented.Women, to a much greater degree than men, must assert themselves in a rule-consistent manner and rely on obligations in their efforts to resolve conflict.

To accomplish this, they must (a) learn to discriminate gender-based social rules and (b) integrate self-interest with a transparently warm and communal interpersonal style. These skills are considerably more sophisticated and complex than the relatively straightforward response that characterises effective assertion by males.

For Rudman and Glick (2001), this means women must be 'bilingual' – simultaneously competent and nice. The greater demands and risks women face constrain their assertion and result in significant real-world consequences such as salary and promotion disadvantages. For instance, women ask for less than men when negotiating starting salary, which has a significant impact on future earnings as small initial differences become compounded over the years into major discrepancies.

In addition, women make fewer requests related to working conditions, and those that they do make are more likely to involve home rather than job concerns. Unfortunately, women struggle to promote their own interests within a culture that even today teaches preschoolers that assertion is a component of social competence and acceptance for bcys, but not for girls.

As adults, men and women who have internalised a traditional view of women's role in society devalue assertion by females. Women, therefore, must discriminate the context fully, including the gender biases of the recipient and the social rules that establish expectations, in order to make an informed decision about the value of assertion.

In this regard, females do appear to be making slow but

steady progress in successfully juggling social demands and costs: they increased their assertiveness in the last third of the twentieth century by a significant though modest amount (0.46 standard deviations), as measured by two common behavioural self-report scales and the dominance scales of three trait instruments.

RESPONSE CLASSES

The studies assessing the perception of various response classes of standard assertion have produced conflicting data. Schroeder and his colleagues determined that expressing unpopular opinions involved the greatest amount of assertiveness, behaviour change requests the next most, and refusals the least.

Behaviour change requests were perceived to be most socially acceptable and expressing unpopular opinions the least appropriate. Lewis and Gallois, on the other hand, obtained contradictory results: behaviour change requests (conflict statement only) were judged most assertive but least socially desirable, while expressing unpopular opinions was perceived most favourably.

Furthermore, expressions of different opinions by friends were more positively evaluated than such behaviour by strangers or refusals by friends. Refusals by strangers were judged more positively than refusals by friends or the conflict statement component of a behaviour change request. Finally, Crawford found no differences in the reactions to the expression of negative feelings, positive self-presentation, and the setting of limits.

However, these three response categories appeared to be variations of behaviour change requests rather than representatives of distinct response classes. The conflicting data obtained may be due to cultural differences between the USA and Australia or to a variety of methodological differences, such as varying response topographies and specification of degree of familiarity of friends.

Furthermore, these investigations evaluated standard assertion only. Friends, as part of their relationship, may very well accept a difference of opinion without explanation, compromise, or empathy, but are likely to expect those elaborations to accompany the refusal of a request. These data, then, are consistent with the emphasis on employing empathic assertion for resolving conflicts in continuing relationships.

Level of Assertiveness

Socially competent persons judge assertive responses to be more likeable, effective, and appropriate than aggressive and non-assertive ones. Because non-assertive persons expect more negative outcomes from assertion, it is not surprising that many studies find that their perception of such behaviour is relatively unfavourable.

However, when non-assertive persons have the opportunity to evaluate a spectrum of behaviour that is broader than a single standard assertive interaction, their evaluation of the asserter is similar to that of assertive persons. Non-assertive persons, with their lower level of conceptual complexity, may moderate their judgement of conflict assertion only when it is portrayed concretely and in concert with other responses that have unambiguous social acceptability.

The activism, pragmatism, rationality, and ethical relativism that legitimise assertion embody middle-class, US, Caucasian male values.

Thus, the specific behaviours and attitudes fostered by this ideology will not be congruent with cultural assumptions of all societies or ethnic groups. In society, for example, the issue of race must be considered directly. A system of cultural values that originated in Africa and the legacy of brutal discrimination (e.g. interracial discomfort, the development of distinct communication and linguistic patterns) raise questions about the social acceptability of assertion by African-Americans.

In fact, the research suggests that there are important differences in the way African-Americans and whites react to conflict assertion. In general, African-Americans perceive assertive behaviour by an African-American as more aggressive than similar behaviour emitted by a white person, and value aggressive and standard assertive behaviour more, and empathic assertion less, than do whites.

When the race of all participants in an assertive interaction is examined, even finer distinctions emerge. The data suggest that the obligation components are appropriate training goals for whites asserting to whites, but that the goals for blacks asserting to whites might place greater emphasis on strategies to foster awareness of, and then to decrease, whites' discomfort with black assertiveness.

Generalisations about the appropriateness of assertive response styles for members of diverse cultural and ethnic groups must be made cautiously. Japanese, Malaysian, and Filipino adults, The adults and adolescents are less likely to engage in conflict assertion than their Western counterparts. Nevertheless, assertion that accommodates cultural norms is an accepted communication style in a wide range of societies. Furthermore, sensitivity to cultural values that are more communitarian and tradition bound than mainstream US can form the basis of successful intervention with a wide array of ethnic groups.

More recently, this approach has been articulated in a novel and idealistic manner: Dwairy proposed that a broad-based effort to train Palestinian-Arab citizens of Israel in conflict assertion skills could help these persons coexist more effectively and harmoniously within the individualistically oriented Israeli milieu, particularly if a companion intervention helped Israelis to understand the communitarian-authoritarian foundation of Palestinian society.

OVERVIEW

Assertion is a situation-specific social skill that has been touted in the pop psychology literature as a panacea for all social frustrations, and then chastised by many researchers as a concept that has outlived its usefulness. Despite these polarised judgements, assertiveness and its accompanying training procedures have settled into a comfortable role in an increasing number of professional settings.

As the peoples of the world experience rapid changes that bring them in closer contact with each other, it is likely that increasing numbers will conclude that their society's long-term interests are served when its members personify assertiveness.

This is because assertiveness is an egalitarian social philosophy that encourages responsible individual action to challenge the legitimacy of barriers (interpersonal, societal, cultural, legal, or whatever) that prevent fair and equitable sharing of power and resources. Human nature being what it is, conflict assertion skills will remain central for all who seek to redress societal inequities.

Chapter 11

Interacting in Groups

INTRODUCTION

A group cannot successfully complete a task unless its members reach agreement about the division of the work that has to be carried out. Group members may realise that their common and private interests coincide with respect to successful completion of the group task, but all of them may nevertheless feel tempted to act in their private interest by, for example, leaving unpleasant work to fellow group members.

The second part of this chapter elaborates on the role of communication in the process of tuning common and private interests. Cognitive tuning and tuning of interests are two basic processes in groups. In both tuning processes, communicating group members exert strong pressures on one another to consider the cognitions and interests that they have in common.

Although essential for successful completion of the group task, strong normative conformity pressure to arrive at a common understanding of the task may have its drawbacks when it comes to innovative thinking. At the end of the first part of this chapter, we will discuss some preventive measures that can be taken to weaken dysfunctional normative conformity pressures.

In the process of tuning of interests, by contrast, normative pressures on group members to consider their common interests cannot be strong enough. As we will see at the end of the second part of this chapter, groups often take additional normative measures to counteract group members' temptation to enjoy a free ride on fellow members' cooperative efforts.

COGNITIVE TUNING

Newly formed task groups or existing groups faced with a new task can formulate solutions only after a common understanding of the task is achieved. There are three basic modalities of cognitive tuning toward a commonly shared frame of reference, namely, normalisation, conformity, and innovation. Normalisation occurs when there is no a priori shared interpretation of the group task. When the task is very ambiguous and fluid, group members mutually and gradually converge on a common frame of reference that serves from then on as a group norm.

Conformity assumes prior normalisation since it involves the attempts of a majority of the group members to maintain their socially anchored representation of the task by putting pressure on deviating individuals to go along, or risk being rejected by the majority. When a persisting minority of deviates tries to introduce a new frame of reference an explicit cognitive conflict is created. Innovation occurs when this cognitive conflict is resolved through persuasion of members of the majority by the minority.

The three modalities of cognitive tuning embody increasing levels of cognitive conflict in a task group. The following three sections will describe some classic studies on the role of communication in group members' attempts to form, maintain, and change their common frame of reference, respectively. These studies are often cited as starting points for more recent research on cognitive-tuning processes in task groups. To illustrate some implications of the research findings, we will use the example of an educational committee.

NORMALISATION

Although all of the members of the committee may share the conviction that the current curriculum needs an update, their participation in the committee may initially feel like a leap in the dark to (some of) them. How will they arrive at a common frame of reference when there is not yet an a priori shared interpretation of the group task? In a very literal sense, darkness has been employed by Sherif in a classic series of experiments on the formation of a shared representation of an ambiguous task.

Sherif made use of the so-called autokinetic phenomenon, a compelling optical illusion to a person who stares at a tiny light bulb in an otherwise completely darkened room. Even though the light is in fact stationary, after the person watches it for a minute or two it appears to move, due to (unconscious) eye movements and neural processes in the eyes of the perceiver. The illusion occurs when the room is pitch-dark and when experimental participants are unfamiliar with the room's size so that they lack any physical standard against which to compare the position of the dot of light. Their task is to estimate the apparent movement of the light after each of a number of exposures.

INTERACTING IN GROUPS

Sherif's first series of studies investigated the formation of a personal frame of reference. Participants were run in isolation and there was no opportunity to communicate. It appeared that a participant's initial responses varied widely from one exposure to the next, but with repeated exposures, a participant's responses gradually converged on a single estimate. This single value that each participant eventually arrived at differed widely across participants, suggesting that each participant built up a stable personal frame of reference to judge subsequent task stimuli. In Sherif's second series of studies, inexperienced participants were placed together in the pitch-dark room and were allowed to communicate with one another. It appeared that, as in the first series of studies, participants' individual estimates showed a pattern of extreme initial variability.

However, as a result of mutual adjustment between group members' estimates in the process of communicating, participants' responses soon converged on a single group estimate. These group estimates differed widely across groups, suggesting that each of the groups developed its own frame of reference. The question arises as to why some groups converged on a high, while other groups converged on a low, group estimate. To address the role of the content of the communication, in some studies Sherif paid experimental confederates, acting as if they were regular fellow group members, to offer extremely high (or low) estimates.

In response to these extreme estimates given by the confederates, the naive group members drastically increased (or decreased) their estimates to converge on a high (or low) group estimate. Subsequent studies observed that, once such a high (or low) group estimate had been established, it acquired a life of its own as a group norm. When the experimenter removed the confederates from the group after a number of trials and replaced them by new naive participants, the artificially high or low group norm still continued to affect the group's judgements in subsequent trials.

In the above studies, the naive, inexperienced participants felt very unsure about the correctness of their own estimates. In the absence of any communication with fellow participants in the first series of studies, the internal cognitive conflict about the correctness of their own estimates had to be resolved by the individual participant himself or herself.

In the second series of studies, the possibility to communicate with fellow group members helped participants to resolve their internal cognitive conflict. Participants were so uncertain about their own initial responses, that they gave much weight to the estimates expressed by their fellow group members.

As a result, they developed a common understanding of the task and a common response: a group. In a subsequent study, a much stronger cognitive conflict was experienced by the participants, not merely at an intrapersonal level (as in the above mentioned studies) but also at an interpersonal level. It appeared that participants that had first been exposed to a number of trials in isolation before they were placed in a group were less willing to adjust their own initial estimates to those of their fellow group members. Many of the participants stuck to their personal way of responding that they had developed in isolation before they entered the group. As a result, the progress of cognitive tuning toward a socially anchored norm, that is, a single group estimate, took much more time and was far less complete than when no personal way of responding had been previously established.

The strongest interpersonal cognitive conflict was felt by participants in yet another study. After having naive, inexperienced participants respond to repeated trials in separate groups so that a socially anchored local group norm had been developed within each group, Sherif took individuals from these separate groups and created new groups for another series of exposures.

Unlike completely inexperienced participants or participants who had already built up a personal norm in isolation before entering a group, these participants were least easily influenced by the fellow members of their present, newly created group. They persisted in the norm that they had developed by communicating with fellow members of their previous group. Taken together, Sherif's studies suggest that once task ambiguity has been cognitively resolved by the formation of an internalised frame of reference, group members attach less weight to new perspectives, which may then be seen as discrepant from their own frame of reference.

These results imply that the communicative process of cognitive tuning toward a commonly shared frame of reference depends on group members' previous experiences. For example, if (some of the) members enter the educational committee with well-developed ideas about the task, which may differ widely from one member to another due to previous normalisation in other social settings (such as student meetings or faculty meetings), the formation of a common frame of reference will not be easily achieved. This is very likely to happen, since one usually does not recruit naive, inexperienced candidates to participate in advisory committees. When (some) members stick to their previously developed, socially anchored frame of reference, the committee should find ways to resolve the cognitive conflict between the group members.

Under these conditions of prior normalisation, the question arises as to whether a group member faced with a number of fellow group members advocating a discrepant perspective that does not seem correct will go along or stick to their previously developed, socially anchored frame of reference. This group member may be displaying attitudes or behaviours that have gained them personal acceptance in other groups to which they belong. In a newly formed group, the person may be met with disapproval. What happens if such an individual is faced with a discrepant majority?

CONFORMITY PRESSURES FROM A MAJORITY

How will a group member respond upon learning that a personal frame of reference, established by previous experience, differs from the one held by the majority of the fellow members of the present group? The classic experimental paradigm for studying this issue has been developed by Asch who asked small groups of participants to make a series of relatively simple judgements.

Their task was to state publicly, and in the same fixed order, which of three comparison lines matched a fourth 'target' line in length. The correct answer was obvious. When making these simple judgements in isolation, participants made no mistakes. In the typical group experiment, only one of the group members was a naive participant, who had to respond next to last in the row after hearing the responses of the preceding group members, who (unknown to the naive participant) were all confederates of the experimenter.

The group judged a series of stimulus sets, and on many of these (the 'critical' trials) the confederates had been instructed to agree on a clearly incorrect response. By having the confederates advocate a clearly incorrect response, Asch assessed an individual group member's willingness to conform to a majority when this individual could be completely certain of being right and that the majority was wrong. Being faced with a unanimous majority that offered an obviously incorrect answer created a strong intra- and interpersonal cognitive conflict for the naive participant. This participant was puzzled by the discrepancy between personal judgement and the unanimous judgement of all of the fellow group members.

Should the person comply with the unanimous majority of the present group or stick to their internalised frame of reference? It appeared that only 25% of the naive participants showed no conformity at all and remained independent of the social pressure from the majority throughout the session. Only a few participants conformed on all of the critical trials to the blatantly incorrect judgement of the majority. However, 33% of all participants conformed to the clearly incorrect majority position on more than half of the critical trials.

What can be learned from these results? On the one hand, they demonstrate the impact of majority influence. One out of every three naive participants solved the cognitive conflict by adjusting their own response to the incorrect responses of the majority on many (but not all) of the critical trials. On the other hand, the same results demonstrate that conformity in a group is not easily achieved when group members are strongly convinced that they themselves are right and that the majority of their fellow group members are wrong. At least one out of every four naive participants remained completely independent of the majority pressure, whereas two-thirds of all naive participants remained independent on more than half of the critical trials. Note that such a reluctance to conform to the judgements of fellow group members was also observed in Sherif's studies, by participants who had previously developed a socially anchored frame of reference before they entered their present group.

The case of one (naive participant) against all other group members (confederates) is a special case, however. Whereas a lone individual will find it hard to resist the pressure of the majority since the one view can be dismissed as a personal idiosyncrasy, the presence of some fellow dissenters in the group may cast doubt on the majority view. In follow-up studies, Asch instructed one of the confederates to give the correct response on some of the critical trials. When the naive participant found that they were not alone in disagreeing with the clearly incorrect majority, conformity rates were much lower.

In yet another variation, Asch arranged for one confederate to disagree with the majority, but also to disagree with the (correct) answer of the naive participant. It appeared that even the presence of such a fellow deviate who did not agree with the majority nor with the participant made it easier for a naive participant to express a personal viewpoint during the group discussion and to withstand pressures from the majority. Apparently, the cognitive conflict of being faced with a unanimous majority is more intense (and, as a result, elicits more conformity) than the cognitive conflict of being faced with a non-unanimous majority.

Subsequent research by Asch revealed that naive participants were less willing to go along with the majority when they were not required to state their judgements publicly but were allowed to state their judgements privately in writing. Thus, conformity to a majority position does not necessarily reflect a participant's true opinion.

Indeed, in private, post-experimental interviews (away from the group), participants who had publicly agreed with their fellow group members in the group session pointed out that they did not believe that the others were correct, but that they themselves did not want to appear different. Their anxiety about appearing different was not unrealistic. In a reversal of the above described studies, Asch replaced the confederates by naive participants, so that there was a majority of naive participants facing one incorrect confederate. Under these conditions, the naive participants expressed strong confidence in the correctness of their majority position and exposed the persisting deviate to amusement and scorn.

The relationship between non-conformity and rejection by fellow group members has also been demonstrated by Schachter. He showed that, throughout group discussions, communication directed toward disagreeing group members tends to increase over time in order to put pressure on these deviants to conform to the majority. At a later stage of the discussion, the amount of communication with deviants decreases, either because initial deviants yield to the majority pressure or because the majority gives up trying to influence a persisting deviant.

In the latter case, the deviant is literally excommunicated. Reviewing the above classic studies and many recent studies that used a large variety of tasks (ranging from perceptual tasks to attitude tasks), Wheeler concluded that the need to communicate in a group increases when the issue has more relevance for the group and when group members feel the need to maintain a congenial group atmosphere. Furthermore, pressures to communicate in the direction of a specific group member are stronger when the perceived likelihood that communication will change that person in the desired direction is greater. Communication with an unyielding deviate will eventually stop.

Applied to the process of cognitive tuning in the educational committee, these studies suggest that its members may feel compelled to conform to the opinions of the majority of their present group, that is, the committee. Learning that a majority of the committee has reached agreement about their understanding of the task that differs from one member's own understanding may lead the individual to doubt whether personal views are valid and whether a deviant will be liked as a group member.

With increasing group cohesion or when the topic of discussion has more relevance for the committee, it will be harder for a deviant to withstand the majority's conformity pressures. Resistance to majority pressure is more likely, however, when there is still another group member advocating a perspective that differs from the one held by the majority. Whereas a single dissenter's arguments can be dismissed as personal idiosyncrasies, more than one dissenter in the group may cast doubt on the validity of the majority's perspective. In the next paragraph, we will elaborate on the potential innovative impact of such a few persisting dissenters.

INNOVATIVE PRESSURES FROM A MINORITY

Members of a minority who challenge the prevailing group norm by maintaining their own discrepant views in a consistent and confident way may not only successfully withstand the conformity pressures of the majority, but may also have innovative impact on the group. Consistency in the responses of the minority in the face of majority opposition (and sometimes even ridicule) may be considered by the members of the majority as a sign of self-confidence and commitment to a coherent idea and thereby may focus their attention on the minority's line of reasoning.

Herein lies the potential of minority influence. It can purposely create cognitive conflict, and doubt and uncertainty about the prevailing group norm, exploiting most group members' dislike of cognitive conflict and their need for uniformity. When the cognitive conflict cannot be resolved by mutual convergence (as participants did in Sherif's autokinetic effect studies), it may be solved either by excommunicating the deviant minority or by an attitudinal shift of members of the majority in the direction of the minority.

Effective minority influence has been demonstrated in a classic series of ingenious studies by Moscovici, Lage, and Naffrechoux. Groups of six individuals were shown a series of blue slides, which varied in brightness. The participants' task was to judge the colour of the slides and to announce judgements aloud.

When the group consisted of six naive participants, 99% of all participants labelled the slides as blue. By instructing two confederates in the six-person groups to advocate an unusual response, that is, labelling the blue slides as green, Moscovici and his co-workers were able to assess naive participants' willingness to go along with a discrepant minority. It was unlikely that the unusual responses by these confederates would be dismissed as blatantly incorrect, as had been the case in Asch's studies, since the colour perception task faced participants with more ambiguity about the correct response than Asch's line-matching tasks.

The results showed that when the judgements of the two confederates were consistent, both over time and across themselves, the four naive participants eventually described the slide more often as green (8% of all responses given by the naive participants were green) than when the judgements of the two confederates were inconsistent, that is, sometimes labelling the slides as blue, sometimes as green (resulting in only 1% of all responses being green). Thus, it appears that a consistent minority may exert innovative influence, whereas an inconsistent minority may have virtually no impact on the group.

Although naive participants in the six-person groups were more likely to agree publicly with the unusual colour judgements when these were made by a majority (four confederates labelling the slides as green) than when these were made by a consistent minority (two confederates labelling the slides as green), their private beliefs were influenced more deeply by minority influence than by majority influence. From private interviews (away from the group) after the group sessions, it appeared that participants who had followed the minority's suggestion that the slides were green had a stronger belief that the slides were green than participants who had yielded to a majority labelling the slides as green.

These results were conceptually replicated with various other tasks, such as discussion tasks. Several studies show that naive participants' private beliefs are more strongly affected by minority influence than by majority influence. When naive participants can express their opinion at the end of the discussion in private, they tend to agree more often with the minority. However, they tend to agree more often with the majority when they have to express their opinion in the presence of fellow group members.

Taken together, majority influence appears to be particularly effective in eliciting public compliance, whereas group members' private beliefs are more strongly affected by minority influence. These results suggest that a small subgroup within the educational committee may create a cognitive conflict by demonstrating a consistent and confident behavioural style in expressing a discrepant perspective. This subgroup may be able to introduce a new frame of reference. Its innovative impact may not be visible right away, however.

Minority influence may not immediately come to the surface during plenary meetings, but only in the absence of the majority of the committee members, for example, during private discussions between individuals after a plenary meeting.

In order to enhance its innovative impact, a minority should encourage group members who have been privately persuaded by the minority's arguments to support publicly the new frame of reference. To increase the size of the minority (and thereby its impact), the minority should persuade individual converts that some fellow committee members have also privately expressed their support for the minority position. The assumed presence of fellow dissenters makes it less threatening for individual converts to adhere publicly to the minority position during a follow-up, plenary committee meeting.

INFORMATIONAL VERSUS NORMATIVE PRESSURES

The preceding sections have dealt with cognitive-tuning processes in groups in which there exists either a broad range of perspectives or in which a majority or minority favours one particular perspective. The three associated modalities of cognitive tuning, that is, normalisation, conformity, and innovation, respectively, can be described in terms of two basic social pressures in groups: informational pressure and normative pressure.

Informational pressure is based on group members' tendency to rely upon fellow group members to acquire accurate information to form an appropriate frame of reference in an ambiguous task environment. Open communication may induce group members to converge on a common frame of reference or social norm.

This process of normalisation has been observed in Sherif's groups of inexperienced participants, who were literally put in the dark and lacked any standard against which to compare the position of the dot of light. Internalisation of such a socially anchored frame of reference may result in individual group members attaching less weight to new, discrepant perspectives, but it does not immunise them, since group members rely on others to acquire not only accurate information but also approval. When faced with a majority holding a discrepant perspective, individual group members may yield to normative pressures of a majority to reward conforming group members and reject persisting deviates.

A comparison between Asch's and Sherif's research findings suggests, however, that conformity in the interest of being liked as a group member has less powerful ramifications than conformity that results from viewing fellow group members for the purpose of gaining accurate information. Many of Asch's participants, who were confident that their own frame of reference was correct and that the fellow group members were wrong (no informational social pressure), publicly conformed to the local majority norm because they were afraid to be seen as different. Their compliance persisted only as long as they felt normative pressure.

Once outside the group, they were more likely to express their private beliefs. By contrast, a local group norm that had been established through communication between inexperienced naive participants in Sherif's studies (on the basis of their informational needs to arrive at an accurate representation of ambiguous task stimuli) acquired a life of its own and tended to persist even in the absence of fellow group members with whom the norm had previously been developed. Not only a majority, but also a consistent minority may induce individual group members to shift their opinion. Particularly when the task environment leaves some room for different interpretations a minority's discrepant perspective cannot easily be dismissed as blatantly incorrect.

Since minorities lack the numerical advantage of majorities and their positions are often quite unpopular, minorities cannot exert normative pressure on individual members of the majority. By intentionally raising doubt about the validity of the prevailing opinion of the majority, minorities may instead set the stage for informational social influence.

To be effective, arguments supporting the minority position must be well communicated. In addition, minorities should evoke elaborate discussions in the group. Such discussions are less likely to be initiated by members supporting the majority opinion. When the content of the minority's persuasive arguments eventually becomes clear, minorities may induce a real change in group members' private beliefs.

Following this line of reasoning, Nemeth argues that majority influence may induce a fixation in thought, because it focuses group members mainly on the normative requirement of conformity. The fear of being rejected by the majority of one's group impedes creative and divergent thinking.

By contrast, given a minority's inability to exert normative pressure, minority influence relies on informational pressure. The cognitive conflict evoked by a persistent minority is likely to promote careful consideration of the reasons for the apparent discrepancy. Nemeth and Kwan demonstrated that group members not only express more, but also more divergent and original, ideas in response to a discrepant minority than group members exposed to a discrepant majority. Thus, a dissenting minority appears to stimulate creativity and openness in the exchange of information rather than adaptation and fixation.

Although normative and informational pressures can be distinguished conceptually, they are closely related. Normative pressures can inhibit informational pressures by determining what information gets exchanged in a task group.

During discussions, group members may be so concerned with receiving social approval from their peers (rather than with careful evaluation of the available information) that some information never gets expressed. As a result, they tend to discuss information that they assume to share in common and fail to mention distinguishing pieces of information that are known only to single individuals within the group or information that might contradict an emerging group consensus. In its most extreme form, normative pressures may lead to premature concurrence-seeking in decision-making groups.

Failure to take relevant alternative perspectives into account may result in serious policy disasters. Given the importance of open-mindedness to alternative perspectives at various stages of task completion, task groups should find ways to row against the current of normative pressures. The next section will elaborate on some formal techniques to push group members past the bounds of restrictive thinking along the lines of the prevailing local group norm.

OVERCOMING DYSFUNCTIONAL NORMATIVE PRESSURES

How can premature concurrence-seeking and biased information exchange be avoided? Brainstorming may stimulate group members to generate divergent ideas. Group members receive instructions from a group facilitator, who introduces several rules to encourage group members to express as many ideas as possible within a certain time interval. Group members should not screen their own ideas. In order to generate even more ideas, they are encouraged to piggyback on ideas expressed by their fellow group members. One person records all the expressed ideas and presents the list to the group as rapidly as possible, without discussion, clarification, or comment.

Evaluation of one's own and others' ideas has to be postponed. In a review of many studies, McGrath concluded that, in spite of the popularity of interactive brainstorming and common beliefs about its efficacy, there is little empirical evidence that groups that follow this procedure generate more ideas of superior quality than individuals working separately. On the contrary, separate individuals may produce even more and better ideas than the same individuals acting as members of an interactive brainstorming group. One of the reasons that conventional interactive brainstorming groups fall short in producing creative ideas seems to be that group members, despite the instruction not to evaluate one another's contributions, fear negative evaluations from their fellow group members.

Normative conformity pressures are often too strong for free expression of one's idiosyncratic ideas. Furthermore, it has been demonstrated that members of a conventional interactive brainstorming group tend to converge on similar amounts of idea expressions. This convergence appears to be biased in the direction of the least productive group members. Real group interaction leads to mutual matching that normalises a low performance level. How can these drawbacks be prevented?

In order to overcome these dysfunctional normative pressures, a modification of the traditional face-to-face brainstorming method has been developed. The so-called nominal group technique (NGT) involves a process with two formally distinct stages. In the first or elicitation stage, individual group members work separately, generating alternative perspectives on the issue at hand. In order to minimise normative pressures, group members are not required to express their ideas aloud in the presence of the fellow group members, but write their ideas down (cf. Asch's research findings, suggesting that normative conformity pressures can be weakened when group members are not required to express their opinions publicly, but are allowed to state them privately in writing).

The second or evaluation stage involves the collective listing and evaluation of the perspectives that have been generated during the first stage. In a series of studies by Van de Ven and Delbecq to compare NGT with conventional interactive brainstorming techniques, NGT was found to produce superior results. This suggests that interaction and communication between members of brainstorming groups may be most useful if individual group members have first generated ideas separately and thereafter get additional social stimulation of other members' ideas.

Some groups may install a 'devil's advocate' to evoke discussion about alternative perspectives. In order to promote the examination of both supporting and detracting evidence, one group member presents any information that may lead to the disqualification of the prevailing frame of reference. Unlike the lone dissenter in Asch's studies, this dissenting group member's popularity in the group is not harmed, since this person is formally installed to play that role. Moreover, the role may be shifted regularly from one group member to another. The cognitive conflict created by having one group member disagree consistently with the majority position sets the stage for informational social influence, as in the case of minority influence.

Severe cognitive stress should be avoided, however, by instructing the devil's advocate to present arguments carefully in a low-key, non-threatening manner. Yet another technique to inhibit dysfunctional normative conformity pressures may be to arrange that members of the group meet in separate subgroups, which will each develop their own frame of reference. The presence of two subgroups in a subsequent combined meeting may elicit discussion and critical examination of the reasons for the differences between the perspectives that have been developed within each of the subgroups. If the subgroups eventually come to agreement, which may not be easily achieved it is less likely that any important considerations will be overlooked or ignored.

The common frame of reference on which the subgroups eventually come to agree may then be adopted with more confidence than if only a single group had worked on it. Although normative conformity pressures can be dysfunctional and may produce erroneous group judgements, one should acknowledge the potential benefits of normative pressure to ensure mutual social control. Mutual control becomes increasingly important when group members are motivated to act in their own way. As long as they are merely concerned with tuning their cognitions, group members' motivation to act in their own way may be relatively weak: they may publicly conform to the local group norm, despite keeping strong private reservations about its correctness.

In later stages of task completion, however, group members may become increasingly concerned with their private positions and interests. When the division of labour becomes an issue, for instance, the costs of giving in to the group (i.e. living up to normative expectations to contribute as much as possible to promote group success) may be more tangible than the costs of conformity in the process of cognitive tuning. To save themselves costly personal contributions, some of the group members may feel tempted to leave unpleasant work to fellow members. As we will see in the next section, the tuning of interests requires very strong normative pressures to complete the group task successfully.

TUNING OF INTERESTS

Once a common cognitive frame of reference has been developed, group members have to reach agreement about the division of labour to complete the group task. The division of labour may give rise to a conflict between common and private interests. Groups have to ensure that members' common and private interests are properly tuned, because the unrestrained pursuit of private interests will cause the whole group to fail or fall apart. Communication plays a crucial role in this process of tuning of conflicting interests.

Entwining of Common and Private Interests

Since a group member's outcomes do not depend solely upon their own performance but also on the performance of fellow group members, members of a task group are mutually interdependent. Two basic types of interdependence can be distinguished, positive and negative interdependence. To the extent that one group member's successful performance directly promotes the interests of fellow group members, group members are positively interdependent. As far as their private interests coincide, group members will be motivated to cooperate to serve their common interest. Cooperation requires coordinated action.

For example, it is in the common interest of all members of the educational committee that each of them submits proposals to change the curriculum before a certain deadline, so that all individual proposals can be assembled and sent to all the members of the committee before the next meeting. Group members' private interests coincide, since it is in nobody's private interest to be late in submitting proposals. Coordination requires clear communication (e.g. about submission deadlines) to structure the interaction process in such a way that group members optimally combine their contributions. If the group falls short in optimally combining its members' contributions, the group suffers from 'coordination losses'. In the next section, we will elaborate on this type of productivity loss.

By contrast, group members are negatively interdependent to the extent that a gain by one group member entails a loss by other group members. Usually, the distribution of benefits and costs among group members increases the salience of this type of interdependence. For example, when the educational committee has to elect a chairperson, a candidate can achieve personal success only at the expense of other group members. Since only one of them can be installed, the election may create a competitive atmosphere between members of the committee.

To give another example of conflicting interests, it may be in the students' best interest to increase the number of seminars and tutorials in the curriculum, whereas faculty members of the committee may advocate student self-tuition in order not to increase their own teaching load. Students can achieve success only if the faculty members give in. As long as problems arising from negative interdependence remain unsolved, the resulting competition within the group may pose a serious threat to group productivity. The above dichotomy is an oversimplification, however, since pure positive and pure negative interdependence are rare. The mixture of positive and negative interdependence in almost any task group evokes a motivation to cooperate (group success can be achieved only by cooperating with fellow group members) as well as a motivation to act in a self-interested way (what is to be gained by one group member in the division of benefits and costs can often be obtained only at the expense of fellow group members).

Even when the motivation to act in a self-interested way seems to prevail, as in the election of a chairperson or in the final phrasing of the committee's recommendations, opposing parties should communicate to serve their common interest. In an attempt to resolve the conflict of interests between the parties, they may start negotiating and bargaining. The present chapter focuses on such so-called mixed motive task situations, in which the motivation to cooperate prevails. But even under predominantly cooperative circumstances, group members' self-interest may lead them (un)consciously to reduce their personal contributions to the group and take advantage of fellow group members' cooperative efforts to achieve group success. Reduced individual contributions in task groups reflect the second type of productivity loss, namely, 'motivation losses'. Before we elaborate on group members' communicative attempts to overcome motivation losses, we will first address the issue of coordination losses.

Coordination Losses

To the extent that group members are positively interdependent, they are eager to contribute to their common interest, since there is no incentive for any of them to refrain from contributing. Cooperation requires good coordination. Group interactions need to be structured in such a way that members optimally combine their efforts. Coordination losses occur when the group falls short in optimally combining its members' efforts. The behavioural requirements may not be immediately clear to all group members. Some tasks, for instance, require simultaneity in group members' efforts. A group whose members are properly tuned to focus simultaneously on one and the same part of the task performs better than a group in which individual contributions are less well tuned in time. Communication is essential to make sure that everyone is aware of what has been achieved so far and to ensure that people will make further contributions that are compatible. Successful committees, compared to those that fail, stimulate task-relevant communication by focusing their members' attention on simultaneity in submitting individual proposals, evaluating these proposals, and reaching agreement upon one particular course of action and its subsequent implementation and evaluation.

The completion of a group task will always benefit from simultaneity in group members' contributions, however. In interactive brainstorming groups, for example, it would be unproductive if all participants were to express their ideas aloud at the same time. While one group member speaks, other group members have to keep silent. Group members have to wait for others to express their own ideas. This type of coordination loss, which is called 'production blocking', may hinder group members in presenting or even remembering their own ideas. One way to prevent production blocking in the generation of ideas is the NGT discussed earlier. Another way is computerised brainstorming, in which individuals are exposed to ideas from others on their computer screen as they generate their own ideas. As in the NGT, the absence of face-to-face interaction in computerised brainstorming may prove particularly fruitful in larger task groups. Unfortunately, group members rarely show much interest in planning the coordination process. Yet, controlling the process by communicating about how properly to sequence group members' contributions has strong positive effects on group productivity.

MOTIVATION LOSSES

Even if the processes in task groups are so well organised that virtually all losses due to faulty coordination are eliminated, group productivity might still suffer from motivation losses. Motivation losses occur because task groups are seldom characterised by pure positive interdependence, but almost always involve a mixture of positive and negative interdependence. The conflict between common and private interests lays the ground for motivation losses, reflecting the (un)conscious tendency to decrease one's personal share in the collective burden by letting one's fellow group members do the work. Motivation losses are more likely if group members can take advantage of circumstances in which their own contribution to the group product is hardly identifiable (such as in large groups) while they still share in the collective benefits of group success.

When motivation losses are more or less unconscious, the decrease of individual contributions to the group is termed 'social loafing'. When group members intentionally let others do the work, we speak of 'free riding'. A very likely reaction in response to the (assumed) presence of free riders in the group is to reduce one's own efforts, too, rather than to take the risk of being exploited (being the 'sucker'). The scientific study on productivity losses started with studies by Ringelmann (his classic paper is reprinted in Kravitz & Martin, 1986), who had young men pull a rope, either alone or in groups of varying size. Participants working alone pulled with an average force of 63 kg, participants working in dyads pulled with a force of 118 kg (i.e. an average of 59 kg per person), participants working in triads pulled with a force of 106 kg (i.e. an average of 53 kg per person), and eight-person groups pulled with an average of 31 kg per person.

Thus, the average individual performance decreased with increasing group size. To estimate the relative impact of motivation losses in the total productivity loss, Ingham, Levinger, Graves, and Peckham employed an experimental method that eliminated all coordination losses (i.e. productivity losses due to faulty coordination, such as a lack of simultaneity of the muscular contractions of the individuals).

This suggests that group members are less motivated to do their ultimate best when the size of their (imagined) group increases. Subsequent research has shown that motivation losses also occur in cognitive and perceptual group tasks. Communication may help to overcome motivation losses, since it sets the stage for normative social pressure on group members to contribute their fair share (or even: as much as they can). Communicating simply to get better acquainted with one's fellow group members is not sufficient, however. So, what might be relevant topics to discuss? In the first place, communication may facilitate group members' understanding of the extent to which they are positively interdependent. When their attention becomes focused on their common interests, group members may come to understand that mutual cooperation is preferable to mutual non-cooperation. Thus, communication may help them to agree on mutual cooperation as a shared goal. However, it is rather risky to cooperate unless you can count on your fellow group members to cooperate.

If others cannot be trusted, those who cooperate run the risk of being 'the sucker'. Therefore, the second important function of communication is to reduce group members' uncertainty about fellow group members' actual contributions. Shared cooperative goals and mutual trust are the two key concepts theory about cooperation in mixed-motive situations. Group members who share a cooperative goal, and expect fellow group members to cooperate, may eventually establish a cooperative group norm. Two group norms are of particular importance, namely, the commitment norm and the norm of equity or reciprocity. The commitment norm prescribes that group members should actually carry out those actions which they have publicly promised to perform. Communication may present an opportunity for group members to establish mutual commitment to cooperate as a binding social contract.

The equity norm prescribes that the rewards of group performance should be in proportion to group members' individual contributions. When all group members have an equal share in the collective outcomes of group success, as often is the case in task groups that provide a common good, the equity norm prescribes that all of them should exert equal amounts of effort. The equity norm may both encourage and discourage cooperation in task groups, however. When a group member learns that fellow group members exert more effort, personal failure to work as hard as these others would violate the equity norm. Equity considerations may then induce this person to cooperate, since free riding would violate the equity norm.

However, if the same group member learns that fellow group members are free riding upon their cooperative effort, the most likely response would simply be to cease cooperating himself. Few group members will endure the inequitable 'sucker' role in their task group. A cooperation-inducing strategy, based upon the equity norm, may be to start cooperating and keep cooperating just as long as fellow group members cooperate; whenever fellow group members act uncooperatively, then refrain from cooperation.

Group members who employ this reciprocal 'tit-for-tat' strategy communicate that they are willing to cooperate as long as fellow group members do the same.

Research findings that normative pressures to conform to group norms are stronger in cohesive groups suggest that the above discussed cooperative norms are stronger when the salience of a common group membership is high. Communication in groups appears to enhance feelings of being a part of the group and creates a sense of group identity or group cohesion.

Communication among group members in mixed motive situations indeed tends to focus on the normative requirement of cooperation and on how angry the group will be at group members who do not take their fair share of the collective burden. Furthermore, the more group members feel part of their group, the less strongly they distinguish between their common and private interests.

Members who strongly identify with their group are also more likely to perceive fellow group members in generally favourable terms as trustworthy and cooperative. Such favourable attributions may lay the ground for trust in the cooperative intentions of fellow group members, even in the absence of information about the extent to which they actually cooperate.

Additional Measures to Strengthen Normative Pressures

Even under these normative pressures to cooperate, a task group remains vulnerable to motivation losses of (some of) its members. If only one of the group members refrains from cooperating, this 'bad apple' may elicit non-cooperative responses from fellow group members, who may feel justified to do so on the basis of the equity/reciprocity norm. Reciprocal cooperation is not easily established in task groups with more than two members. Many studies suggest that cooperation declines as groups become larger.

Other factors inhibiting the evolution of cooperation in large task groups may be the perceived efficacy of one's own contribution, the extent to which one's own contribution is identifiable and can be evaluated, and the extent to which one feels responsible for the achievement of the common interest. A second reason for task groups' vulnerability to motivation losses is that the beneficial effects of enhanced group identification on individuals' willingness to conform to cooperative group norms may be weakened by subordinate group boundaries. For example, members of the educational committee may refrain from taking their fair share of the work to be done because they may be more concerned with their particular subgroup (students or staff) than with work that has to be done in the interest of the committee as a whole.

Therefore, communicative attempts to promote cooperation often have to be combined with additional measures. Since cooperative behaviour is the result of normative pressures to serve the common interest, cooperation can be further promoted by enhancing the salience of cooperative norms and/or increasing the severity of social sanctions for non-cooperation. Several lines of research confirm this assumption. First, enforcement of any social norm requires the ability to monitor inputs and outcomes so that norm violations can be detected. Social loafing (more or less unconsciously hiding in the crowd) and free riding (its deliberate pendant, when one expects that fellow group members will do the necessary work) are less likely to occur when identification and evaluation of one's own contribution are more likely.

Group members appear to be very sensitive to the risk of being detected as an underperforming group member. As a result, higher levels of cooperation are achieved when group members have to make their contributions publicly than when their contributions remain unidentifiable (cf. Asch's findings, suggesting that participants are more likely to comply with the local group norms when they have to state their opinions publicly than when they are allowed to express their opinions in the absence of any social control by their fellow group members). Record keeping, for instance, allows group members to check whether each of them does their fair share of the work. It promotes social control that encourages group members to conform to cooperative norms.

Second, a group may increase social control over its members by the use of explicit promises to reward cooperators or threats to punish non-cooperators. Promises seem to yield more beneficial effects than threats, as the latter communicate that fellow group members cannot be trusted to be internally motivated to cooperate. However, even promises may arouse reactance and prove counter-effective if group members perceive the rewards as an attempt to bribe them. Third, when group members learn that soft interventions do not suffice to ensure satisfactory levels of cooperation and fairness in individuals' share in the collective burden, they are quite willing to hand their decisional freedom over to one of the (cooperative) group members to make decisions on behalf of all of them.

OVERVIEW

By communicating, members of a task group exert strong normative pressure on one another to consider the cognitions and interests that they have in common. However, in the process of cognitive tuning, normative pressure is a double-edged sword. On the one hand, normative pressures lead group members to converge on a common understanding of the task, necessary to achieve group success. On the other hand, normative pressures make group members so concerned with receiving social approval from their peers that innovative perspectives that might contradict the emerging group consensus never get expressed. Since premature concurrence-seeking constitutes a serious threat to group success, some formalised communication techniques (such as NGT or installing a devil's advocate) may be employed so that important alternative perspectives are less likely to be overlooked.

When group members are tuning their interests, normative pressures to consider common interests cannot be strong enough. Normative expectations that all group members will contribute their fair share may promote cooperation, but may at the same time increase the temptation for some of them to free ride upon other's cooperative efforts. Therefore, task groups often take additional measures to sanction non-cooperation. In sum, preventing or overcoming productivity losses is a continuous concern for task groups. Even if group members realise that time and energy must be devoted to find effective solutions to these threats to their common interest, many of them may prefer not to become involved in the activities necessary to implement these solutions and leave this task to (one or some of the) cooperative fellow group members.

Chapter 12

Negotiation and Bargaining

ANALYTIC MODELS

Analytic models of negotiation are formal models which use simple and elegant notations to describe the process of negotiation in abstract and, therefore, very general terms. They are used to analyse the ways of thinking that may occur in negotiation and bargaining, and to explain why they may have certain effects. It is a matter of controversy to what extent such models are useful in guiding our understanding of particular cases.

There are two main kinds of abstraction. They are connected by considerations of what it means to act rationally in certain contexts. In the first case, the context is defined by an abstract statement of 'the bargaining problem' developed in contexts of interest in microeconomics. In the second case, the context is defined by models of strategic interaction in the mathematical theory of games.

BARGAINING PROBLEM

The phrase 'the bargaining problem' should give some indication of the generality of the analysis that is involved. It is intended to apply to any example of bargaining or negotiation. The abstraction works – if it works – by assuming that the way to understand the problem is to start by considering a two-person or two-party negotiation and then to generalise (or to think about generalising) such results to any multiperson or multiparty negotiations.

Such models (often called utility models) begin by

describing a contractor, P, and a client, O. It is assumed that they have wants which conflict to a greater or lesser extent, and that bargaining is a process of deciding on an allocation of goods. The process is one in which they exchange bids, where each bid is a proposal to allocate some goods to P and others to O. It is assumed that P and O will each estimate the various costs and benefits each will expect if the other agreed with the proposal on the table. It is also assumed that each will estimate the costs and benefits they would each face in the event of a failure to agree. An agreement is reached when the process of bid and counter-bid converges on to a proposal both P and O find acceptable and both think is the best they could have obtained in the circumstances.

Such models have two advantages. They capture the idea that each proposal has a net worth (expected utility or expected value) for each of the bargainers, so that the process of bargaining may be described as an allocation of utility (or value) between P and O. They also suggest that competition and cooperation are not at opposite ends of a continuum. Formally, the bargaining problem is represented on a set of orthogonal axes: the vertical axis representing the utility to P (from high to low) and the horizontal axis representing the utility to O (from high to low). The high-high quadrant contains those agreements that are positively valued by both P and O; the low-low quadrant contains those that both P and O wish to avoid; and the other two quadrants represent options P will want but O will not and that O will want but P will not. The location of agreements within and between quadrants represents the allocation of utility.

If we superimpose a new set of orthogonal axes such that the new axes divide the old quadrants into two equal segments, we will have a line that, firstly, bisects the high-high quadrant and the low-low quadrant and a line that, secondly, bisects the high-low quadrant and the low-high quadrant. Both P and O wish to gain outcomes in the high-high quadrant and avoid outcomes in the low-low quadrant so that the first line represents an axis of common interest. By contrast, the second line represents an axis of competition.

The main lesson is that cooperation and competition are not at opposite ends of a continuum. Rather, there are two perpendicular axes: from low cooperation to high cooperation and from low competition to high competition. Consequently, utility models capture the very important idea that conflicting interests always occur in the context of common interests.

Some writers focus on the high-high quadrant and translate talk about utilities into talk about aspiration zones, contract zones, and settlement ranges. For example, Walton and McKersie argue that P and O each form an aspiration zone with a target and a resistance point. The target is determined by their highest estimate of what is needed, by their most optimistic estimates of what is possible, and by their most favourable estimates of their bargaining skill. The resistance point (sometimes called the minimum necessary share) is determined by their lowest estimate of what is needed, by their most pessimistic assumptions about what is possible, and by their least favourable estimates of their bargaining skill. The four points may be plotted on a single line, known as the conflict line.

The distance between A's resistance point and B's resistance point is known as the settlement range. When these points are compatible, there is a contract zone or positive settlement range (because both prefer some agreement to their best alternative to a negotiated agreement). When these points are incompatible, there is a negative settlement range, and agreement will be impossible until either A or B or both change their minimum terms. Analyses of this kind have been used to gain insight into historical cases. To take one example, it has been shown that the Berlin Wall was built because it was the only option preferred to no agreement by both Soviet and Western negotiators. Although there is a common statement of the bargaining problem, there are many different solutions.

- Some describe constraints that proposals must satisfy if they are to be turned into outcomes that are fair, acceptable, optimum, etc. Such constraints are known as arbitration schemes.

- Some locate the main impetus for concession making in estimates of the risks of disagreement, but give different treatments of the nature of those risks.
- Some view the process of bargaining as a learning process in which various expectations are revised. Each kind of solution points to different kinds of skill.
- The focus on arbitration schemes has prepared the way for a consideration of principled bargaining.
- The focus on perception of risk has prepared the way for a more general consideration of negotiators' reputations for resolve.
- The focus on learning has prepared the way for more detailed explorations of how negotiators define issues, interpret feedback, and revise expectations.

THEORY OF GAMES

The mathematical theory of games was an ambitious theory that attempted to define rational action in contexts where the outcomes for each person depended partly on their own actions and partly on the actions of others. Negotiation was seen as a game of strategy in which P and O make separate choices: either to make concessions or to maintain their current level of demand, or to choose between cooperative or competitive approaches. The outcome of the game depends on the choices made by P and O so that what P gets depends on O's choices, and vice versa.

The logic of the game may be represented in the form of a two-person, two-choice matrix with four cells: both P and O stand firm; both P and O make concessions; P stands firm but O does not; O stands firm but P does not. When some estimate of utility or value is entered into each cell for each player, it may be possible to identify some of the reasons why negotiators act as they do. Two of the games, known as the prisoners' dilemma game and chicken, have been related to dilemmas in the process of negotiation.

EVALUATION

It is clear that analytic models treat only some aspects of

negotiation. The models are intended to be simple but powerful. Thus, bargaining is described in terms of a small number of processes, capable of mathematical treatment. Other activities are either ignored, or somehow interpreted in terms of the variables included in the model. Such drastic simplification is not without value. It helps us to realise that negotiation begins when someone sees change, or the possibility of change, in the status quo; and it helps us to realise that different people might look at the status quo in very different ways.

Once negotiation begins, it is important to realise that the process is one which engages mixed motives. The description of lines of conflict and lines of common interest given above has encouraged some writers to draw a distinction between distributive bargaining and integrative bargaining. In the two-person case, distributive bargaining is competitive bargaining in which P and O struggle to get as much as they can of something that they each desire. Integrative bargaining is collaborative bargaining in which P and O actively search for new agreements from which each will gain.

Because distributive bargaining is competitive and integrative bargaining is collaborative, negotiators face certain strategic dilemmas. Typically, distributive bargaining is bargaining in which negotiators struggle to exploit asymmetries in power. However, to the extent that they misrepresent their own positions, they make it difficult to explore ways in which the requirements of the parties might be reconciled. Such dilemmas may be particularly acute when negotiations are complex. Raiffa's own solution is to advise negotiators to keep secret their minimum necessary terms, but otherwise to behave openly and honestly. Nevertheless, models of this kind have very important weaknesses. The way they simplify the bargaining problem is too drastic. Consequently, they provide inadequate models of people, parties, processes, and contexts.

- They provide inadequate models of people because they take the character of the conflict for granted.

- They provide inadequate models of parties because they treat parties just like people (so that P and O stands just as well for person and other, or party and opponent). In reality, party and opponent are usually loose coalitions in which negotiation within sides is as important as negotiation between sides.
- They provide inadequate models of processes because they neglect the ways in which parties identify issues, develop solutions, choose between alternatives, and implement policies.
- They provide inadequate models of contexts because they abstract away from the historical relationship between the sides. They neglect the fact that agreements have to be justified as rules that make sense – because they link what is happening now to what has happened in the past, and to what needs to happen in the future.

Despite such criticisms, some analytic models deserve to be taken very seriously, notably those of Walton and McKersie – who deal with industrial negotiations – and Snyder and Diesing – who deal with international negotiations. Both have recognised the importance of dilemmas in negotiation; both have recognised the intellectual demands placed on negotiators, and both have realised the importance of bargaining within and between groups.

The identification of four separate systems: namely, those concerned with distributive bargaining, integrative bargaining, attitudinal structuring, and intraorganisational bargaining. The first three systems are concerned with relationships between groups and the fourth is concerned with relationships within groups.

Talk about distributive bargaining and integrative bargaining is used to identify strategies and tactics designed to move opponents along the line of conflict or the line of cooperation, respectively. Attitudinal structuring is activity designed to change the basic 'bonds' between the negotiators. Intraorganisational bargaining is internal negotiation designed to achieve consensus about what to do in the external negotiations between groups. Walton and McKersie's theory is a very welcome attempt to provide better analytic models of people, parties, processes, and contexts, but it has not been without critics and, most fundamentally. It was argued that almost all bargaining involving representatives of groups is distributive bargaining, but agrees that negotiators may take a more competitive or a more cooperative approach.

From his perspective, 'attitudinal structuring' is not a separate system of activities, but a set of tactics available to those who wish to take a collaborative approach. Furthermore, intraorganisational bargaining is not a new kind of bargaining. It is to be explained in just the same ways as external negotiations that take place between organisations. I shall follow Anthony in his attempt to understand internal and external negotiation in the same general kinds of way.

BEHAVIOURAL MODELS OF NEGOTIATION

Behavioural models attempt to describe what negotiators do. In this sense, the theory is a behavioural model because it is an attempt to classify the activities observed in collective bargaining with distinctions from utility theory and from the theory of games. In this section, I include four kinds of research.

On the one hand, there are attempts to predict the outcomes of experimental negotiations by examining the process of negotiation and its preconditions, background factors, and concurrent conditions. On the other hand, there are attempts to describe 'phase sequences', 'critical transformations', or 'turning points' in negotiation by experimental methods, category schemes, or comparative analyses of individual cases.

OUTCOMES OF EXPERIMENTAL NEGOTIATIONS

The various experimental tasks which have been used include: matrix games (such as prisoner's dilemma and chicken); distribution games, in which participants negotiate the division of a quantified scarce resource; games of economic exchange, in which participants take the roles of buyers and sellers; role-playing debates, in which participants learn the details of a particular dispute, and then negotiate as if they were representing a party in that dispute; and substitute debates, in which an encounter which occurs in laboratory conditions is substituted for one which might have occurred elsewhere. It is still the case that the vast majority of experimental research has used matrix games or tasks in which negotiation is limited to little more than the exchange of bids, although there are some signs that research is becoming more likely to recognise the complexities of real life.

THE PROCESS OF BID AND COUNTER-BID

The most popular experimental task simulates a situation of bilateral monopoly in which there is integrative potential because there is more than one issue. Sometimes a buyer (P) and seller (O) have to agree on the price–quantity combination at which a particular product will be traded. Sometimes there are several products, for which P and O agree a price for each, regardless of quantity. Sometimes there is a single product, but P and O agree prices for linked elements such as delivery time, discounts, and finance.

Typically, the buyer and seller have complete information about their own profits but none about those of their opponent. Two features of the profit tables are important. First, P and O are able to offer a variety of possible contracts at a given level of profit. Two contracts that are of equal (or near equal) value to P may differ considerably in their value to O, and vice versa. Second, the profit tables contain some agreements which are Pareto optimal – meaning that they maximise the joint gain or profit (MJP) available to the participants. The most important finding from this research is that P and O often fail to find agreements which are Pareto optimal. This means that there is some other agreement which would give either P or O or both significant gains, at little or no cost to the other.

According to Pruitt and his associates, the main predictor

of MJP outcomes is that P and O each adopt a problem-solving strategy. One obvious possibility is that this will occur when P and O each exhibit high concern for their own outcomes and high concern for the other's outcomes. The model which specifies the factors which lead to this combination of motives is known as the dual-concern model. It has been used to integrate findings which deal with negotiators' assigned goals, with their relationship to their constituents, with the possibility of future interaction, and with the effects of mood. One suggestion that seems to have a more general significance is that MJP outcomes are more likely when negotiators are motivated to engage in systematic trial and error.

However, the possible reasons for this are not clear. If prospect theory is correct, negotiators who are most concerned to maximise gains rather than minimise losses are more likely to reach MJP outcomes. This suggests that it is often important to adopt a problem-solving or collaborative approach. Furthermore, such a conclusion is compatible with a great deal of evidence that 'powerful and persistent images of a mythical fixed pie' lead to an 'incompatibility bias' and mean that negotiators in experimental negotiations fail to extract maximum value from negotiations.

At the same time, there is evidence that negotiators will fail to reach MJP agreements if they are too anxious to reach agreements. In these respects, the results of experiments are consistent with the analyses of real-life negotiations, meaning that it is important both to disagree and not to let the disagreement go too far. More recently, there has been an emphasis on group process and on social norms – both long overdue. The emphasis on group process has been conducted mainly within the context of social decision scheme theory. One of the main findings has been that majority rules and sequential agendas lead to compromise rather than integrative agreements.

Consideration of the effects of social norms has led to a critique of Fisher and Ury's account of principled negotiation. Fisher and Ury urge negotiators to insist from the beginning that any agreements be based on norms of fairness. They also urge them to seek objective evidence to show that their claims are consistent with those norms. While some see principled negotiation as part of a problem-solving strategy that offers an opportunity to make mutual gains, others see it as limited to special cases. The reader will find a useful summary of the arguments in Johnson and Pruitt and Carnevale.

Recent analyses have confirmed the view that most experimental studies of integrative bargaining do little more than scratch the potential for integration between the sides. In the end, I think that they fail to give participants sufficient detail of the historical contexts in which they are supposed to be operating. Because of this, they do little to illuminate why negotiators have to 'look beyond interpersonal process to the underlying substance of the problem, seeking to figure where potential value exists and how to embody it in sustainable agreements'.

THE ANALYSIS OF REAL-LIFE NEGOTIATIONS

With hindsight, it is possible to integrate much of this research by describing its purpose as the identification of those transitions that are necessary and sufficient if negotiation is to succeed. Two methods have been used. The first involved the use of category schemes to describe units of discourse2 identified according to 'objective' rules3. Such coding schemes were used to identify transitions within negotiations.

The earliest research used Bales' interaction process analysis and saw the key transitions as those that shifted between task problems and social-emotional problems. Next, research identified the key transitions as those that involved a shift between interparty and interpersonal aspects of the negotiation task. When the interparty role was salient, the negotiators were forced to come to terms with the imperative of representing their parties. When the interpersonal role was salient, the negotiators were forced to come to terms with imperatives of maintaining personal relationships with their opponents.

Later research was concerned with the ways in which

transitions were linked to arguments in negotiation. To quote Putnam and Geist: 'What emerges from presenting proposals and counterproposals are significant issues that must be discussed to uncover or create interpretations that lead to a settlement' Recently, Putnam has suggested four 'mechanisms' or 'shifts in levels in abstraction' that may be crucial turning points in such discussions. The first is a shift from the specific to the general; the second is a shift from part to whole; the third is a shift from the individual level to the system level; and the fourth is a shift from the literal level to the symbolic level. My own preference would be to relate what Putnam says to descriptions of dilemmas in any decision-making process, such as those identified by Friend and Hickling.

The second kind of analysis has involved the systematic comparison of individual cases to identify 'precipitants' of turning points (whether procedural, substantive, or external), 'departures' (what happens next), and longer-term 'consequences' has reviewed some of the 'social and psychological dimensions of departure' by reviewing 'changes in individuals, interactions, and collectivities'. His paper provides some new ways of looking at old literature and makes some interesting suggestions about the forces for change (primarily external when security issues are at stake but primarily internal in other cases). Other research is not so much concerned with transitions in the process of negotiation as with comparisons between negotiators with or without a track record of success. The coding schemes involved are essentially a development of Bales' interaction process analysis, adapted so that the categories form more convenient contrasts, and may be applied to speech units larger than a simple sentence. The net effect is that the categories are easier to use reliably in real time.

EVALUATION

Behavioural models have been applied to both experimental and real-life negotiations. Much of the experimental literature is individualistic in the sense that it ignores historical variables at the level of the small group or the larger organisation (or even the culture), and perhaps it has to do so in the search for abstractions that are simple but powerful. On the other hand, social psychologists are paying much more attention to the ways in which experimental studies may be integrated with studies of naturalistic decision making, and this is to be applauded.

Attempts to describe the process of real-life negotiations are important because they make it abundantly clear that there is more to negotiation than a process of bid and counter-bid. Negotiation is a kind of argument even if the argument does not always conform to the canons of academic debate. Such argument is not only possible but almost inevitable given that all social actions are ambiguous, cannot be completely described, and will be described from a particular point of view. To understand the nature of this argument, it is important to link it to wider psychological concerns that arise within cognitive psychology and social psychology.

INFORMATION-PROCESSING MODELS

So far, negotiation has been treated mostly as an exercise in bargaining, dominated by strategic or tactical concerns. However, as negotiations become more complex (e.g. because of the number of participants, information overload, or uncertainty), it seems likely that questions of strategy (how can P outwit O, or vice versa?) must be subordinated to questions of structure (how to find a definition of the bargaining problem that compels assent). The reason is that negotiators may find that their capacities to process information are insufficient to cope with the demands of the task. In consequence, they may find it difficult to understand the issues (the 'language' problem), and because of this they may find it difficult to find practical ways of handling them, so that they are able to justify commitments to particular lines of action (the 'action' problem).

MAKING SENSE OF CHANGE

To make sense of change, negotiators must organise a

collective process in which they identify issues, develop solutions, choose between alternatives, and implement policies. There is evidence that more-skilled and less-skilled negotiators structure these processes in different ways. Let us suppose that some change in existing circumstances has created a circumstance in which P must confront O. P and O must plan suitable responses. Furthermore, they must plan those responses in contexts which are ambiguous and cannot be completely described.

This means that negotiators interpret changes in the status quo in terms of more or less well-organised systems of attitudes, values, and beliefs, and pass on those interpretations to others, What is important is that, through the experience of negotiation, skilled negotiators have been able to build up more or less systematically organised knowledge of the negotiation task, and how to work in it. This means that they have schooled and highly specific ways of perceiving, and are able to see relatively quickly what other people may never see at all. Thus, the skilled negotiator is a skilled perceiver, for further discussion of the role of perception in skilled performance).

There are good reasons to believe that learning about the world requires people to use organised systems of belief to anticipate the future and to explain the past4. However, if they are not to see only what they expect to see, they must also be sensitive to new information. There is a dialectical contradiction between these two requirements and this means that some negotiators find it extremely difficult to learn from the process of negotiation. Early research located the problems in the structure of the belief systems. Later research has implicated a wide range of cognitive, social, and contextual factors;

Probably, negotiators will always disagree about how tc describe events, and how they contributed to the development of social settings. They will maintain general images of their opponents which are not likely to change. However, a combination of cognitive, social, and contextual conditions combine to produce two kinds of activity, which Snyder and

Diesing have articulated in terms of a 'rational bargaining module' and an 'irrational bargaining module'.

Two features of the rational bargaining module are important in the present context. First, Snyder and Diesing found that rational bargainers had low confidence in their initial diagnoses of what had happened, and why. They used the process of bargaining to test hypotheses: to root out ideas, which were plausible, but false or incomplete. Second, they initiated an active search for information to find out which aspects of others' positions were flexible, and to what extent.

MATCHING CAPACITIES TO DEMANDS

This is a part of cognitive psychology that we just cannot ignore from an applied perspective. Much of the early work in cognitive psychology was intended to establish which features of our cognitive systems limit our ability to process information. One clear implication of this work is that effective performers find ways of working that allow them to match their intellectual capacities to the information-processing demands of the task.

A second implication is that those who are effective performers in social domains recognise the processing problems faced by other people. Consequently, they use a variety of techniques designed to reduce ambiguity, clarify communications, and slow things down. Methods of behaviour analysis have been used to identify some of the ways in which effective negotiators tailor their performances to help their opponents deal with the information-processing demands of the negotiation task. Effective negotiators recognise that social actions are inherently ambiguous. Consequently, unless special care is taken, it is all too easy for people to see only what they want to see.

So, effective negotiators take pains to label their actions, making frequent use of verbal forms such as, 'May I ask you a question?', 'If I could make a suggestion...', and so on. They are significantly more likely than average negotiators to test understandings, often by summarising what has been said. Much of the work which has contributed to the Harvard

Programme on Negotiation fits within the framework of matching capacities to demands. This is one reason why those within the programme have often emphasised that the cheapest concession which can be made is to show that you are actively listening to what is being said.

There are actually two sides to this. First, it is important to be able to see the negotiation as others see it, because, if you want to influence them, it is important to see the appeal for them of their point of view. Second, it is important to communicate that understanding to members of the other side. Otherwise, when you try to say something, they will not be listening. They will, instead, be using their limited processing capacity to complete a different task.

To be specific, they will be considering how to rephrase their argument so that this time you will understand it. For similar reasons, a good rule seems to be: 'Present your proposals as solutions to problems. State the problem before you give your answer.' If you begin with your own proposal you may find that the other side will stop paying attention. They will not be listening to what you have to say. Instead, they will devote their mental resources to the task of working out their own responses.

Evaluation

Information-processing approaches give negotiators the respect they are due as intelligent social actors. They force us to consider aspects of complexity in negotiation which other theories ignore.

They show that skilled negotiators are skilled perceivers. Negotiators have well-organised and well-schooled systems of evaluative beliefs which allow them quickly to see what less skilled negotiators may never see at all. They avoid the problem that they may see only what they expect to see by making active attempts to root out ideas which are plausible, but false or incomplete. Studies which have compared the performance of effective and less effective negotiators, using techniques of behaviour analysis, are consistent with Welford's theory that skill is the use of effective strategies which match the capacities of performers to the demands of their task. The best of the 'how to negotiate' texts include practical advice which follows from the application of information-processing perspectives.

CHARACTERISTICS OF EFFECTIVE NEGOTIATORS

It is commonplace to find that those who write about the psychology of negotiation include checklists of negotiation skills. Much of the literature is anecdotal, but some is based on questionnaire studies which ask experienced negotiators to identify the personal characteristics which make negotiators effective. If this is done in a very general way, it is likely that results will do little more than reflect some of the central characteristics of the negotiation task, or respondents' general theories about the nature of negotiation. In this literature, one study stands out: that of Williams. His sample was limited to legal attorneys in civil cases, but he compared negotiators identified as effective, average, or ineffective by Q-sort techniques.

The main contrast was between cooperative and competitive approaches. Each kind of negotiator wanted to get the best for his or her client. The cooperative negotiators were more constrained by ethical considerations and wanted to reach agreements that were fair. The competitive negotiators were more concerned to make a profit for themselves and to outdo or to outwit their opponents. Williams was able persuasively to suggest that the two kinds of negotiators do not understand one another because they have quite different ideologies. One is problem solving; the other is aggressive.

The cooperative negotiators had some traits in common, regardless of their level of effectiveness. They were all seen as trustworthy, ethical, fair, courteous, personable, tactful, and sincere. The effective negotiators within the cooperative group were seen as fair-minded, with realistic opening positions. They did not use threats, were willing to share information, and actively explored their opponents' positions. In contrast, ineffective negotiators within the cooperative group were seen as trustful, gentle, obliging, patient, forgiving, intelligent, dignified, and self-controlled.

In some ways, the contrast between effective and ineffective negotiators was even more marked when negotiators were competitive. The effective negotiators were dominant, forceful, and attacking. Their strategy was simple: to push their opponents as far as they would go. To do this, they were willing to stretch the facts, take unrealistic opening positions, and withhold information. The ineffective negotiators were seen as irritating, argumentative, quarrelsome, aggressive, rigid, egotistical, headstrong, arrogant, intolerant, and hostile. They had not learned to cope with the 'negative side of efficiency'.

According to Williams, the combination of cooperator and competitor causes the majority of the psychological problems in negotiation. This is too strong a claim, but there is little doubt that each may misinterpret the intentions and actions of the other. Williams has shown that both strategies can be effective, and argues that skilled negotiators should be able to use both. This is important if negotiations cycle through competitive and collaborative stages, and if the difference between the stages is more marked in those negotiations which end in success.

It seems likely that ineffective negotiators will find it extremely difficult to switch from one stance to the other as the situation demands. Even so, we may have to recognise that negotiating style has much less impact on effectiveness than personal characteristics such as being prepared (on the facts and on the law), being self-controlled, observing the manners of the Bar, and taking satisfaction in using legal skills. Such conclusions are supported by the more recent research of Lynch and Evans, and to some extent extended into the domain of criminal law, via consideration of plea bargaining. In addition, Lynch and Evans made an attempt to see how such effective negotiators were perceived in terms of the 'Big Five' dimensions of personality.

They concluded that it did not matter whether negotiators were extrovert or introvert, nor whether they were aggressive. What mattered, apparently, was whether they were 'emotionally stable, and to a lesser degree creative, conscientious, and likeable'. This research is interesting and potentially important, but is limited because the authors did not collect comparative data about average or ineffective negotiators.Questionnaire studies of the personal characteristics of effective negotiators have to be treated with care. Nevertheless, studies such as those of Raiffa and Williams reinforce the argument that there is much more to negotiation than a process of bid and counter-bid.

The top five characteristics were reported were, in order of importance: preparation and planning skill, knowledge of the relevant subject matter, ability to think quickly and clearly despite pressure and uncertainty, ability to express thoughts verbally, and listening skill. Williams' evidence suggests that there is no one ideal negotiation style, but that skilled negotiators need to be able to switch from a competitive to cooperative stance as the situation demands. (This is consistent with behavioural studies of real-life negotiations outlined earlier.) Williams' work has also helped to increase our understanding of the dynamics which occur when someone with a cooperative stance negotiates against someone with a competitive stance. Much of the other research that falls within this category needs to be treated with a very great deal of care.

DISCURSIVE MODELS

It has been argued that, as negotiations become more complex, there needs to be a shift from a concern with strategy and tactics to a concern with messages and meanings a shift from talk about manipulation to talk about what makes sense in particular historical contexts. Discursive models rely on some sort of language-action perspective. They are concerned with those collective processes by which participants make sense of change (the 'language' part) and decide how to act, given that something has to be done and commitments have to be made (the 'action' part).

One of the main concerns of Morley et al. was to link

talk about negotiation with talk about narrative decision making. The central idea was that talk about stories or scripts functioned to identify paradigm cases of threats and opportunities and how they might be handled. It was admitted – indeed insisted – that endorsement of a paradigm case by a particular group of people depended on a series of arguments in which different people tried out different arguments and commitments to different lines of action. What I have tried to show is that the kind of reasoning involved is both 'partisan and highly stylised: dramatising what has happened in the past and what will happen in the future'.

It is this kind of reasoning that instantiates how negotiators collectively struggle over intellectual problems (what to count as facts, and how to interpret what is going on) and over political problems (what to do, and why). Hence, the attraction of some sort of language-action approach to be distinguished from some sort of approach based on individual information processing (instantiated in most of cognitive psychology). There are a number of such approaches. The one described here is probably the most general. There were a number of immediate consequences of applying some such perspective:

- Bargaining within groups was seen as similar in kind to bargaining between groups.
- Judicial or quasi-judicial procedures involve much more than the presentation and examination of facts. Arbitrators, like negotiators, 'create order by reconstructing a story from reports which are partisan and incomplete. They use this story as a basis for making a judgment'
- There is more to negotiation than bargaining. Negotiators do not reach bargains, nor do they resolve conflicts. Rather they struggle to reach agreements that manage conflicts – because to manage a conflict is to show that what has happened in the past may be used to justify what should happen in the future.

Let us take this last point seriously. It implies that

negotiation is a process in which people meet to define the terms of their relationship, or that of reference groups they represent.

The participants are concerned to establish whether certain changes are possible and, if so, at what cost. The outcome of their deliberations is a set of rules, defining the terms on which the persons, or parties, will do business in the future. This is why negotiators have been described as writing social history. The writing part of the metaphor is used to remind us that negotiations are conducted in the context of existing rules, and that the effect of an agreement is to change those rules.

The social part of the metaphor is used to make the point that, in formal negotiation, the changes have to be explained to other people and accepted by them. This is why one of the major tasks of negotiation is to find a formula, linking what is happening now to what has happened in the past, and to what will happen in the future. The formula provides a rationale showing that people have developed lines of action which make sense in particular social and historical contexts. Without such a rationale, negotiation is likely to be prolonged or to break down. Unless the rationale is accepted by those not at the negotiation table, the rules will be broken when attempts are made to put the agreements into effect.

From this perspective the central problem in negotiation is to forge collective commitments that make sense within and between groups. This will require participants to build close relationships with opponents, whether it involves information exchange, collusion, or 'appreciative moves'. Kolb's concept of appreciative moves is perhaps one way of thinking about what Walton and McKersie call attitudinal structuring. As she says, appreciation includes 'recognizing' O's 'concerns' and giving O 'space' to talk, by retailing 'stories or histories' and 'doing the invisible work of connecting and trust building'. It also requires leadership to enable participants to handle cognitive and political dilemmas that are inherent in the process of negotiation. I shall consider each of these three problems in turn.

Forging Collective Commitments that Make Sense

Those processes by which we make sense of our world are regarded, pre-eminently, as the province of cognitive psychology (see above: 'Information-processing models'). But there are two crucial elements missing from such models. The first is that our cognitive beliefs are socially 'tuned', because 'What we learn, and how we express that learning, is very much affected by those we meet, where we meet them, and by our relationships with them'. The second is that cognitive psychology has failed to realise the crucial significance of disputation and change in the intellectual and political aspects of our social lives.

Language-action perspectives have the merit that they bring such issues to the fore. Negotiators have to describe change, or the possibility of change, and reach a working consensus, within each party, that the changes are changes of a certain kind. Because of this, they face an intellectual struggle. Equally, they face a political struggle because people with different levels of investment in the issues, different sources of power, and different levels of skill, have to forge commitments based on those descriptions, and show that they make sense. This means that negotiators will attempt to find arguments which make sense of what they are doing, and disseminate them to others. It is no accident that successful teams send more information to members of their reference groups, and take greater pains to put that information in an appropriate context.

From a discursive point of view, one of the most interesting recent developments has been a growth in commentaries by participants from each of the sides in industrial and international negotiations (followed by debate between them). With respect to industrial negotiations, the key text is still that of Friedman and Meredeen. Each was a major participant in the Ford sewing machinists' strike for equal pay at the Dagenham River Plant.

The power of the analysis came from what might be called a 'thick-textured' analysis of the process of disputation and change, partly through negotiation and partly through action external to negotiations (grievance procedures, working to rule, and strikes). In part, we read an account reenacting the central themes of the negotiation, explaining what each side wanted, and revealing major problems of internal adjustment (intraorganisational bargaining) within each side. We are given an insight into the kinds of rhetorical argument that were effective and the kinds that were not.

We are also given major insights into the ways in which the success of proposals may depend on the way in which claims may be linked to other claims or to bureaucratic procedures.

In many respects, what we see is discursive psychology at work – from particular and partisan points of view.It is easy to see that more research is needed, and that we will have to treat it with caution. So we shall. But there are signs that there is much to be gained from serious and systematic analyses of such debates between participants, as seen in a recent issue of the Negotiation Journal.

BUILDING CLOSE RELATIONSHIPS

Kanter (1984) has argued that the basic commodities of organisational power are the abilities to build relationships based on the exchange of information, resources, and support. This implies that those negotiators who put more effort into building relationships with other people are more likely to be successful, although much of the literature emphasises the size of the network rather than the quality of relationships with focal persons.

There are two aspects to this. It is important to be in contact with a sufficient number of people to triangulate the different points of view of those people close to the action, because this is how to gain authentic information. At the same time, one reason why some people are more influential than others is that they are linked into networks of relationships through which arguments may be tested or promoted. Thus, networking serves two functions: that of collecting organisational intelligence and that of building commitments to particular lines of action.

Dilemmas in the Process of Negotiation

Dilemmas arise when negotiators search for acceptable ways of handling issues, whether within or between groups or both. They may all be described under a general rubric of judgements of balance with respect to intellectual or political concerns. All concern structure in the process of negotiation: sometimes at the sociological end of social psychology and sometimes at the psychological end. The more sociological concerns are evident in contrasts such as that between leader and delegate roles or between that of the need for leadership and the need for democracy.

It is axiomatic in certain versions of folk psychology that unanimity is hard to achieve, but majority rule is not without its problems, especially if the rule is a simple majority rule (more than 50% of the franchise). The more psychological concerns are evident in judgements about whether to make the scope of negotiations more focused or more synoptic; whether to make the treatment of complexity simpler or more elaborate; whether to be more proactive or more reactive; whether to try to reduce uncertainty or to increase uncertainty; and whether to explore options or to close them down. A careful reading of case studies of negotiation will reveal examples of each kind of dilemma, and illustrate some of the ways in which they shaped the process and outcomes concerned.

One example, taken from Morley, may illustrate the potential power of the analysis. It concerns the treatment of progress. The dilemma arises because internal and external negotiations may be seen as the planning and action stages of a single process. The balance of strategic judgement is between: (1) a view of an ideal planning process as one in which people become increasingly committed to plans as they narrow the options from broad lines of development to specific proposals and (2) a recognition that it may be costly to delay too long because it may allow other people to articulate their own definitions of the situation, and seek support for partisan positions, perhaps narrowly defined. There is a clear example of a failure to make a balanced strategic judgement of this kind in the pay and productivity negotiations described by Warr. Case studies show that many problems follow when teams lack an experienced leader, so that they are unable to cope with cognitive and the political aspects of the negotiation task.

Pruitt and Carnevale have been generous enough to suggest that the language-action perspective may eventually lead to a fundamental shift in the way we think about negotiation. Certainly, it draws attention to aspects of negotiation which are not given sufficient attention in other models. One aspect concerns the shift from talk about strategy and tactics to talk about messages and meanings; a second aspect concerns the metaphor that negotiators write social history; a third aspect concerns the axioms which underlie a discursive psychology; a fourth aspect concerns negotiation considered as a form of joint decision making. Overall, the effect is to insist that studies of the skills of negotiation need to locate negotiation within its socio-historical context.

OVERVIEW

The analytic approach has the merit of assuming that negotiation involves mixed motives and indicates some intellectually sophisticated ways of looking at some of the skills of negotiation. Unfortunately, and despite some honourable exceptions, such as Walton and McKersie and Snyder and Diesing most of those who work within this 'paradigm' seem to assume that there is little more to the process of negotiation than the exchange of bid and counter-bid. Because of this, most behavioural studies are equally impoverished: while some deliver some important conclusions, most do not.

Behavioural studies of real-life negotiations help us to discover some of the skills involved in negotiations between representatives of groups, but suffer from limitations of sample size. Information-processing models take seriously the proposition that 'as negotiations become more complex participants may find it increasingly difficult to work out what is going on, and why', so that questions of strategy (how to outwit an opponent) increasingly become subordinated to questions of structure (how to work out what is going on, and why). Both information-processing models and models of the personal characteristics of negotiators help us to show why this may be so.

They also help us to elucidate some of the skills employed by the participants. Discursive models show how, and why, negotiators may be described as writing social history. At the moment, the most useful framework theory for describing the skills of negotiation seems to be some sort of language-action approach. I regard this as one form of social constructionism. It has the merit that it treats both the intellectual and political skills of negotiators seriously, and shows some of the ways in which they may be related. The model of skill that is articulated follows from the work and helps us to understand those individual and collective processes by which negotiators relate their intellectual capacities to the many demands of the negotiation task.

Chapter 13

Relational Communication

GOALS AND PURPOSES

The first issue concerns the purposes for which people might enter relationships, such that one can then assess whether their goals are achieved. Without such an assessment, one cannot set standards by which successful or skilful achievement of those purposes could be known or measured. Weiss laid out some principles for judging the needs that are satisfied in relationships in the West. It was proposed that there are seven provisions of relationships and one could assume that the ability to serve these goals would count as skilled. This should be so not only from the point of view of self fulfilment but also, more subtly, as the sense of fulfillment is judged by others, an important issue for assessments of skill, which can be viewed as an inherent characteristic or else as an attribution made by others. Such judgments can come from the outside observers as well as being made from the inside as persons assess their satisfaction of cultural norms and so qualify themselves for successful and skilled performance of their relationships in their own eyes.

PROVISIONS

- *Belonging and a sense of reliable alliance:* The sense that others are available to support one in times of need is an important feeling for people, and it creates a sense of membership in a stable context. To the degree that such a sense of belonging is established and conveyed in relationships, the person has been skilful in fulfilling this need. Many studies have used the extent and depth of a person's membership in a community as a measure of the person's skill in relating.

- *Emotional integration and stability:* Derived in part from Festinger's considerations about social comparison, this provision asserts that people seek a sounding board for their emotional responses to life's eventualities, and that the commentary provided by others is a needed addition to their own personal reactions. In assessing skill in relation to this provision, therefore, some expressiveness of emotions is presumed.
- *Opportunities for communication about self*: Weiss supposed that people have a desire to talk about themselves and expose elements of their experience and condition. A skilled relater should be one who does this in appropriate ways, neither too much nor too little.
- *Provision of assistance and physical support*: Given that most models of social support unequivocally suppose that physical and emotional support are requirements of relationships, it is not surprising that Weiss placed emphasis on this self-evident provision of relationships. It might be possible to assess a person's abilities in relationships according to the extent to which the person is successful in eliciting delivery of such support.
- *Reassurance of worth and value*: Weiss assumes that people have a desire to evaluate themselves positively and to be reassured that they are valuable members of the community in which they exist. Again, this sort of provision could be readily assessed as a measure of the success of a relationship. Indeed, the skills of establishing it help to develop personal wholeness or stability of self-esteem, and increase trust.
- *Opportunity to help others*: Weiss regards this as a

separate provision but it might also be seen as a subcomponent of many of the other components. For example, provision of assistance and physical support can be a way of satisfying a need to help others and thereby maintain one's own and others' views of a person as helpful. However, the voluntary expression of support for others and the provision of help are known to be a rewarding and self-fulfilling experience for both recipient and donor and are clearly more readily available to the extent that the person has skilfully sustained a network of relationships.

- *Personality support*: Seen in terms of traditional views of personality, this provision simply means that actions of friendship and closeness represent the supporting of a person's personality needs and values, an assumption that has been foundational in relationship research for several decades. Personality support is distinct from reassurance of worth and value in that personality support is accomplished through verification of one's existing identity, while the reassurance of worth and value is based on the enhancement of that identity.

Such individual provisions are fundamental explanations for the existence of relationships, and each offers a way to assess the success or skill of an individual in relating. Yet, as Simmel noted, any couple tends to judge its satisfaction and performance not only relative to satisfaction of the internal feelings that the participants have about their own relationship but also against cultural and normative standards against which their success or failure may be assessed. Couples from the nineteenth century might judge their personal relationship as satisfying in ways that would horrify couples in the twenty-first century, giving preference to the dominance of the husband over the wife and to an assessment that the judgement of the husband about the relationship amounted to a final truth about it status.

Although a couple may be satisfied with the internal

dynamics of their relationship, therefore, some reference of their outcomes to social norms might be expected as a legitimate judgement of the skill of their performance. The modern 'Cosmo questions' about the relative performances in their relationship compared to norms of '10 essential behaviours in relationships' or '15 things your relationship needs' might contribute to a couple's overall satisfaction with their relationship. Indeed, many couples now compare their sexual performance and experience with such standards before judging that they are sexually normal.

Such activities and feelings suffice to indicate that the individual analysis of one's own performance is not an adequate measure of the satisfaction in the relationship and hence that the judgement of skill in a relationship does not rest with the couple alone but also with their performance relative to some societal norms. Likewise, an individual's behaviour may be judged skilful or unskilful from different vantage points.Weiss's provisions, then, may apply only in the ideal but they are a recognisable standard that is used by (and which is derived from) Western standards for skill and performance levels. In the West, the satisfaction within a relationship is judged partly in relation to such norms, and so skill in relationship must also be measured against the existence of norms within a particular society rather than judged simply in terms of the claims of relational participants.

As Montgomery teaches us, then, the communicative standards applied to assessments of 'quality' in relationships have their roots in a society's assumptions about 'personality' and the role of relationships in fulfilling self in relation to communicative standards. Moreover, outsiders may apply socially relevant norms of assessment to the behaviours observed in relationships, and, as Davis has powerfully noted, even the sexual behaviours in an intimate partnership are subject to the evaluative commentary of others at times. Hence, the issue of the relationships between judgements of 'skill' and actual relationship behaviours is somewhat complex even if one can properly acknowledge the limits on the categories of behaviours to be included. In order to advance our case, therefore, it is necessary to know something about the behaviours regarded as basic to relating in order to set standards for their skilled performance.

BEHAVIOURS, THOUGHTS, AND RELATING

Some have sought to define relationships in terms of the underlying patterns of behaviour that occur between interactants. For example, Hinde defined a relationship as 'a series of interactions between two individuals known to each other.' Hinde used the following set of eight criteria for describing relationships and distinguished them from otherwise unconnected interaction series:

- *Content of interactions:* the things that the partners do together.
- *Diversity of interactions:* those relationships that are multiplex are more likely to be closer and more intimate than those which involve only one type of activity, such as customer–server relationships.
- *Qualities of interactions:* involving such assessments as intensity of interaction, content of discourse, and sensitivity of one partner to the behaviours of the other.
- *Relative frequency and patterning of interactions:* for example, the sequencing of negative and positive responses to a partner.
- *Reciprocity versus complementarily:* relationships are different if an action evokes a similar, reciprocal response, such as 'Hi' to a previous 'Hi', rather than a different but supplementary, complementary one, such as an answer to a question. Some interactions require reciprocity, as in the courteous greeting rituals that are a mark of skill in most superficially polite interactions, whereas others require complementarily, and people are not skilful unless they recognise and use this difference.
- *Intimacy:* different sorts of relationships differ in the amounts of touch and verbal intrusion into the other's psychological space that are appropriate.

- *Interpersonal perception:* individuals in different sorts of relationships differ in degree of balance between their perceptions of each other. Satisfying relationships occur successfully only when the perceptions of one partner with another are appropriately meshed.
- *Commitment:* degrees of commitment not only to the relationship and to the partner but to the likelihood of future interactions can differentiate relationships.

It is clear from the delineation of these categories that there is a host of ways in which they could be relevant to consideration of skill in relating, and we will consider them more closely below. At this point, it is sufficient to note that variation within these categories – and difference in performance from the expectations associated with each of them – could be critical in the determination that a person is a skilled relater.

Inappropriate levels of commitment, intimacy, or sought frequency of interaction could register someone as over-intrusive rather than intimate, or as inappropriately distant rather than friendly and open. It rapidly becomes apparent, however, that patterning of interaction is a necessary but not a sufficient condition for labeling action as 'relating'.

Some form of psychological interdependence is clearly necessary as an adjunct to behavioural interdependence, whether measured in terms of perceived common fate or mutual interest or concern over the outcomes of the other (for example, whether they are equitable and satisfying). Some scholars have noted that relationships exist in the absence of repeated or frequent interaction, whether through the influence of long distance or because of estrangement of some sort (as between parent and errant children) or through death.

Some have argued that relationships are partly mentalistic concepts and that the difference between a string of interactions and a relationship is what the parties think about those interactions. Indeed, some have pointed to the negative consequences of people's mere thoughts about relationships, such that they could lead to charges of harassment or stalking when one person believes that the relationship exists in a form that the other partner does not see or agree to.

Sigman noted that people exercise various means to continue the mental element of their relationship in the face of absence or lack of interaction, since: 'Relationships are "larger" than the physical presence or interactional accessibility of the participants'. Sigman thus successfully explains how relationships may be continuous despite periods of separation. The discontinuous aspects of social relationships are managed by using relational continuity constructional units (RCCUs) – behaviours that partners use before, during, or after an absence and which function to construct the continuity of the relationship during periods of absence.

TYPES OF RCCUS

- Prospective units are those behaviours that relationship partners perform before physical separation and 'define the meaning and duration of the impending separation and of the likely return'. Examples are fare wells, setting agenda for future meetings, and the use of tie signs or tokens of relationships, such as the offer of engagement rings, or 'spoors' (objects left behind and which indicate a likely return, such as a toothbrush in one's lover's bathroom).
- Introspective units represent the relationship's continuity during periods of absence and are exemplified by photographs of the partner on a desk at work, or a greeting card pinned to a personal space.
- Retrospective units mark the ending of a period of relational separation and can be seen in conversations that allow the partners to 'catch-up' on what happened to each other during the period of absence, such as end of day debriefing or catch-up conversations.

In this context, then, it is notable that skilled behaviours in relationships are not necessarily connected to the present alone, and so it becomes critical to Hinde's definition that relational communication is joint discourse that points to past and potential interaction. In this definition, a relationship emerges from interaction, but is not reducible to it. In other words, relationship is created on the basis of a combination of behavioural skills, but this synthesis exceeds those behaviours. This excess is what renders communication relational: relational communication.

Skilled performance is likewise tied not only to the present performance but also to management of future expectations. Thus, relational communication is behaviour that not only develops interactors' shared history but also suggests future interaction. In the following section, we will review various types of relational communication and discuss the value of viewing these behaviours as skills, given the need to consider management not only of behaviour but also of expectations and continuity.

The distinction between behavioural and psychological factors points us to the difference that might be made in assessments between outsiders (limited to the behavioural and to inference about the psychological) and insiders (who have access to the psychological as well as to the behavioural) in assessing skill as a performance or as an attribute.

SKILLS AND THE QUALITY OF RELATIONSHIPS

The Dictionary defines skill as 'the ability to do something well'. A chapter on relational communication for a book on communication skills therefore must include discussion of relationship behaviours (doing something), the bases of communicative quality (well), and the relation between the two, since not all relational skills are necessarily intentionally communicative. This chapter will identify some skilled behaviours reckoned to be fundamental to successful social relationships and will then consider some themes that have historically been understood as quality communication in the relationships literature and discuss the basis for these understandings. There is both a performance element (based perhaps on skilful application of relevant rules) and an experiential element here (since satisfaction must imply some skilled ability to extract outcomes desired by the individual reporter). Overlaying both, however, is a strategic element indicating that the ability to make choices between competing or inconsistent rules itself amounts to a skill.

SKILLS AND RULES

The first focus must be on whether the very communication of the existence of relationships is a first sign of skill. It is a truism of Western culture that the number of friends that a person can claim is seen as a measure of social success and the implicit rule to demonstrate connectedness is a powerful one. Liberace once sent out invitations to 5000 of his closest and dearest personal friends. The very ability to 'attract' others is treated as significant and a measure of skill and one's social value. In like manner, the ending of relationships is treated with pity and negativity such that there are no 'successful divorces' but only 'failed marriages'.

Ending of close relationships is stigmatic for their participants and is generally treated with remorse and disapprobation. Hence, existence of numbers of relationships is not sufficient to apply a label of skill but rather the implicit rule requires a demonstrated capacity to work and sustain those relationships. Accordingly, the emphasis in the literature taking this line has fallen on the microbehaviours that are used skilfully to demonstrate warmth and openness in relationships, beginning with the non-verbal and later extending to strategic success in the long term.

A skilled relational performance is first connected with needs and provisions that we outlined earlier, as well as with the ability to fulfil the requirements of social prototypes of relating. Davis and Todd (1985) listed the paradigm case features of friendship and noted that such performances as acceptance, respect, trust, and spontaneity were prerequisites of friendship, such that their absence disqualified the relationship as an instance of friendship. Hence, the ability to perform the behaviours associated with such features is a necessary skill and raises the question of the means by which such features are communicated. The catalogue of behaviours that are counted as skilled here is quite large and covers a considerable range of activities, some of which are clearly 'relational' and some of which are less clearly connected to relationship activity and more obviously associated with smooth but simple social interaction.

Argyle originally observed many skills of social interaction that essentially convey attention, warmth, and friendliness, and without whose presence the continuance of a relationship may be jeopardised. Familiar examples are eye contact, gaze, smiles, nods, and open postures, but the contribution of these behaviours to the establishment and growth of relationships seems to be 'hygienic' rather than substantial. Herzberg differentiated hygienic factors in organisational contexts from motivational factors.

Motivational factors make workers work harder; hygienic factors do not, but their absence makes people work less hard (examples are such things as adequate heating and lighting, whereas motivational factors are pay and respect from supervisors). In like fashion, some of the above non-verbal behaviours seem destined to have effects only in the breach, and to damage the prospects for intimacy when they are absent without substantially increasing them when present. Nonetheless, the ability to perform such behaviours at all will count as skilled, and hence as a prerequisite of skilled relational behaviour in the above senses.

In addition to such microbehaviours, a larger issue is connected with strategic skills of recognition of the rules of certain situations, and later work attended to the designation of social situations and the appropriateness of attendance to the prerequisites of such designation. For example, a skilful relationship with a friend requires recognition of the rule to tell the truth and be open about one's emotional state, so that one expresses warmth or affection and provides emotional support. Argyle and Henderson later broadened the notion of rules to relationships in general and concluded: 'Rules are a very useful guide to many aspects of socially skilled behaviour. We have taken as one criterion of relationship rules whether or not [the breaking of them] results in disruption of a relationship.

Social skills are commonly identified by a comparison of the performances of successful and unsuccessful practitioners. The concepts of rules and skill thus have a good deal of overlap'. It is, however, also apparent that some relationships can survive rule breaking. Furthermore, there are important variations in rules depending on the specific relationship involved, not only across cultures but also within groups, as a function of the needs that are supposed to be fulfilled by the relationships in each case. For example, family life and work relationships are expected to fulfil some of the needs fulfilled by friendship.

Given the strengths and relevance of the rules approach to skill in relationships, one must ask a number of questions in order to position the problems raised by the above comments in relation to the general value of a rules approach to skills. It is clear that there can be different layers of rules, some of which prescribe specific actions in particular circumstances (e.g. smile when you greet someone) and yet others which are of a higher and more abstract order ('be tolerant of friends'). It is also clear that judgements are required about the sets of rules to apply in particular circumstances, and whether it is, for example, more important to expect a smile from friends at each new encounter or to tolerate their bad moods.

Such judgements indicate that a skill rests not only on the application of specific rules but in the ability to make wise assessments of the relative importance of applying the rule and ignoring it or supplanting it with some other rule. In short, knowledge of the rules is necessary but not sufficient to warrant a judgement of skilled relational communication, and perception of situational awareness/parsing of situations or even an awareness of cultural and situational norms is an asset that has power only when used with strategic good sense. Larger goals of relating can supplant the microperformances that would otherwise be regarded as skilful, just as social norms about relational conduct within an organisation could be different from those available in a culture more broadly or in society outside the organisation.

Such larger skills of relating might indicate successful affective management on top of the microbehaviours, and there is sometimes a tension between relating effectively (for example, assertively) and relating skilfully. Clearly, integration of goals and needs is a big issue in skill, and the ability to deploy specific tactical skills in a situation is a lower-order analysis. Some critics have therefore asked whether skill resides in the ability to adjust and adapt to situations or in the recognition that a specific rule applies to the relationship presently under consideration. Spitzberg noted that the ability to adapt to rules is itself a skill and indicates that competence may be understood as an ability (to perform well) or a quality (an attribution made by observers). Competence has three roles in relationships.

First, it has a direct role that facilitates development and management of relationships (skill = success of outcomes). Second, competence mediates how others respond to the actor's behaviour, so managing the appearance of competence is important. (This is the reason why we hear so much about spin doctors these days). Third, competence is a self-inference that affects motivation.

Important theoretical and practical issues flow from these observations. If competence is an ability to make choices between options, then there is a dialectics of motives (for example, politeness versus assertiveness; communality versus instrumentality; adaptation versus control the issue of when to adapt to situation and when to be self – attention to short term versus long-term objectives; the decision to show openness versus closedness/ privacy). If competence is an attribution by observers, then there is a dialectics of attributions (context-facilitated versus context-impaired; self-deception versus alter deception; predictability versus novelty; success versus obsolescence – where one can have too much of a good thing or where repetition of a behaviour becomes adaptively.

JUDGING RELATIONSHIP SKILL

Montgomery (1988) argues that our judgements about relational quality are based on ideal standards for relational communication. These standards are located in particular contexts: they can be based on cultural ideologies, shared relational meanings, or individual idiosyncrasies. While not universal, these ideals do have an a priori nature in that these cultural, relational, and personal interactional codes form the basis for particular social behaviour. That is, our judgements about the skilfulness of a relational behaviour are based on its correspondence with ideal relational standards, or scripts. In actual interaction, the criteria for judging quality communication are pluralistic; cultural, social, and individual criteria all bear on the assessment of communicative quality.

For example, it was demonstrated that the ritual performance of the wedding ceremony (cultural), interactions with other wedding guests (social), and personal understandings about commitment (individual) all contributed to the quality of lesbian, bisexual, and gay family members' experiences at weddings. In their discussion of inappropriate relationships, Duck and VanderVoort presented the negotiation of cultural and relational codes for 'competent' but 'inappropriate' relational behaviour along a continuum from unconventional, notable, and scandalous, to forbidden. This scheme suggests that when criteria for quality relationships conflict, relational behaviour is based on the relative weight that relational partners give to cultural and relational standards.

While standards for the quality of relational communication serve as yardsticks to measure the valence of relationships, scholars also attest that these standards render social relations recognisable and meaningful in a more global sense. Surra and Bohman assert that people understand their relationships (and judge their quality) by comparing them to relational norms. Fletcher and Simpson echo that ideal standards for close relationships serve these interpretive and evaluative functions for relationship members, adding that they also serve an adaptive function: when relational scripts do not match the relationship itself, they serve as guidelines for change. Furthermore, it propose that in romantic relationships when partners' personal scripts for enacting and interpreting romantic relationships correspond to normative scripts, couples experience greater relational well-being. These studies suggest that because we understand our relationships on the basis of ideal standards, our understanding of relationships is inextricably bound to our perceptions of their quality.

To deal with such questions, one must reflect on the matter of judgement of quality within a culture. This requires us to explore relationships at the macrolevel and consider how they knock against larger social structures that unobtrusively influence daily existence or deal with the innumerable ways in which everyday social encounters make our experience for us. In different ways, theorists have focused on the means by which social relationships reflect larger social forces and so embody the ways in which 'society' is experienced at the mundane level of experience.

If society has a face, it is in the face that attends our daily interactions with each other and constrains or empowers certain forms of social action and experience. Relationships in everyday life therefore embody and manage our connection with 'society' as a larger concept.

COMMUNICATIVE STANDARDS

Montgomery identifies three values implicit in relationships literature that serve as standards for quality and hence obliquely as bases for judgements of skill: positiveness, intimacy, and control. These assumptions remain implicit in the majority of relationship studies. Montgomery goes on to note that competence in relationships is judged in terms of the same criteria of positiveness, intimacy, and control. They must of course be understood as having a number of components, stressing the positive in relationships and the elicitation of positive experiences from others, but also being grounded in general psychological tendencies (in the West at least) to achieve self-fulfilment through relationships.

POSITIVITY [H

The relationships literature demonstrates an overwhelming prosocial bias mostly indicated through the sorts of literature with which we opened this chapter and which regards positivity as the main signal of relational engagement. There is a growing literature on the importance of positive relationships at work but there is also a growing literature on the 'dark side' of relationships, which demonstrates an increasing turn from the field's predominant focus on the prosocial nature of relationships.

While these studies increasingly represent the negative side of relationships, they serve to reinforce the relational ideal of positiveness. On the other hand, a compelling arguments for the importance of both centrifugal and centripetal relational forces, suggesting that centrifugal forces, such as closedness (privacy), change, and autonomy (independence), also have value for relationships. All the same, the recognition that there are two sides to relationships that are always present together in experience simply shifts the focus of discussions of 'relational skill' from the performance of those behaviours that are rated positively and toward the issue of the management of the competing negative and positive forces that can be guaranteed to be present in all relationships.

Rather than focusing on positivity, then, the important development of recent literature is to note the importance of the daily management of the different elements of relationships as well as the contribution of different forms of 'community' in which the management can be practised and held to account.

INTIMACY

As is evident from the literature reviewed so far, and from many other sources, the assumption is that successful and skilled enactment of relationships revolves around the establishment, increase, and maintenance of intimacy. Indeed, the title of the Hendrick sourcebook is Close Relationships. It appears to be heretical to suggest that skilled relational communication could involve successful maintenance of distance or non-intimacy, despite Delia's telling observation that by far the majority of our interpersonal relationships not only are distant but persistently remain so. Kirkpatrick, Duck, and Foley note that relationships at work can embody several different and competing goals; the relational goal of intimacy may be unadvisable in a context dedicated primarily to achieving extrarelational tasks. Here, team-playing can be seen as an important criterion of skill which would not be similarly applied to long-term relationships based on intimacy. The bias in assessments of relationship skill in terms of an intimacy assumption must nevertheless be acknowledged.

POWER/CONTROL

Most assessments of relationships assume that self-control and power over others are desirable features of relational life. Dominance is a trait preferred to submission, and authority is preferred to subservience. Problems in relationships at work are assumed to exist when equality of power shifts in friendly roles, with, for example, the promotion of one friend over the other. There are no inherently good ways to conduct a relationship, and indeed cultures and contexts differ widely on the performances that are judged to be appropriate and skilled.

Hence, any discussion of the 'skilled' performance of relationships necessarily nods toward the existence of cultural and situational norms and standards that apply in one's assessment of relationships and which might not apply to assessment of relationship quality in other cultural or situational contexts. Skill at work or in organisational settings where hierarchies of power are formally operated does not necessarily equate to skill in interpersonal relationships within the family, for example. Brisk and authoritative behaviour in one setting may be 'skilled' where soft, warm, and intimate behaviours would be judged 'skilful' in the other.

Hence, judgements about the skilled conduct of relationships must be tempered by the recognition that such judgements are embedded in the acceptance of a cultural and contextual standard for judging both the nature of the relationship between participants and the performance of relationally relevant activities, as well as the outcomes from relationships that are regarded as positive or appropriate in the circumstances. Ultimately, the reduction of relationships to a set of performable skills is both useful and misleading.

Is the 'skill' to be found in a list of performable behaviours or is it found in the ability to adapt and to act in ways not obviously predicted and forced by the situation? Is the truly skilled performer one who follows the rules, or one who shows ability to adapt, change, and modify those general rules? More significantly for our following discussion, can one person ever be judged as 'skilled' in the absence of knowledge about the interaction partner and his or her behaviour? For the entirety of its existence, the research literature on relationships has been criticised for attending to the actions, feelings and reports of only one person in the relationship. In like manner, it seems absurd to focus on the mechanical behaviours of only one person in a pair and to judge the person as 'skilled' or 'unskilled' without making any assessment of the appropriateness of their activities with respect to the attitudes, feelings, and responses of the other person present.

SKILL AND THE STRUCTURALIST PARADIGM

The claim that we enact and interpret relationships on the basis of ideal standards rests on a structuralist paradigm. Here, relationships are treated as parallel to Saussure's explanation of language: parole, or speech, is an enacted, performed instantiation of langue, an abstract and a priori system of signs (for example, 'grammar'). Analogously, in the relational structure paradigm, our relational behaviour is an instantiation of a system of relationship standards. As such, relating is understood as synchronic; that is, it takes a 'snapshot' of relational skill at a single point in time, rather than understanding standards for skilled relational behaviour as unfolding over time. According to the relational structure paradigm, social practices that fail to meet the system of relational standards fail to be legitimated as 'good', 'quality', or 'skilled'. If no social practice outside the system of relational standards can be understood as legitimate, alternative social practices lack the force to transform the system of relational standards.

Thus, while the concept of ideal standards (whether cultural, relational, or personal) is useful, it is insufficient to explain relational skill. By itself, this perspective does not account for a mechanism that allows for change in the fundamental structure of relational values. The relationships literature shows that our understanding of relationships does indeed change on the basis of social practice.

While this does take place on the levels of cultural ideologies and individual idiosyncrasies, the relationships literature most clearly illustrates the transformative power of social practice at the relational level. It was explained that relational partners' accounts of their behaviour serve not only to legitimate it, but also to construct the terms by which relational behaviour can be legitimated. Duck explains: Engagement in interpersonal communication [re]calls forth speakers' daily lives to other people for evaluation. By the same conversational means, people are able to evaluate their rhetorical visions of life, of other people, of themselves, and of a host of other things that have been variously called personality, meaning systems, or culture.

Following this view, we argue for an adjusted conception of relational structure. Relationships are not judged in comparison to static, unchanging abstract and standard structures; instead, relational practices in the living everyday world – the relational paroles as it were – create the basis for their own evaluation.

In other words, relational practices are self-structuring. Elias suggests that the monolithic but abstract conception of social structure is illusory. He argues that social structure comes down to figurations of everyday social relationships; the abstract notion of 'society' is really something substantial that is enacted in a set of relationships between people and their associates. An argument structure that guides social practices emerges from those social practices themselves. It was declares that the structure of the utterance is sociological; that is, it 'obtains between speakers'. Simmel similarly positions structure as contingent on sociation, or social interaction. For Simmel, 'the content – the materials, so to speak – of sociation [is] everything that is immediately present in individuals', while social forms are abstractions 'through which, or in the shape of which, that content attains social reality'. While Simmel maintains a conceptual distinction between social content and social forms, he explains that in sociation the two 'constitute one reality'.

It is important to note that we are not proposing a mere reversal of the binary between social structure and behaviour. We are not arguing that instead of social structure guiding behaviour, behaviour guides social structure. We introduce relational co-performance, the interstice between behaviour and structure, as a third term that evades the binarism on which the relational structure paradigm relies. In short, we advocate performance as an alternative to structure as the basis for relational signification.

Hence, we advocate co-performance as an alternative to skill as the basis for relational signification. In other words, we claim that the notion of skill in relating has fallen prey to the same flaw present in the relational literature as a whole – reliance on the reports and examination of the responses of one person in the dyad. By focusing on co-performance, we emphasise the fact that relationships and all forms of social behaviour are founded on the notion of (at least) two interactants. Accordingly, it is necessary to be aware of things other than the feelings of one person that are 'present' in any interaction that is located relationally – that is, in a flow of history.

Unlike the synchronic skill paradigm, co-performance is rooted in a diachronic conceptualisation of relationships that accounts for both their historicity and their generativity. Our earlier discussion of Hinde indicated that relational communication is joint discourse that points to past and potential interaction. In this definition, relationship emerges from past co-performance (history), but is not reducible to it (generativity). As link between past and future, co-performance can be understood as a limen, or threshold, of becoming.

Relationships are continually recreated through this process of play, where the old and new collide and collude. Any jointly performed discourse is both generative and historical. First, co-performance is generative: it resignifies the shared history of a relationship by performing new contextual frameworks for interpretation. Bauman and Briggs argue that participants contextualise their performance (e.g. produce interpretive frameworks) through the contextualisation cues in the performance itself: 'textual details... illuminate the manner in which participants are collectively constructing the world around them'.

This contextualisation of voice is constructive, rendering relational meanings new, though contingent on their historical grounding. Likewise, it was noted that the behaviours and talk of two relational partners with each other are both grounded in the partners' awareness of past interaction between themselves. The interpretation of an instant remark depends to some degree on the location of that remark in the relational history between the two interactants and the interaction sequencing as well as in the personality and past record of the speaker. The more one knows of the speaker's history, the more subtly one can interpret the significance of a particular comment.

However, the co-performance not only serves to transform (contextualise), but also to preserve (entextualise) existing voices. By calling attention to the form by which the performance is organised, the performance takes itself as its own object, rendering it extractable from its interactional setting. While contextualisation cues can be understood as an emergent structure that organises and situates discourse, contextualisation cues are also markers that call attention to that organising form. Thus, the same performative features account for both (a) the contextualisation or transformation of relational meaning and (b) entextualisation or reification of relational meaning. Thus, relational meanings are always in generative flux, yet at the same time rely on and promote an understanding of shared relationship history.

While we suggest that the structuralist underpinnings of the term 'skill' are problematic for a conception of relationships as processual, the literature overwhelmingly demonstrates that the valence of relational practices is significant. Studies consistently show that relational satisfaction is a meaningful way in which social actors understand their relationships. In addition to this personal experience of relational value, we also recognise the importance of identifying the ethical value of relationships. The literature on intimate partner violence demonstrates the importance of avoiding a relativistic stance where judgements of good and bad have no place.

In proposing co-performance as an alternative to competence, we are not claiming that relationships cannot or should not be evaluated. Instead, we take issue with the means by which relationships are understood to be evaluated in rule-based constructions of skill, in which relational evaluation takes place on the basis of ideal standards. The alternative of co-performance advocates judging relational performances by the criteria the performances themselves construct, rather than against a priori criteria. Because relational performances are historical and generative, they can be judged on the basis of their appropriation of the past to create new performances.

Rather than positioning relational standards as some ideal structure separate from performance, the conditions for evaluating relational behaviour exist within those behaviours themselves. Each utterance contains a palimpset, a trace of previous actions against which that utterance can be judged. Duck applies the metaphor of hypertext, explaining that relational history is indexed within social interaction, 'linking' the past to the present. We evaluate our relationships on the basis of the indexed past, or present constructions of the past. It is not unusual to claim that relaters continually renegotiate their relational histories, arguments over the usefulness of retrospective data being an excellent example of the entailments of reformulating the past. We further argue, however, that the relational past unveils itself only insofar as it is indexed in interaction.

This presentation of the past, which may masquerade as the invocation of a given structure of relational standards, is the basis for determining the value of relational behaviour. In other words, we do not judge a behaviour's value on the basis of extant relational ideals, but in the idealisations that emerge from that behaviour itself. Locating the criteria for relational skill in the ongoing flux of conversation disrupts the understanding of a behaviour as 'skilled' or 'unskilled', or an individual as 'competent' or 'incompetent'. Incompetence is not just the lack of competence: there is more going on when that label is applied. An attribution of lack of skill is a way of pointing to deficiencies in performance as judged from the cultural, contextual, and situational embedding of the relationship.

To label someone as incompetent is to refer to a contextualised speech situation, not a quality of the individual in isolation. Kirkpatrick et al. suggest that those who are often construed as 'difficult' people are not difficult in themselves, but in relation to others; relational difficulty sits instead in the multiple competing roles that individuals enact. Incompetence, then, is not a matter of personal or performative deficiency, but instead a problem of performative excess. That is, it is difficult to navigate continually shifting criteria for skill as they emerge through interaction. For example, as individuals are rewarded in relationships, they come to expect increasing rewards. Because criteria for skilled performance are realised within those performances themselves, skilfulness is a moving target. Incompetence is not the lack of competence, but a function of the generativity of relational skill.

IDEAS FOR FUTURE CONSIDERATION

The above concerns bring us back to some issues noted at the beginning and focused on the matter of whether skill is appropriately sited in microbehaviours or macro-action. In other words, do our assessments of 'skill' properly attach to short-term or long-term elements of relational communication? Equally relevant is the issue of whether relationships (especially long-term relationships) are to be seen as inherent or instrumental, such that skill should be assessed relative to 'warm and fuzzy' qualities or to specific outcomes. A third issue of relevance to judgements of skill focuses on the strategic versus the routine aspects of relating. Much has recently been made of the non-strategic mundane and ordinary behaviours of relationships, and the removal of emphasis on strategic activity renders the consideration of pedestrian and apparently insignificant (even phatic) activity much more relevant to judgements of skill. A fourth consideration is whether relational skill can be taught, and a final issue concerns the definition of incompetence and its impact on the health status of the person in ways relevant to the conditions with which we opened the chapter. We will now take these in turn. term or short-term relating as the basis for assessing skill?

Given that personal norms of creditable performance are not sufficient to judge the success of a relationship and that social norms about skill may be differently applied, one must make a further distinction between types of relationships for which an assessment of skill or lack of skill may be applied: the long-term versus short-term distinction. It is important to note that the goals of (and hence measures of satisfaction with skill in) long-term and short-term relationships are different. Short-term relationships are judged successful when there is an easy rapport, when first impressions are favourable, and when liking is evoked from someone who did not have any reason to feel it before, being a stranger.

Long-term relationships require more than this and are found to require deep similarity and management of established intimacy and of long-term commitment as well as development of significant trust in a variety of contexts and relative to a range of concerns, as well as other things. The distinction in the literature between short-term and long-term relationships readily suggests, therefore, that different skills and criteria for skilfulness apply in each case. We have already considered the specific case of long-term strategic overlay on the dialectics of (in)competence, for example, but there are many other cases where the confusion of short- and long-term goals – and hence of short- and long-term criteria for skilfulness – are quite markedly different.

For example, a person who is shy but capable of intimacy might be judged incompetent in one sort of relationship, but not in another. Hence, the notion of skill is not a simple reference to personal ability but to a person–situation interaction at the very least. The issue of skill also implies an ability of two kinds of observers, both external reviewers and participants, to differentiate the goals and requirements of short- and long-term relationships. The literature on long-term relationships suggests strongly that an underlay of similarity of attitudes is a prerequisite of successful long-term relationships and that different skills might underlie short-term relationships. Such similarity may be judged differently by insiders and outsiders because they have available to them different sorts of information about internal states.

One obvious difference lies in the knowledge of private relational history and the fact that whereas similarity of underlying 'rhetorical vision' (personal view of the world) is essential to the success of the relationships on the enduring future, in short-term relationships, the basis of the relationship may be independent of such history and could depend only on the fulfilment of instrumental needs and goals which are specific and perhaps even time-limited. What is the parallelism between long-term and short-term relationships? Perhaps short-term relationships work best if they mimic the goals and styles of long-term ones, but, given that they most often have time-limited objectives and are strictly performative in character, this mimicry may not matter.

'Uses' of long-term relationships as an analogy for deciding what short relationships should be offering might point to the errors in too simple a conclusion about the extension of one type of relationship skill to another. It could be argued that short-term relationships are successful to the extent that they may be able to mimic the effects and styles of long-term relationships, but this is actually questionable and the two sorts may better be seen as related but independent forms. Thus, for example, the fact that long-term relationships are based on trust and intimacy might be heard as a clarion call for all those seeking successful short-term relationships to imitate such features, but it is also apparent that short-term relationships can be quite successful without such features being present.

Hence, a primary restriction on the notion of relationships as skilled performances relates to the distinction between long-term and short-term relationships. In the workplace or organisational context, one can see relationships as closer in form to short-term than to long-term relationships, and so different criteria for skill and success in outcome should be applied.

ARE RELATIONSHIPS INTRINSIC OR INSTRUMENTAL IN PURPOSE

One difference between long- and short-term relationships is that the former are normally expected to fluctuate in outcomes, whereas the emphasis in the latter is immediate and expectant homogeneity. Where a short-term partner may leave the relationship if rewards are not immediately positively balanced against costs, a long-term partner might be more willing to sustain the relationship in the face of (temporary) difficulty, on the grounds that the immediate rewards are not the point. The larger questions, then, are whether relationships are inherent/intrinsic or instrumental and how the answer to this first question affects the idea of skill. It has long been argued in the relationship field that relationships should not be reduced to a calculus of profits and losses but have instead some inherent and intrinsic self-referent qualities that make them desirable in and of themselves.

Although some wiseacre once said, 'Sincerity is the key to successful relationships and if you can fake sincerity then you have got it made', the emphasis falls here on such an instrumental use of the features of long-term relationships that the claim makes us instantly aware of the merits of Wright's point. Drawing from Duck the ability to create and sustain shared meaning systems is the basis for relationship maintenance in the long term and so should be accounted in the assessment of 'skilled performance' in any longer-term association whether strategically or routinely sustained (see next section). In this case, the situation may be complicated in that it is not only that competent communicative performance creates and sustains relationships, but also that relational communication allows us to create shared ideals about relationships and relationshipping. This allows us to maintain the same conceptual scheme, but flip from an outcome-based to a process-based model of competent relationships.

An emphasis on skilled performance for relationships suggests an instrumentality that may not apply successfully to long-term relationships. The ability to achieve goals and to derive specific satisfaction from relationships may be more valuable as a perspective from which to understand short-term relationships where goals are more specific and limited than is true of long-term relationships whose strategic maintenance may require the forgoing of a specific instrumental personal goal at this moment in order to sustain the relationship in the long term in intrinsic form.

ROUTINE VERSUS STRATEGIC ASPECTS OF MAINTENANCE AND RELATING

Throughout the chapter, we have followed the predominant emphasis of the relationship literature in stressing the importance of cognition, awareness, and strategic action in relationships. However, more recent research has focused also on the everyday routine and mundane performances that surround relationships. The issue that arises in assessing skill, then, is whether the relationship is constituted by the skills or whether skills are necessary but not sufficient for relationship formation and maintenance.

The matter is complicated by the fact that performance of relationships requires certain necessary mechanical skills, such as the performance of warmth, acceptance, and friendliness and, in some cases, intimacy, exclusivity, and trust, but that these are not necessarily skills that are transferable from relationship to relationship or situation to situation.

In intimate or romantic long-term relationships, exclusivity is more relevant and important than in short-term business relationships or in friendship, for example, and so the features that characterize skilled performance of exclusivity cannot be readily generalised from one relationship form to another. Furthermore, communication is not skill-based alone – at least not as 'skill' is normally understood and represented – and cannot be essentialised to different relationship forms, but is more naturally routinised in the activities of daily life that make up particular relationship forms.

Everyday conduct of conversation can itself be skilled but does not typically register in the literature because the focus of research is basically on the unfamiliar and extraordinary cases of intimacy growth rather than on the everyday patterns that matter in continuing relationships. Relationships can be skilled in the short term, but that is not their essence for long-term relationships. In short-term relationships, by contrast, a person can be 'skilled' by reason of the person's ability to complete relevant tasks and to sustain whatever basis of familiarity is necessary for that to be accomplished, but in long-term relationships a strategy devoted to the long-term maintenance of the relations despite short-term cost could be more important and hence more skilled.

Moreover, given the variable nature of long-term experience of any kind, the skills of discretion weighed against valour, for example, may make a person better able to handle the inevitable instabilities and ups and downs of relationships even over and above any skills necessary to handle actual conflict. Translations from maintenance of long-term to maintenance of short-term relationships are therefore not easy because the implied, and in some cases the explicit, goals are different. The maintenance of a successful short-term business relationship may be different from the goals that confront people in long-term relationships. Even in organisations and business relationships, these goals could be specified in different ways. Hence, the ways in which 'skill' might be characterised in short- and long-term relationships could be quite radically different, depending on whether one sees the maintenance of the relationship as a goal or not, relative to other tasks.

CAN RELATIONAL SKILL BE TAUGHT?

Underlying most considerations of 'skill' is the implicit question of whether skilled conduct of relationships can be taught. Yet, in common language, the notion of 'relating' runs counter to any sense of strategic management or, worse, manipulation. The essence of common-sense notions of relating is in genuineness and spontaneity rather than manipulative or strategically managed actions. In short, the goals of it are perceived to be more in line with those of longer-term relationships and there is some suspicion about people who are able to produce immediate or decontextualised disclosures and openness, particularly where there are power differences between speaker and listener.

A further twist on this dilemma is provided by the observation that some of the mechanical 'social skills' are taken to be a barrier to the authenticity and 'true communication' that are preferred in this society, since the mechanical production of smiles, nods and other encouragements or signals of interest is presumed to mask an underlying lack of interest in the comments of the speaker, and hence to fail the test of authenticity.

Although, clearly, this is not always the case, the fact that psychotherapists are taught to manage these cues to warmth and intimacy as part of their professional training can be seen to show that the point cuts both ways. It does indeed mask professional distance but simultaneously has the effect of encouraging the speaker to continue to disclose and explore experiences within the safety of a therapeutic context.

Hence an appearance of warmth in the listener can, even if masking some other feelings, lead to benefits for the speaker and to a sense of being accepted. However, it is probable that the sense of acceptance is tested against things other than the immediate non-verbal behaviours associated with one short interaction; hence, the standard for assessing skill is once more a long-term one. It is insufficiently clear at this point whether these long-term skills can be trained in the ways in which short-term ones may be.

IF WE KNOW 'SKILL', THEN WHAT IS INCOMPETENCE

As we have suggested above, incompetence is not just the lack of competence: there is more going on when that label is applied. The obvious point is that an attribution of lack of skill is a way of pointing to deficiencies in performance as judged from the cultural, contextual, and situational performance of the relationship as it is normally embodied in the culture. However, our points above also suggest that the context for assessment provides different outcomes of judgements depending on whether the relationship is seen as primarily instrumental, short term, and routine, for instance.

To label someone as unskilled is to refer to a cultural and situational context as well as to denounce them in some way. In a broader context, it was noted that many terms that appear to characterise someone actually make attributions: that is to say, they do not identify an inherent personal characteristic so much as they place a person in a social category whose operation cannot be understood apart from the social context. For example, a 'shy' person cannot be shy in the absence of other people and a 'difficult' one does not demonstrate difficulty alone. Thus, difficulty and lack of relational skill are essentially terms that require the incorporation or imagining of other people. The perception of a person as a 'difficult person' is based on a set of assumptions about the ultimate goal of a work relationship (namely, the achievement of extra-relational tasks).

In conclusion, the consequences of skilled and unskilled performance are therefore hard to pin down until one decides what level of skill one is interested in. The ability to sustain long-term relationships that are genuine and open is probably the aspect of relating that is tied to the long-term health issues noted in the opening paragraph of this chapter, although, of course, people who are lonely and isolated may lack the short-term skills that bring them to relationships in the first place. Whatever the health implications of relationships, the basic skills of connection of individuals to society are central to both health and social success.

Chapter 14

Employment Interview

THE INTERVIEWER'S PERSPECTIVE

In terms of the definitions previously cited, interviewers, by way of social interaction, attempt to achieve their identified goals: that is, to make successful predictions of job/organisation suitability across a range of applicants and to ensure that sought-after applicants take up offers to join the organisation. It is incumbent upon interviewers to make considered choices pertaining to the type of interview(s) to be employed and the use of appropriate interpersonal skills, which together enhance the likelihood of the employment interview achieving its selection and/or recruitment objectives. Analysing employment interviews as social encounters, Stevens confirmed that they can be viewed as moving through a number of sequential scenes, originally labelled by Tullar as greeting and establishing rapport, interviewer questioning, applicant questioning, and disengagement.

The type of interview format adopted dictates the precise nature of the communication skills required, and, as a consequence, the amount of freedom and discretion afforded the interviewer varies. Interview structure One of the major dimensions along which interviews can be differentiated relates to their degree of structure. It was suggested that the main structuring criteria 'relate to the degree of interviewer flexibility with respect to the content of the interview, what is included, how it is sampled, in what sequence and how much freedom is offered to interviewees with respect to their answers (i.e. open ended or multiple choice formats)'.

Campion et al. defined structure very broadly as 'any enhancement of the interview that is intended to increase psychometric properties by increasing standardization or otherwise assisting the interviewer in determining what questions to ask and how to evaluate responses'. As a consequence of their extensive literature review, Campion et al. identified 15 components of structure representative of two main categories: the actual content of the interview and evaluation of the content.

In a relatively sophisticated approach, each component can reflect a degree of structure, which ranges from highly structured to completely unstructured, and for any individual interview the permutations are considerable. Nevertheless, adopting a categorical approach may serve to structure a discussion of types of employment interview.

UNSTRUCTURED INTERVIEWS AS A SELECTION TOOL

The unstructured interview format has been reported as a very popular approach for personnel selection. The unstructured interview tends to devolve considerable power and freedom to interviewers to make important procedural decisions concerning the conduct of the interview itself and subsequent evaluations of information communicated. One of the more central aspects of interview conduct concerns the role of interviewer-led questions.

According to Campion, the derivation of questions employed in typical unstructured interviews is likely to be focused on personality traits or self-descriptions, traditional open-ended questions inviting candidates to talk about themselves and their strengths and weaknesses or indeed about anything the interviewer deems relevant, based on intuition or 'gut feelings' found that 34.5% of interviewers said they were free to ask anything they wanted to, and a further 49% selected questions flexibly from a prepared list of topics.

Unstructured interviews specify no standardisation of questioning sequence but rather delegate such control to the interviewer's discretion. It is usual for interviewers to be given complete freedom to decide whether follow-up, probing, or elaboration-type questions are required or not. Stevens reported that 55% of interviewers' questions were categorized as 'secondary follow-up probes', and Van Der Zee et al found that non-standardized follow-up questioning was employed by 78.2% of interviewers. Given that follow-ups are intended to clarify initial responses by candidates to interviewer questions, their use in the employment interview may serve a very important function in removing confusion and developing greater understanding. To this end, the employment of so-called neutral probes and elaborations, such as 'Go on', 'Could you say a bit more about that?', or 'Could you give me an example of ' may reduce information deficiencies yet not introduce irrelevant material.

As indicated earlier, interviewers working within an unstructured format are free to ask whatever questions they think are relevant to the purpose of the interview. Often questions are focused on seeking opinions, attitudes, goals, aspirations, self-descriptions, and self-evaluations. In general, such questions tend to be somewhat ambiguous and not always clearly related to purpose, although they are commonly employed. However, they do afford candidates ample opportunity to express themselves, present their credentials, and argue their case to the full, by what Kohn and Dipboye all giving candidates 'voice'.

Turning to the process of evaluating the responses elicited, unstructured interviews typically conclude with overall or global impressions being recorded. Van Der Zee et al reported that 89% of their interviewers did not utilise any rating scales for evaluating responses, and an overall global rating approach was adopted by 64%. According to Ganzach et al., such a procedure is less accurate than employing rating scales and some form of structured combination. When considering the effectiveness of unstructured interviews in the selection process, the literature reports inferior validity to more highly structured formats. There are a number of reasons for the poorer psychometric properties of unstructured interview formats as a means of selecting job applicants.

The inconsistent use and variable sequencing of primary questions and follow-ups about topics, which may not be job-relevant, conspire to reduce both reliability and validity of the procedure. Assessments made by unstructured techniques are more likely to focus on general mental ability, background credentials (educational and work histories), personality traits (such as agreeableness), social and communication skills, and physical attributes, some of which are poor predictors of job performance. However, interviewers using low structure formats do make trait assessments (for example, conscientiousness and emotional stability), and these subjective assessments are related to their evaluations of applicant suitability.

Interviewers need to be acutely aware of the immense difficulties in making accurate assessments of candidate personality, and of the pitfalls in making subsequent inferences from trait judgements to job performance. Moreover, interviewers may reach different conclusions based on similar applicant responses by applying varying judgement standards or by viewing the salience of specific traits differentially.

It is by no means clear whether job-related personality traits can be accurately assessed by unstructured interview formats, a fact which in turn reduces the predictive validity of this type of interview as a means of making selection decisions.Taking a slightly different approach to personality assessment, Blackman and Funder have focused attention away from the assessment of personality traits regarded as predictive of effective job performance and onto those traits that they termed 'counterproductive'. Rather than focusing on those attributes of knowledge and skills that are very specific to a particular job, attention is turned to a range of behaviours and attitudes that are largely unwanted in potential employees irrespective of the job in question.

For example, most employers would prefer their employees to be careful rather than careless in their work, and not to engage in theft, harassment, and even violence in the workplace. Early results from Blackman and Funder suggest that estimates of such unwanted traits and behaviours are better accomplished in unstructured interviews where the context facilitates a greater expression of quality information by the candidate.

A major consequence of using unstructured interview formats, which also may help to explain their poor psychometric properties, is the increased likelihood of introducing errors or what Campion describe as 'contamination'. Stevens identified six main types of selection error that serve to contaminate the content of information elicited in interviews and the evaluations made of it by interviewers.

- Halo effect, whereby interviewers tend to rate applicants highly on every dimension because they scored highly on one
- Central tendency, whereby interviewers rate all applicants as average and fail to use the whole of the scale
- Leniency, whereby interviewers rate all applicants favourably, again failing to discriminate effectively
- Strictness, whereby interviewers rate all applicants unfavourably
- Contrast effect, whereby the rating of applicants is influenced by how they compare to a previous applicant
- Stereotyping, whereby interviewers rely on initial impressions or schemas, set about confirming these impressions, and subsequently rate on this basis.

UNSTRUCTURED INTERVIEWS AS RECRUITMENT TOOLS

According to Posthuma, there is growing acknowledgement that the interview serves a recruitment as well as a selection function. The evidence to date suggests that interviews with less structure seem to be more suited to achieving the recruitment function. When unstructured interview formats are employed, applicants tend to rate the organisation and the interviewer more positively and indicate a greater willingness to accept any job offers that may ensue. It is possible that the more free-flowing conversational nature of unstructured interview formats creates a reaction in applicants that provides them with a greater sense of having had a chance to 'sell' themselves, of having been listened to, and determines a more positive reaction to the experience. Favourable impressions may have important outcomes such as enhancing the organisation's reputation, attracting more future applicants, and reducing the likelihood of lawsuits.

Therefore, in considering the psychometric qualities of interviews in the employment context, it seems crucial to do so with clarity of purpose to the fore. Investigations into the social processes involved in employment interviews have revealed a range of psychometric weakness related to poor reliability and low content and predictive validity, especially with respect to the selection function. As a result of these findings, research has focused on reducing the 'human' errors by developing alternative approaches to the unstructured interview. The direction of these developments has witnessed the introduction of increasing amounts of structure, and to varying degrees, the reduction of human discretion in the process.

STRUCTURED INTERVIEWS AS SELECTION TOOLS

The development of the structured selection interview emanated from attempts to design an interview in such a way as to reduce the possible influence of individual biases and errors on interviewer decisions. All major reviews have reported significant increases in both the reliability and validity of more highly structured approaches. As stated earlier, structuring may take many forms.

A number are specifically related to the question content of the interview. It is commonly agreed that all questions should be derived from a current job analysis, making all questions highly job-related. Gollub-Williamson et al. purport that this leads to 'increased content validity and reduces reliance on idiosyncratic beliefs about job requirements and reduces the likelihood of bias'. Furthermore, all job-related questions should be presented in a completely standardised manner and asked of all candidates in the same wording and invariant sequence. Campion et al. (1997) suggest that adopting standardised procedures serves to increase interview reliability (both internal consistency and interrater) and might ease the comparison between candidates and therefore improve validity. The reliance on highly job-related questions may further reduce the intrusion of irrelevant information and minimise the likelihood of interviewer biases adversely influencing selection decisions.

In the highly structured format, interviewers are prohibited from engaging in any prompting, probing, or elaboration questioning, but are simply required to present the primary questions and may, if necessary, only repeat the question for the candidate. However, Van Der Zee et al.found only a minority of their interviewers (20%) engaged in no follow-up questioning, and the majority (78%) largely omitted tandardisation of follow-up questioning. With structured interviews, it is possible to relax the degree of control and to permit a limited but agreed number of preplanned follow-ups worded in the same manner; for example, 'Is there anything else you would like to tell us'.

Considerable effort has been expended on developing particular types of questions for use in the highly structured selection interview context. As a result, two main types of questions have been developed, those that focus on past experience and those that orient the candidate toward the future. Each is hypothesised to possess predictive qualities, as the former is based on the assumption that past behaviour is the best predictor of future behaviour, and the latter is based on the assumption that goals or intentions are the best predictor of future behaviour. The two main question types have been characteristic of two related, structured-interviewing approaches, namely, the future-based 'situational interview' and the past-based 'patterned behaviour description interview'.

However, both approaches base the interview on a series of questions derived from job analyses and therefore the level of job-relatedness of the question content is high, possibly contributing to enhanced face, content, and predictive validity, and perceptions of fairness. In essence, the two approaches ask candidates to state either what they did do or what they would do when presented with predetermined work scenarios. Van Der found that interviewers reported employing hypothetical type questions least often, closely followed by past behaviour-oriented questions. Both types were included much less frequently than questions that focused on motivation, goals, ambitions, and previous work experience.

It may be useful to be selective in terms of choosing which approach to adopt, partly on the basis of the type of applicant being considered. If an applicant has little or no past work experience to draw upon, it might be more appropriate to use the situational interview approach, whereas, in the converse situation, the interviews that use reflection back to previous work experience and speculation forward to hypothetical scenarios are both possible.Within the highly structured approach, interviewers are required to employ highly structured rating procedures, facilitated by the use of specially designed rating scales provided for each interview question.

The rating scales constructed to 'score' the applicants' responses should be anchored scales with the anchor points identified through discussion with personnel and job experts. Completing specific rating scales for each question may serve to reduce the cognitive overload demanded of interviewers. The gains for reliability by using multiple ratings are strongly endorsed by Conway et al.

The evidence to date provides strong support for the validity of both types of structured interview in the selection process. Much of the research fails to find any significant differences between the approaches in terms of predictive validity, although an arguement that if the question types for the situational interview are properly constructed (that is, contain within them a work-related dilemma) and rating scales are utilised for evaluation, this approach demonstrates superior psychometric properties. Structured approaches were developed primarily to reduce subjectivity and inconsistency, to increase reliability and validity, and to guard against infringing legal guidelines pertaining to fair employment practice and reduce the likelihood of litigation. Although, as indicated above, structured approaches have demonstrated superior levels of reliability and validity with respect to selection decisions, there are some disadvantages associated with their use.

As observed, 'Highly structured interviews can appear to the applicant a bit like an interrogation, and may place too much emphasis on the selection objective at the expense of the attraction objective.' There is a growing body of evidence to suggest that highly structured approaches tend to decrease the attractiveness of organisations for candidates According to Kohn and Dipboye candidates may 'perceive an interview that is job-relevant and highly standardized as overly narrow' and incapable of enabling them to reveal their unique characteristics or to present fully their case for employment.

The belief that using highly structured interview formats may harm an organisation's ability to recruit has been one of the reasons offered by personnel for resisting their inclusion. Given the prevalent preference for recruiters to base applicant evaluation on 'intuition', 'feelings', 'experience', or 'body language' and to retain freedom and control over important decision-making and communication processes, the use of structured interviews may also create difficulties for these types of interviewers. They may not, according to Daniel and Valencia, wish to be viewed as 'a robot, an impersonal unfeeling scientific instrument', but prefer to be viewed as warm, attentive, likeable, and socially perceptive.

EMPLOYMENT INTERVIEWS AS SELECTION AND RECRUITMENT TOOLS

The extent to which employment interviews are able to meet both selection and recruitment functions seems more complex and somewhat conflicting. The drive toward greater psychometric qualities through higher levels of structuring serves the selection function admirably but may influence the recruitment function in a quite contrary manner.

However, there have been some suggestions that highly structured interviews do not assess all pertinent constructs in the selection process. For example, estimates of counter-productive work-relevant traits seem better achieved by adopting less structured interview formats.

Similarly, accurate assessment of person–environment fit constructs has been viewed as more likely if less structured interview formats are used. The selection versus recruitment dilemma has been widely studied. What seems to be the case is that choosing to adopt either a highly structured or an unstructured interview format will fail to meet some of the objectives of employment interviewing. In order to offer the best compromise, where predictive validity for selection can be adequate and applicant reactions mainly positive, greater flexibility of approach is necessary.

As observed, 'some balance is needed between concerns about the psychometric integrity of interviewer assessments and providing applicants the opportunity to present fully their qualifications.' In general, there are two major possibilities. The first is to modify the degree of structure within a single interview.

Here the rigid standardization of administration is reduced, thereby allowing candidates more opportunity to 'sell themselves'. This includes encouraging interviewees to ask more questions by, for example, incorporating a less formal and more interpersonal discussion stage at the end of the interview. Campion et al. suggest, 'In practice, it is not likely that the sole use of just one question type is desirable. As long as different types have adequate validity, a range of questions offer variety for both the candidate and interviewer.' These modifications may soften the impression of rigid structuring, increase perceptions of fairness, and reduce negative candidate (and interviewer) reactions.

The second major alternative is to carry out more than

one interview, each with its own specific purpose. Even with selection in mind, there may be a case for at least two interviews, each carried out for different purposes. For example, Blackman and Funder (2002) suggest that employers should initially screen applicants by a more structured interview format to predict future job performance and, for those who are successful at this stage, to add a second unstructured interview to estimate their job-related personality attributes, including counter-productive traits.

There have also been suggestions to separate the selection and recruitment functions and offer two employment interviews, each adopting differing levels of interview structure.It was suggested that by using two interviews, 'one designed strictly for prediction and the other designed to allow an informal question-and-answer session to meet the needs of applicants'.

Whatever type of interview format has been utilised, it is always important to consider the disengagement scene or closure of the interview. The nature of selection interviews, where decisions have not yet been formally taken about the suitability of the candidate for the job, requires a cautious closure. It would seem important that this phase of the interview should acknowledge the effort invested and participation by the interviewee in the interview, yet this must be achieved in a 'neutral' way so as not to raise expectations.

Conventional practice typically allows applicants the opportunity to ask questions at this stage, although highly structured approaches recommend that this be carried out in a separate interview with a personnel representative to ensure that only job related information is considered for the purposes of reaching a selection decision. In somewhat less structured methods, applicant questions may be regarded as an important source of information and exert a positive influence on candidate impressions.

In summary, the role of selection interviewers requires them to assume substantial responsibility for convening and conducting the interview. Therefore, it is vital that they are knowledgeable about interview tactics and skilled in the utilization of interpersonal communication skills. Indeed, less structured interview formats often consist of what call 'free-flowing exchanges between the interviewer and applicant'. Effective interviewers need to focus attention on both the technical qualities of their procedures and on the social context in which candidate recruitment and selection takes place. The extent to which objectives are attained is not simply a function of interviewer competence but is also influenced by the effectiveness of applicants in playing their role. It is to this aspect that we now turn.

APPLICANT'S PERSPECTIVE

Given that the employment interview remains the most widely used recruitment tool for applicants, an inescapable part of the route to future employment. As a result of the information gained during personal interaction with each applicant, interviewers make decisions about the person best suited to the available post. It has been shown that what applicants do and say in an interview has an impact on interviewer's ratings. Therefore, it is understandable that individuals will want to use the opportunity and the time allotted to them in the interview to create as positive an impression as possible. Here, the applicant's role in impression management is reviewed.

Impression management in the employment interview Impression management has been defined as 'the conscious or unconscious attempt to construct and portray a particular image by controlling the information available to others (i.e. targets) so that they will view the actor as he or she intended'. According to Ralston and Kirkwood, 'Whenever we attempt to influence how others see us, we are engaging in impression management.' Nowhere are self-presentation or impression-management strategies more prevalent than in the employment interview.

IMPRESSION-MANAGEMENT STRATEGIES

Many factors contribute to candidates' attempts to shape and control the image they project in the interview context.

Both verbal and non-verbal impression-management tactics can be crucial to success or failure in the employment interview. Impression management may indeed be a necessary part of employment interviews; if applicants are to ensure that their subjective qualifications are perceived positively, 'impression management techniques play an even greater role in the interview process than previously suspected'.

In general, there appear to be two main categories of self-presentation behaviour, namely, assertive and defensive. The terms 'offensive' and 'defensive' were adopted by Liden and Parsons to reflect a similar dichotomy. Assertive tactics can be either self-focused, whereby attention is focused on the interviewee, or other-focused, whereby attention is focused on the interviewer. In terms of assertive, self-focused tactics, those who wish to embellish their qualifications and minimise their weaknesses will use:

- Self-promotion: engaging in positive self-descriptions about skills, knowledge, and abilities
- Entitlements: exaggerating responsibility for positive life experiences and achievements
- Enhancements: giving an event pronounced value or significance to enhance its importance.

Other-focused assertive strategies described by Ellis et al include ingratiation tactics utilised by applicants when they wish to cultivate interpersonal liking and attraction between themselves and the interviewer. These include opinion conformity (expressing opinions, beliefs, or values that are thought to match those of the interviewer) and other enhancement (praising or flattering the interviewer in order to raise their self-esteem). Referring to defensive tactics, Ellis et al. outlined three that are designed to save face or bolster an individual's image. That is, when they find their mage under threat from the interviewer, interviewees will offer excuses (claim no responsibility for a negative outcome), justifications (accept responsibility but diminish the negative aspects), or apologies (accept responsibility and acknowledge the need for restitution).

Accordingly the advantage in adopting self-focused tactics is that 'applicants can focus the direction of their interviews' content on areas which will allow them to excel, hence creating as positive an impression as possible'. Perhaps the applicants use positive self-focused tactics (self-promotion) more frequently than other impression-management tactics, and supports the assertion by Gilmore and Ferris and Kacmar that self-promotion produces positive outcomes in the interview situation.

For example, Kristof-Brown found that self-promoting behaviours led interviewers to see applicants as a good fit and potentially more hireable. Given that interviewers attempt to assess the degree of fit between the applicant and the organisation, applicants who cultivate the perception that there is congruence between their values and that of the organisation are more likely to receive job offers.

In addition, it show that the type of question posed by the interviewer influences the type of impression-management tactic selected. For example, the use of self-promotion is more likely in response to experience-based questions than situational-based questions (e.g. 'Suppose you were... How would you address this situation?'). In this case, situational-based questions incurred more ingratiation tactics, particularly opinion conformity.

Candidates should be aware that the overuse of self-promotion tactics can backfire. The evidence indicates that interviewers may regard those who over-indulge in such tactics as disingenuous. In particular, Kacmar and Carlson warn applicants against the use of other-focused impression-management tactics, because such tactics receive lower ratings than self-focused tactics in the interview situation.

Highlighting the importance of what is said in the interview, Silvester found that successful candidates were those who made stable and personal attributions for previous negative events, whereas less successful candidates used defensive tactics in the same situation. The impact of impression management on fairness in the employment interview

Consideration needs to be given to whether successful execution of impression-management tactics could lead to unfairness in employment interview outcomes. Commenting on the harmful consequences of impression management, Ralston and Kirkwood (1999) argued that deceitful or inaccurate information that is intended to mislead interviewers can undermine the value of the interview. On one hand, self-promoting behaviours could be regarded as harmless and positive when they represent a true picture of the applicant's nature and character. At the other end of the continuum, attempts to create an impression through deceit will have negative consequences.

For example, feigning motivation, other-directedness, or interpersonal attraction, unless spotted by the interviewer, will lead to error in the selection process. While they may not be setting out to deceive, by engaging in these tactics, applicants portray the appropriate image for the post, and if they are appointed on the basis of their performance, the behaviour may lead to an error in interviewer judgement.

In order to increase fairness in employment interviews, was suggested that impression-management tactics that are 'deceptive, manipulative and insincere' need to be 'detected, minimized and discounted'. The paradox is that, while image building is an inherent part of the interview process and is to some extent a requirement for success, it is necessary for interviewers to be sensitive to self-presentation tactics if they are to make sound judgements about candidates who attend for interview.

MEDIATORS AND INFLUENCES ON THE EMPLOYMENT

The employment interview as a method of selection and recruitment provides applicants with the opportunity to interact personally with a potential employer and, based on their experience of the interview, make decisions about the company. However, many factors affect this experience and can have an influence on the process and outcome for the interviewee. These include personal characteristics such as personality, physical appearance, and speech style. The impact of each of these factors on applicants' experiences in employment interviews is now considered.

Personal Characteristics

Before candidates present themselves for interview, recruiters already have established a 'picture' of the individual from the information available to them, usually by way of the application form and/or curriculum vitae. The interview itself is the opportunity for candidates to present themselves in person to the recruiter. Many personal factors of the candidate are then 'visible' and under the scrutiny of the interviewer. It is these factors and their influence on the employment interview that we now turn to, including personality, physical appearance, speech style and confident communication.

Personality

Turning first to the influence of personality, Cook stated that the 'personality characteristics of the interviewee play an important role in the evaluation of the interviewee's performance and the outcomes of the interview'. For example, personality characteristics such as type A/achievement, extroversion, and internal locus of control are associated with positive interview performance and outcome.

Examining the relationship between personality and success in interviewing, Caldwell and Burger utilised the 'Big Five' personality markers (neuroticism, extroversion, openness, agreeableness, and conscientiousness) and found a link between personality and the likelihood of being employed. Firstly, inferences are drawn about an applicant's personality from how they behave in the interview. Secondly, research supports the notion that the personality of candidates influences how they prepare for an interview, and 'this preparation was related to interview success'.

Applicants perform better when interviewers exhibit a 'warm personality'. That is, as a consequence of positive non-verbal interviewer behaviour (head nods, smiling), applicants make a better impression and receive higher ratings. Similarly, the findings of Papadopoulou indicated that applicants perceived interviewers who were willing to provide information as 'warm and thoughtful'. In turn, it was the provision of information about the job and the company that influenced applicants' decisions to take up a job offer.

Physical Appearance

Physical appearance has an impact on hiring decisions, in that recruiters make decisions about candidates based on appearance. In this respect, two aspects, body decoration and obesity factors, seem to be important. Attempts to portray a particular image can have negative consequences for the individual. Shepperd and Kwavnick (1999) pointed out that body piercing (and tattoos) may be viewed as symbols of rebellion or recklessness. Even the most trivial of cues (a small piece of jewellery, such as an earring) or body piercing (especially noserings) may disadvantage candidates through their being rated as less sociable, trustworthy, and hireable. Furthermore, perceptions of men with jewellery may be more negative than those of women.

It seems that how an applicant's image is regarded and evaluated depends on the attitude of the recruiter. Referring to non-work-related factors (e.g. personal appearance) that are evaluated in the interview, Shannon and Stark stated: 'If the interviewer has any previously acquired dispositions to evaluate certain characteristics with a positive or negative bias, these acquired dispositions, or attitudes, could influence the interviewer's overall evaluation of the applicant.' Perhaps the increasing popularity of piercings will lead to more acceptability in the workplace, and applicants choosing certain image markers will be less disadvantaged since, as expressed 'Fashion changes over time as do attire rules and expectations.'

It could be argued that employers who do not revise their policies on personal image and dress codes may risk losing potentially excellent employees. Meanwhile, the indications are that candidates in the process of seeking employment should be aware of the expectations of recruiters in terms of dress code and appearance in order to avoid the negative consequences of lower ratings in the interview – or make choices about which firms to apply to.

The belief or perception that overweight or obese people are responsible for their condition could help to explain why overweight applicants are often rejected for jobs. Pingitore found that interview ratings for obese (versus non-obese) applicants were more likely to be unfavourable, particularly if interviewers (male or female) were conscious of their own body.

Polinko and Popovich suggested, 'Obesity discrimination may occur, first, from the lack of fit between the expectation of an overweight individual's abilities and second, the perceived reality of the job's requirements in terms of skills and abilities.' However, the findings overall indicate a positive shift in discrimination against hiring overweight applicants, despite more negative work-related attributes being attributed to them (e.g. lazy, unattractive). This may be due to a greater awareness of legislation relating to discrimination in employment interviews.

Speech Style and Communication Apprehension (CA)

In the highly evaluative conditions of the employment interview, competence in communicating has a bearing on how applicants are perceived by the interviewer. Specifically, perceptions of communication ability are influenced by factors such as non-standard accents, and style and confidence levels of the candidate.

In relation to non-standard accents, Cargile stated: 'Language attitudes research has consistently demonstrated that individuals with non-standard accents are judged to be less suitable for high-status jobs and more suitable for low-status jobs.' Despite this expectation, Cargile found that Chinese-accented and Anglo-American speakers were rated equally suitable for a (technical) job, and the lack of discrimination was particularly evident for one high-status job in particular – information systems trainee.

However, Chinese-accented speakers were judged to be less suitable for posts in human resources.In terms of speech style, powerful versus powerless speech was examined by Parton et al. (2002). Professional (and undergraduate) respondents evaluated interviewees' dynamism, social attractiveness, superiority, control over self, control over others, and employability. Evidence suggested that those with a powerful speech style were rated more favourably, particularly by professionals. Parton argued that, as 'impression formation is vital to interview success', interviewees should receive training in verbal presentation including powerful speech.

Such training may also be helpful to those who have difficulty in communicating due to anxiety. In the interview situation, characteristics that are rated highly include confidence, fluency, controlled energy, and body language.

Applicants who are unable to demonstrate these characteristics, that is, those with high communication apprehension (CA), may be disadvantaged in the employment interview. High CAs employ verbal and non-verbal avoidant behaviour (talk less, have reduced eye contact, are less fluent, and ask fewer questions) compared to low CAs; hence, they may be judged as ineffective communicators and consequently unsuitable for the job. If, found, high CAs think about and prepare differently for interviews from their low-CA counterparts, perhaps training for high CAs would help to minimise the impact of CA in critical situations such as the employment interview and help applicants to strengthen their communication skills.

THE EXPERIENCES OF SPECIFIC GROUPS IN THE

Research in employment interviews has addressed the experiences of specific groups, such as candidates with disabilities and applicants from various racial and ethnic backgrounds. Consideration of such groups is warranted here as research findings relating to interview outcomes are inconsistent. Difficulties in employment interviews still persist for people with disabilities. While some research has shown that those with a disability are viewed as less employable than those without a disability, others have found that disabled applicants have been rated equal or better than their non-disabled counterparts. For example, Bordieri demonstrated that, regardless of being equally qualified, an employee with depression would be less likely to be recommended for promotion, while Rumrill found that applicants with insulin-dependent diabetes would be rated similar to other applicants when rated by rehabilitation counsellors.

Examining the factors that led to interviewers' hiring decisions for applicants with and without disabilities, Hayes and Macan (1997) found that similar factors were used to determine outcomes with both groups (i.e. preinterview impression, attractiveness, likeability, qualifications, self-presentation, employability).

In particular, employability seemed important in decision making about both sets of applicants. However, for the disabled group, preinterview impressions were significantly related to perceptions of self-presentation in the interview. That is, how disabled persons present themselves on paper and in person in the interview relates to interviewers' post-interview evaluations. For instance, Wright and Multon identified the positive influence of candidate non-verbal communication skills for ratings of traits related to employability, such as assertiveness.

The phenomenon of positive bias toward those with disabilities has been explained in a number of ways. For example, Marchioro and Bartels qualified their finding that no differences were found in attitudes to disabled or non-disabled job interviewees, in terms of social appropriateness. That is, in their desire to provide socially acceptable answers, participants may have 'overcompensated' for negative attitudes toward disabled candidates by giving higher ratings. Similarly, Bell and Klein suggested that the 'norm to be kind' theory could explain the positively biased outcome for disabled applicants. As they stated: 'This norm suggests that one should never do anything that would be unpleasant to persons with a disability'.

That little has changed for the disabled applicant in terms of discrimination was confirmed by Duckett: 'discrimination in employment interviews is very much apparent in the experiences of disabled people'. When he interviewed disabled applicants about their experiences of employment interviews, he found that they described the process in terms of a 'struggle' or 'battle' with the 'odds stacked against them'. Therefore, the indications are that neither the positive bias toward people with disabilities highlighted by research nor the introduction of legislation, as for example in the USA and the UK to protect the rights of disabled people, has yet to affect the experiences of disabled applicants in search of a career. In competing for jobs, candidates with disabilities may be tempted to withhold information that they perceive as potentially damaging to their chances of success in an employment interview.

However, discussing disabilities during the interview could contribute to relationship building and hence lead to more positive impressions and improve the likelihood of being selected for the post. Therefore, educating an interviewer about the nature of a disability through open and honest discussion may be more beneficial than non-disclosure. In the light of this, the indications by Arvonio that applicants are likely to provide information about their disability in job applications and during job interviews is a step in the right direction and may improve the selection process for both interviewers and interviewees.

RACE AND ETHNICITY

The findings of studies investigating the experiences of racial groups in employment interviews are varied. For example, in a meta-analysis of 31 studies, Huffcutt and Roth (1998) found ratings for both black and Hispanic applicants to be only marginally lower than those for white applicants. Additionally, the more highly structured the interview, the lower the group differences. Similarly, Collins and Gleaves found no differences for blacks and whites on measures of personality structure and mean scores on agreeableness and conscientiousness. While studies show a lack of racial bias in hiring decisions, prejudice against minority groups still exists. In a previous study assessing promotion potential across race and gender, Landau found blacks and Asians to be rated lower than whites, and females to be rated lower than males. Hence, interviewer/interviewee racial similarity influences interview outcomes. In addition, racial similarity will have a significant effect on applicants' evaluations of the recruiters.

INTERVIEWER TRAINING

Given that the recruiter plays a critical role in the process and outcomes in employment interviews, it is important that human-resource managers or those involved in selecting or promoting should be trained for the role. Interviewing is a cognitively demanding process requiring interviewers to self-regulate (monitor thoughts and actions) (Nordstrom, 1996). Therefore, it would seem likely that the more prepared interviewers are for the task, the better they will execute it. Training can have a positive effect on recruiters' perceptions of their interpersonal effectiveness.

The power and influence of recruiter behaviour on applicants' perceptions has been demonstrated. Recruiter behaviour affects perceptions of the organisation and attractiveness of the job and on decisions about whether to accept a job offer. However, more than any other aspect of the interview (e.g. structure or focus), recruiter behaviour influences applicants' perceptions of the employer. Training could ensure that recruiters are aware of the impact of their behaviour on job applicants and perhaps help them to become more fully informed about procedures and issues pertinent to employment interviews, including impression management, discrimination, and legislation.

It has been suggested that providing interviewers with training may contribute to enhanced interview validity, because trained interviewers tend to make better use of their interview time by asking more relevant and discerning, and less irrelevant, tangential, or potentially discriminatory questions, and this in turn elicits more high-quality information upon which more sound judgements can be based In addition, it seems important that interviewers learn to utilise selection and recruitment procedures and methods correctly, whatever system is adopted.

Looking at impression management, it was suggested that 'Even intelligent, critical interviewers can be duly influenced by applicants who display impression management behaviour.' However, Howard and Ferris support the notion that training could help interviewers to distinguish between insincere and genuine applicants. Perhaps Rosenfeld's suggestion of interviewer training in 'tactical and strategic impression management' would help achieve this goal.

That is, if interviewers placed more emphasis on strategic impression management (i.e. candidate's work history, abilities, and achievements that relate to characteristics such as credibility, competence, and trustworthiness) than on the instant, short-term tactics used by candidates to create a positive image (smiling, eye contact, etc.), it would help recruiters to make fairer decisions. Therefore, if the interview focused on applicants' accounts of themselves to determine their suitability for the job, interviewers' decisions would be less distorted. Additionally, it has been suggested that job-related questions and probes about past and future performance may help to create a balance and help interviewers to overcome applicants' overzealous use of impression-management tactics.

Training could also address a call for interviewers to re-evaluate their attitudes to impression management. Such a re-evaluation would help interviewers to see an applicant's ability to employ tactics as a skill rather than an obstacle and that it might be an indication of their ability to do the job. From this perspective, an applicant's self-presentation behaviours could be a reflection of future performance in the working environment. As suggested that in terms of making judgements about applicants with disabilities, interviewers require training that would help to increase their knowledge of disabilities and disability legislation.

Training could also help to develop positive attitudes toward applicants with disabilities and help interviewers' comfort levels with disabled people, given that perceived interviewer discomfort has been found to exacerbate anxiety and nervousness on the part of disabled people. It is important also that training should address interviewers' 'acquired dispositions' or 'attitudes' that affect interview outcomes. Finally, comment is required on legal and ethical issues as they relate to employment interviewing.

LEGAL ISSUES

Considerable and increasing focus has been placed on the extent to which recruitment and selection procedures have complied with legal requirements. Issues appear to be related to two aspects of employment interviewing. First, the extent to which candidates are treated the same as all other applicants, with no discriminatory intent or disparate treatment. Second, the extent to which applicants are regarded similarly to other comparison groups with no disparate impact. Although specific findings are sparse, as indicated, that interview procedures that display characteristics of a structured approach tend to be more related to successful court rulings in favour of employers.

In keeping with procedural justice literature, those aspects of employment interviewing that increase the chances of defeating a legal challenge are principally to do with its job-relatedness, objectivity, question type and structure (preferably situational or behaviour description), rating criteria and response scales, and use of trained interviewers. Second, standardisation and consistency of the administration processes, which provides strong guidelines and minimal discretion to interviewers, is also significant in the eyes of judges. In conclusion, the 'Empirical findings together with the conceptual analysis suggest that structuring the interview might enhance the ability to withstand legal challenge.'

ETHICAL ISSUES

Despite the drive to enhance validity related to the

selection function and improve the chances of successful defence against litigation, the employment interview as experienced by applicants also requires attention from an ethical point of view. Issues of openness, self-disclosure, and invasion oı privacy constitute important sources of ethical questions. A major function of interviewers is to collect as much relevant applicant information as possible prior to making selection decisions. However, what comprises relevant and non-discriminatory information must be carefully considered lest interviewers infringe not only the individual rights of applicants but also the law. It is here that careful structuring approaches, described earlier, may be invaluable in focusing on job-related domains and preventing interviewers from straying into highly subjective and potentially biasing areas.

However, according to Poteet and Wilson, the use of illegal questioning persists and indeed may be widespread, the most common topic areas being criminal record, age, and disabilities. Less common areas are related to marital/family status, religion, sex, national origin, and race. Wilson also noted that many candidates are unaware that certain questions are illegal and generally acceded to the interviewers' requests for information. If applicants perceive such questions as relevant and receive a favourable interview outcome, the request for such information is less likely to be regarded as an invasion of privacy.

For applicants unhappy about the use of certain illegal and potentially discriminatory questions, Wilson set out a number of possible applicant strategies, all but one of which seeks to do 'the least damage to the interviewee's candidacy'. The choice of strategy depends on the perceived use of the information, the importance of revealing the information to the interviewer, and the desire to secure the job, and ranges from terminating the interview or directly refusing to answer, to expressing concern about the question and then responding to the question itself.

The extent to which applicants assert themselves and feel that they have provided what they regard as salient personal information may also be crucially dependent on the power relationships in the situation. Generally speaking, the distribution of power in selection interviews is not equal, the greater power residing with the interviewer. This may be particularly evident where highly structured procedures are employed, whereby applicants are required to respond to interviewer-initiated questions, to choose from interviewer-provided response alternatives, and never to put any personal questions to the interviewer.

As noted, 'Inevitably, where there is power there lies the potential for its abuse and hence for unethical behaviour that violates the rights of the individual.' Interviewers who, inadvertently or not, treat applicants in ways that would be detrimental to their performance by inducing states of discomfort, lowered self-esteem, stress, or anger are behaving unethically. This, ultimately, will prove to be counter-productive in the sense that applicants will be unable to display their potential qualities, will be unimpressed with the organisation's representative, and may be less likely to accept offers of employment.

OVERVIEW

This chapter presented research pertaining to the employment interview as a specific example of a complex social interaction governed by a number of rules and regulations to which participants are expected to conform, and which seeks to serve the dual purpose of recruitment and selection. The focus of the material initially dealt ith the employment interview from the interviewer's perspective, setting out the issues relating to the various approaches found to be relevant for practice. This was followed by a similar focus on the role played by the applicant in the employment interview, particularly the influence of impression management. Finally, a brief consideration was given to additional influential factors, the issue of training, and selected legal and ethical issues as they relate to the employment interview context.

Chapter 15

Appraisal Interview Reappraised

APPRAISAL INTERVIEWS

Performance appraisal has been optimistically defined as the process of identifying, observing, measuring, and developing human resources in organisations. It is often sold as a means of promoting two-way communication, showing employees respect by demonstrating that their opinions count, and helping to uncover and resolve conflict. Feedback is intended to provide employees with information to improve their personal performance and effectiveness. Thus, historically, appraisal interviews were intended to focus on three areas – development, motivation, and recognition of achievement.

Formal performance appraisal, at its best, has therefore been defined as 'a means for managers to identify and reward positive performance, promote a unified focus on the achievement of business goals and provide support for the personal development needs of employees'. In practice, organisations tend to have a host of other aspirations for their appraisal systems, including differentiating between employees to establish individual remuneration, the identification of training needs, and assessing suitability for promotion.

In fact, this constitutes one of the biggest problems with traditional appraisals – like a truck overloaded with freight, and thus prone to capsize, the range of expectations invested in them has imbalanced the entire enterprise. For example, it is difficult to convince people that an appraisal interview is primarily developmental in purpose if promotion decisions also depend on the outcome. It is therefore unsurprising that Rees and Porter note, 'Unfortunately, the available evidence is that most schemes do not work effectively.'

Traditionally, and in most of the literature, the term 'performance appraisal' has generally come to mean 'the annual interview that takes place between the manager and the employee to discuss the individual's job performance during the previous 12 months and the compilation of action plans to encourage improved performance'. It is, at any rate, an innocuous-sounding ambition.

The idea that performance appraisal interviews are valuable remains a seductive notion for many managers. In part, this is because evaluating the performance of others is a pervasive activity in which all people routinely engage during most of their interpersonal interactions. Organisational appraisal systems are often regarded as nothing more than 'an attempt to formalise these activities for the benefit of both the individual and the organisation'.

This chapter will shortly appraise the extent to which this hope is realised in practice.Meanwhile, the scope of appraisal has developed rapidly. A Superboss report, which surveyed over 120 businesses in the UK, found that 89% had a formal performance appraisal system in place. It has been estimated that over 94% of US companies use some form of formal performance appraisal. A survey of 280 Midwest companies in the USA found that 25% used annual upward appraisals, 18% peer appraisals, and 12% what are known as 360-degree appraisals, in which people evaluate themselves and then receive feedback from their immediate peers, managers, and subordinates.

They have become a global phenomenon. For example, appraisals have been widely used in China since the country initiated a programme of economic reform. Zhu and Dowling (1998) concluded that 74.8% of Chinese firms carried out annual performance appraisals, presumably because they imagined that these had contributed to economic growth in the West. It is a wonder, with so many appraisal interviews being conducted, that anyone finds the time to make sure that the real work of the organisation gets done.

Designed to overpower some of the bugbears associated with traditional appraisals, 360-degree appraisals have also become a huge growth area in recent years. It has been argued that they offer multiple benefits, since multisource feedback is assumed to provide better performance information, more reliable ratings than what can be obtained from a single supervisor, and improved satisfaction by appraisees after the process is complete. Key companies, such as AT&T, the Bank of America, Caterpillar, GTE, and General Electric, have been pioneers in this latter approach. Given these tendencies, estimate that appraisal interviews are used in about 80% of organisations – although they also estimate that about 90% of appraisers and appraisees are dissatisfied with them.

APPRAISAL INTERVIEWS – THE CRITIQUE

As already noted, research suggests that appraisal interviews are generally ineffective. Many, probably most, are demotivational, divisive, pseudo-scientific, and counterproductive. One typical study, investigating performance appraisal in a public sector organisation, found over 40% of staff dissatisfied with the system, including many who received good or outstanding ratings as a result of it. Among the most common problems are a lack of strategic focus, too much subjectivity on the part of appraisers, an insufficient level of skills on the part of managers, an accumulation of power by potential tyrants, who relish the opportunity to pass judgement on others, and a tendency to deliver criticisms of poor performance too long after the event to have an appreciable impact on outcomes.

Appraisal interviews also tend to focus on individual performance, despite the fact that more work is now conducted in teams and that responsibility is therefore more widely diffused than in the past. Edmonstone identifies two other crucial problems with appraisal interviews and systems. Firstly, managers are encouraged to focus on current performance rather than future potential, through an emphasis on short-term results. Secondly, appraisals discourage multiskilling in favour of tight specification and detailed evaluations. In today's business environment, it is necessary for people to demonstrate behaviours consistent with such notions as flexibility, willingness to take charge, and tolerance for uncertainty, beyond their immediate tasks in a job description. It is ironic that managers used to chafe at trade union insistence on rigid demarcations. Appraisals may well reinstate such demarcations, by encouraging people to focus their efforts only on those aspects of performance likely to be recognised and rewarded in appraisal interviews.

A further difficulty lies in determining precisely what employees have done, and hence the extent of their contribution to organisational success or failure. For example, long-distance appraisals in multinational corporations encounter the problem that 'the staff involved at headquarters may have difficulty forging a precise image of the circumstances in which the various subsidiaries have had to operate to achieve their results. Consequently, the context of performance may be lost'. With the elimination of many middle-management posts over the past few decades and a consequent widening in the numbers of direct reports that most managers are now responsible for, this problem goes beyond MNCs.

Put simply, many managers are in no position to deliver cogent, well-informed evaluations of the performance of others. Moreover, it is probable that any attempt to do so undermines the sense of autonomy and intrinsic task motivation that is essential in many modern workplaces.Given the fact that line managers are often under-prepared to handle the interview process, and are confused about how to give critical feedback, the interview (theoretically, the climax of the appraisal process) is also widely regarded as its Achilles heel. It is little wonder that 'appraisals have become one of the most avoided experiences in organisational life. Supervisors do not like to give them and employees do not like to receive them'.

Appraisal interviews are often linked to evaluation of

performance in the form of 'rating systems'. Here, performance is graded on a scale, normally of 1 to 5, with 5 representing excellent performance and 1 representing grounds for dismissal. Problems with this are legion. They include:

- The grave difficulty in accurately assessing the details of someone's performance. Results are frequently a team effort. How do we disentangle the extent of each individual's contribution? What happens if we credit one person with all the achievement, when others may think that they put in the same or greater effort? If ratings are awarded which people think are unfair, the 'unfair rating' will become the issue, rather than necessary improvements in performance. Moreover, such approaches threaten to detract from other team-building efforts that may have been made. It is difficult to reconcile team responsibility and commitments with an emphasis on individual responsibility.
- How does one measure intangible factors such as motivation, creativity, team spirit, responsibility, and loyalty? Subjective impressions of performance on these issues tend to govern the ratings that are awarded. As discuss below many of the biases that illuminate why subjectivity is endemic to appraisal interviews – in my view, inescapably so. Typically, the impossibility of escaping subjective assessments makes the eventual 'grade' appear arbitrary to the person receiving it, and so leads to destructive conflict over the assessment awarded, rather than an emphasis on identifying developmental needs.
- When everyone knows that a grade is at stake, the emphasis of the meeting shifts from an open discussion of performance (in which both strengths and weaknesses can be honestly discussed) toward the optimum presentation of the self, the covering up of errors, and inflated claims for one's own performance. Naturally, this will involve a greater

reluctance to accept feedback on areas where performance needs to improve. The outcome of appraisal interviews has also often been linked to the award of performance-related pay. Many of the points made in opposition to the use of rating schemes also apply here. In the first place, such practices contradict what is known about motivation. Intrinsic motivation, which is most closely correlated with superior performance, flows from the satisfaction obtained by performing the task at hand, rather than doing it to obtain rewards extrinsic to the task itself. Performance is likely to deteriorate when the emphasis shifts from intrinsic motivation to the gaining of extrinsic rewards. There is, therefore, no evidence that tying performance to pay actually improves performance – rather, the opposite is the case.

Linking appraisal to pay in this manner generally transforms feedback into confrontation. Consider the following. In practice, organisations find it difficult to pay more than a limited proportion of people much more than the budgeted average for any given job. The financial gains on offer from such systems therefore tend to be nominal and/or restricted to a small number of people. The majority of an organisation's employees are more likely to emerge from what almost inevitably becomes an adversarial process nursing wounded egos and bearing feelings of resentment. One reason is that most people do not rate their own performance as either average or below average – in fact, they exaggerate their contribution to organisational success.

The use of performance-related pay as part of the appraisal process means that managers use appraisal interviews to inform the majority of their people that their performance is much weaker than they themselves imagine it to be – an outcome which may also activate a large number of destructive, self-fulfilling prophecies. For these reasons, the evidence suggests that a system of performance-related pay demotivates people, that it does not help organisations to retain high performers, does not encourage poor performers to leave, and creates widespread perceptions of unfairness. It heightens status differentials between managers and employees, and threatens working relationships. In consequence, and perhaps counter-intuitively, performance-related pay (particularly when linked to appraisal) generally fails to improve organisational effectiveness. At the very least, the evidence unambiguously suggests that any discussion of training and development issues should be entirely separate from whatever mechanisms are used to determine remuneration.

An illuminating example of what happens when this research is ignored may be in order. Enron was an organisation that combined both a ranking system and the linking of performance to pay. Its bankruptcy in 2001 stands (at the time of writing) as the biggest in US corporate history. As with many other aspects of its internal culture, its approach to appraisal is a valuable case study in what not to do. An internal performance review committee rated employees twice a year. They were graded on a scale of 1 to 5, on 10 separate criteria, and then divided into one of three groups – 'A's, who were to be challenged and given large rewards; 'B's, who were to be encouraged and affirmed; and 'C's, who were told to shape up or ship out. Those in the 'A' category were referred to internally as 'water walkers'.

The process was known as 'rank and yank'. The company's propensity to disproportionately reward those who were high achievers and risk-takers was widely acclaimed by business gurus. Faculty from the prestigious Harvard Business School produced 11 case studies, uniformly praising its successes. However, problems multiplied. People chased high rankings because the potential rewards were enormous, while low rankings imperilled both their salaries and eventually their jobs. The appearance of success mattered more than its substance. In addition, internal promotions due to the appraisal system reached 20% a year. This made further evaluation more difficult and inevitably more subjective – how could one honestly rank someone's performance when they did not hold a position long enough to render sound judgement possible? Paradoxically, Enron had a punitive internal regime ('rank and yank') but loose control (those adjudged to be top performers moved on too fast to be pinned down). In this case, ratings and performance pay formed a lethal mix. Internal staff churn and a relentless emphasis on achieving high performance ratings in the interests of obtaining ever-greater personal rewards contributed to the lax ethical atmosphere that precipitated the company's downfall.

Versions of rank and yank have been used by many organisations, including General Electric and IBM. IBM, in the early 1990s, actually required that one out of every 10 employees be allocated a poor rating, and given 3 months to improve or be fired. The research evidence overwhelmingly suggests that such practices produce only defiance, defensiveness, and rage. As Kohn has noted, 'Threatening people can make them anxious about the consequences of doing poorly, but the fear of failure is completely different from the desire to succeed'. Praise can be used to emphasise that a culture of retribution belongs to the past, and is therefore much more likely to have a positive impact on performance. It is, however, important that praise is not overdone.

If it is, people may begin to perform tasks for the praise involved, and so find that their intrinsic motivation goes down. Its main value is a signal that authoritarian management holds no sway in the organisation concerned. The main enemy of innovation, effort, and achievement in the workplace is fear. In short, there is absolutely no evidence that either threatening to cut people's pay, or offering to increase it significantly, improves the quality, as opposed to possibly the quantity, of what they do.

However, illusions still linger, and some organisations now seek sustenance in technology. It has been argued that new software systems enable companies to monitor individual productivity more accurately (and less subjectively), and so target rewards on genuine top performers. Among the

companies taking this route are Hewlett-Packard, General Electric, and DuPont. Moreover, it has been suggested that people experience less evaluation apprehension and less emotion when they receive feedback via a computer system.

Such systems can also focus the attention of raters on job-relevant behaviours, thereby reducing interpersonal biases. However, it has also been found that self-ratings are more inflated and less accurate in electronic communication than face-to-face interaction. Greater objectivity could be at the expense of sensitivity, since it removes the direct opportunity to monitor the reaction of recipients. Thus, appraisal remains primarily a human issue. People's feelings about it are unlikely to change at the sight of managers brandishing spreadsheets. Technology has yet to overcome the problems associated with rating systems, the linking of performance to pay, and the challenge of providing people with meaningful feedback that enables them to change their behaviour.

BIASES IN INTERPERSONAL PERCEPTION

It can be argued that 'the biggest challenge that impedes an effective performance review is the biases we all have'. Biases are so pronounced that their existence alone warrants a reappraisal of traditional practice in appraisal interviews. I review, here, the most important biases that have been identified as problematic in the context of appraisal, from the standpoint of both interviewees and interviewers. There is plentiful evidence to suggest that appraisees are likely to have a different and more optimistic view of their work performance than the person appraising them.

Self-efficacy biases predispose us to believe that we personally are better on various positively rated dimensions of social behaviour than most other people. Furthermore, we tend to assume that others see us in the same rose-tinted light in which we see ourselves. The phenomenon can be observed in any reality TV show seeking to identify the next pop sensation, and in which tuneless warblers exhibit the conviction that they are destined to be as influential as Elvis or Madonna – whatever the judges say. Positive feedback

therefore feels intuitively valid while critical feedback that conflicts with our idealised self-image feels erroneous. Perhaps for these reasons, appraisees who receive high evaluations tend to perceive the appraisal evaluation as fairer than those who received a low evaluation. Thus, critical feedback is viewed as threatening. People are therefore likely to reject it, so that the feedback received is more likely to stimulate conflict between appraisee and appraiser than serve as the basis for improvements in performance.

In particular, most of us think that we contribute more to group discussions than the average input of everyone else involved, and that more people agree with our opinions than is actually the case. A major reason for this may be that we are intrinsically motivated to develop a positive evaluation of ourselves, as a means of shoring up our sense of identity. This is easily achieved when we exaggerate our role, general level of influence, and contribution to group discussions. Again, it means that people who work in teams tend to have a heightened impression of their role in delivering team successes, and look askance at feedback to the effect that their performance is average, ineffective, or poor.

Attribution processes play a crucial role in heightening such effects. We are inclined to explain the behaviour of the people around us as the result of global (that is, what is true of them in one situation is true of them in all) personality characteristics which are also assumed to be permanent, while we excuse our own behaviour as the result of the situation we find ourselves in. The tendency to overestimate the role of personality in the behaviour of others while exaggerating the role of situation in our own has been termed 'the fundamental attribution error'. Thus, we attribute our failure to the situation, but our successes to personal factors ('I had a good appraisal because I am bright: I had a poor appraisal because this organisation is terrible').

This also tempts us into a process of blame realignment, in which our primary concern is to establish our innocence in the face of organisational problems, while putting complete responsibility for the situation on someone else's shoulders.

Truly, failure is an orphan, while success has many fathers. Again, this implies that appraisees are likely to have a very different view of their performance from that of an appraiser, stimulating further conflict.Thus, people are especially sensitive to negative input – what has been termed the automatic vigilance effect. Its effects in the workplace have been well documented. For example, a study found that attempts to assist people by pointing out improvement needs in their work were perceived as threatening to employees' self-esteem and resulted in defensive behaviour.

In any event, 75% of people saw the evaluations they received as less favourable than their own self-estimates and therefore regarded appraisal interviews as a deflating experience. Follow-up studies found that those aspects of performance most criticised showed the least improvement. Another experimental study offered people feedback after completing a survey, while withholding feedback from others. It found no significant positive changes in those receiving feedback. It is critical to remember that employees who do not trust whatever appraisal information they receive tend to discount its value and usefulness. Discounted feedback cannot serve as a guide to either employee development or improved organisational performance. It seems that, overall, negative feedback creates resentment, places obstacles in the path of personal development, and diminishes rather than enhances organisational effectiveness.

It may be argued by defenders of appraisal interviews that the focus should therefore be on the celebration of positive behaviour, and a discussion of how it can be repeated more often. Thus, many texts recommend that when criticisms have to be made they should focus on specific behaviours, be linked to realistic action plans capable of achieving improvements, and occur in the context of a supportive organisational culture. In any event, the main emphasis should be on positive feedback. This is more likely to create focus, clarity, and a bias in favour of action to secure significant change. Wise as this approach appears, it seems unlikely that it can be accommodated within the framework of traditional approaches to appraisal interviews. The automatic vigilance effect suggests that even modest criticisms will predominate in the mind of the recipient, and come to be regarded as more typical of the interview than may have been the case. Moreover, the biases which also afflict appraisers may create an inbuilt tendency to deliver imbalanced, inaccurate, unfocused, and unhelpful feedback. It is to these biases that I now turn.

Most of us have a tendency to slot people into categories based on immediately obvious stereotypical traits, such as the colour of their skin, height, accent, and mode of dress. Appraisers also categorise in this manner. This inevitably means that they often perceive people based on their own personal prejudices, rather than as their job performance warrants. In particular, a number of biases have been identified that seem particularly active during traditional appraisal interviews, and which derail most of them. These include the following:

- Appraisers frequently fall victim to the halo effect. There is a tendency to assume that a positive attribute or a job-related success in one area automatically implies success in others. Enron, the most analysed case study of failure in business history, serves here also as an excellent example. Its traders were rated mostly on their ability to generate the appearance of high profits from their transactions. It was assumed that this was representative of a wider business acumen of long-term value to the company. In fact, their ability on this front signified a lack of sounder business judgement and a spirit of ethical incontinence that helped bring the organisation to bankruptcy.
- Personal liking bias means that when supervisors like subordinates, for whatever reason, they generally give them higher performance ratings, their judgement of subordinates' work performance becomes less accurate, and they show a disinclination to punish or deal with poor performance. As was

noted earlier, there has been a significant growth in recent years in 360-degree appraisals since, drawing feedback from multiple sources, it has been assumed that it is less likely to be handicapped by such biases. However, the evidence suggests that this expectation is unlikely to be fulfilled. Interpersonal factors, such as liking and similarity, have been found to be more important in determining ratings in 360-degree appraisals than the technical proficiency of the person being appraised. We also now live in an increasingly litigious age. There have been a growing number of lawsuits claiming that poor appraisals relative to those of others were influenced more by the personal biases of managers than by the actual performance of the employee.

- The horn effect arises when a problem in one area is assumed to be representative of defects elsewhere. If we see a scratch on the bodywork of a new car it might well be that everything else is perfect, but it is unlikely that we will be able to set aside our initial poor impression. As an old Russian proverb puts it: 'A spoonful of tar spoils a barrelful of honey.' In turn, we feel compelled to focus our attention on such negatives rather than positives. Moreover, we are especially sensitive to negative information. This means that it is difficult to set aside a negative impression, once it is formed. For example, it has been found that negative self-disclosures are regarded by most people as much more informative than positive ones. The implications for interviews of all kinds are striking. One study of selection interviewing found that, on average, 8.8 items of favourable information were required to change an initially unfavourable impression, but only 3.8 items of unfavourable information were required to alter an initially favourable impression. Moreover, it takes more than twice as much positive as negative information to change an initial impression of a candidate. Thus, in practice, it proves difficult for people to focus most of their attention on examples of positive behaviour, at least in terms of the judgements they form. One consequence is what has been termed the 10–90 effect, in which 90% of time in an appraisal interview is spent discussing the 10% of the job where the employee is performing badly.

- The consistency error suggests that we have an exaggerated need to feel consistent in our opinions and judgements, and to assume that people and circumstances are more stable than they actually are. Thus, when we form an initial impression of someone, it is very difficult to change it. This predisposes us to interpret new evidence in the light of our existing assumptions, while ignoring anything that contradicts our most cherished beliefs. We have a tendency to seek out and remember information that confirms our prejudices, while ignoring or forgetting anything that suggests we might be wrong. This has been described as the confirmatory bias. For example, if we expect someone to be a poor performer in their job, it is likely that we will see only evidence of this when we examine what they do. Furthermore, this perception is communicated to the person concerned by our overall bearing, and the tension created results in actual poor performance. Our expectation has created a self-fulfilling prophecy, which, of course, only confirms our view that what we thought at the beginning was right all along. These latter authors have dubbed this 'the set up to fail syndrome'.
- The fundamental attribution error, discussed above, means that an appraiser tends to attribute poor performance to the personality of the interviewee rather than to the situation. For example, it may be assumed that there is low ability to begin with, perhaps compounded by lack of effort. However, if the employee has successes, managers are likely to

conclude that it is their own inspired leadership, judgement, and competency that have caused it. The notion that it reflects the talent of the employee is downplayed. Employees, meanwhile, are likely to have exactly the opposite perception.

- The similarity bias means that we are attracted to people who look like us, sound like us, and form a convenient echo chamber for our own ideas. Thus, dissenters in organisations are generally penalised for voicing their views. They are at an obvious disadvantage during appraisal interviews. During appraisals, we therefore often observe a crony effect, in which yes-men and -women have a natural advantage in the competition for promotion, and the doppelgänger effect, in which appraisal ratings reflect the similarities between the person being appraised and the appraiser.
- The 'what is evaluated problem' arises when the behaviours being evaluated differ from those required to obtain organisational goals. For example, Abraham found that companies often identify a variety of competences as essential for managerial effectiveness, such as communication skills, a propensity for risk taking, and team working. However, they persistently fail to use the identified competencies as criteria for assessing performance during appraisal interviews. Under such conditions, rather than driving improved performance, appraisal institutionalises a disconnection between strategic intention and what is rewarded – and therefore what gets done. Such misalignments frequently derail and incapacitate the whole enterprise.
- Each of these problems is exacerbated by ingratiation effects. People with lower status habitually seek to influence those of greater status by exaggerating how much they agree with their opinions, policies, and practices, and so ingratiate themselves with the powerful. There is plentiful empirical evidence to

suggest that most managers are unaware of the extent to which they personally are at the receiving end of these practices, while they also engage in behaviours (again, often unconsciously) which discourage the transmission of critical feedback. The effect is that managers become ever more inclined to surround themselves with those who share their views, ape their mannerisms, and uncritically endorse their opinions. Those of a critical disposition are viewed with suspicion and are less likely to advance in the organisational hierarchy. Similarity and liking biases, already endemic, become ever stronger, making accurate and honest appraisals even more difficult to deliver.

Overall, these perceptual biases suggest that we have a high confidence in our judgements of other people, but that many of these judgements are inaccurate. What can be done to improve them? It is often argued that training must be given to help both managers and other employees with the appraisal process and hence to overcome the problems posed by the biases discussed above.

Training may indeed help managers, for example, to focus their feedback on behaviours rather than personalities. However, it is unlikely, in my view, that managers and staff can be trained to overcome the formidable range of obstacles to effective appraisal interviews identified in this chapter. The example of people's inbuilt resistance to critical feedback, and the enormous difficulties this creates in transmitting it, best illustrates the problem. 'Regression to the mean' effects describe the inevitable tendency for behaviour to cluster around a central midpoint of performance on any given variable.

It suggests that most people will be closer to the average, or mean, level of performance than they are to depart significantly from it. Given that appraisal interviews are designed to be implemented by the majority of a population in any given organisation, it can therefore be assumed that their average level of performance will be closer to the mean than it will be to depart from it – that is, the level of performance is likely to be so weak as to be dysfunctional. For example, one survey of 200 large companies found that 70% of employees said they were more confused than enlightened by the feedback they had received.

This suggests that most managers are poor at delivering effective feedback and most employees are poor at receiving it. Thus, it may be unwise to assume that training will substantially move the performance of most people from the mean scores of behaviour likely to be found on these issues.

Index

N

O

P

R

S

V